THE JFK ASSASSINATION

THE JFK ASSASSINATION

CONSPIRACIES AND COVERUPS

M J TROW

PEN & SWORD HISTORY

AN IMPRINT OF PEN & SWORD BOOKS LTD.
YORKSHIRE - PHILADELPHIA

First published in Great Britain in 2024 by
Pen & Sword History
An imprint of
Pen & Sword Books Ltd
Yorkshire - Philadelphia

Copyright © M.J. Trow, 2024

ISBN 978 1 39903 757 0

Typeset in INDIA by IMPEC eSolutions
Printed and bound in England by CPI (UK) Ltd.

Pen & Sword Books Limited incorporates the imprints of Archaeology, Atlas,
Aviation, Battleground, Digital, Discovery, Family History, Fiction, History,
Local, Local History, Maritime, Military, Military Classics, Politics, Select,
Transport, True Crime, After the Battle, Air World, Claymore Press, Frontline
Publishing, Leo Cooper, Remember When, Seaforth Publishing, The Praetorian
Press, Wharncliffe Books, Wharncliffe Local History, Wharncliffe Transport,
Wharncliffe True Crime and White Owl.

For a complete list of Pen & Sword titles please contact

PEN & SWORD BOOKS LIMITED
47 Church Street, Barnsley, South Yorkshire, S70 2AS, England
E-mail: enquiries@pen-and-sword.co.uk
Website: www.pen-and-sword.co.uk

or

PEN AND SWORD BOOKS
1950 Lawrence Rd, Havertown, PA 19083, USA
E-mail: uspen-and-sword@casematepublishers.com
Website: www.penandswordbooks.com

Contents

Author's Introduction

In the past twenty years of true crime writing, I have identified a plausible suspect for Jack the Ripper; found a far more likely killer of the princes in the Tower than their Tudor-maligned uncle, Richard III; identified a realistic solution to the Hagley Wood and Meon Hill murders in wartime England and come as close as I can to the maniac who butchered eight prostitutes and disposed of their dismembered bodies in the River Thames in the nineteenth century. What I cannot do is to tell you who killed John Fitzgerald Kennedy, the 35th president of the United States. Why not?

First, because the official enquiries into the murder, the Warren Commission of 1964 and the House Select Committee on Assassinations, were whitewashes dominated by men with something to hide. Subsequent enquiries – the Rockefeller Commission (1975) and the Assassination Records Review Board (1992) – have tried slightly harder, but as time has passed, memories fade and witnesses die. What has developed are two armed camps: those conservatives who support the Warren Commission and bend science for their own ends; and those who jump on any tall story, no matter how unlikely, to weave a complex conspiracy where none exists.

Second is the gullibility of the public. In 1963, America was personified as Camelot – the land of the free led by a young saint. What emerged, partly as a result of the assassination, revealed a darker, uglier side to government, the existence of what today is called 'the deep state'. In 2013, authors Belzer and Wayne wrote, '90 per cent of the American people believe there was a conspiracy to assassinate

John F. Kennedy. The other 10 per cent work for the government or the media.'

Very few people emerge from the story of JFK's assassination with either credit or dignity. It is impossible to know who to trust, from the hapless eyewitness in Dealey Plaza to the White House itself. Everybody has an agenda; most people have something to hide. All we can do is find a middle ground, based on common sense and a fair evaluation of evidence. I hope this is possible. And I hope this book presents it. It is depressing to read a throwaway line written as recently as 2021 in an essay on John Kennedy written by Sir Simon Burns, a British politician with vast experience of both sides of the Atlantic, that 'On balance, I suspect that the conclusions of the Warren Commission are correct.'

See if you agree.

Chapter 1

Umbrella Man, Badge Man, the Babushka Lady and the Secret Service Agent

Conspiracy theorists have given conspiracy theories a bad name. The American attorney Vincent Bugliosi wrote *Reclaiming History* in 2007 in an attempt to stop the ever-burgeoning nonsense of amateur researchers who were prepared to go to any lengths in pursuit of their pet theory in relation to the Kennedy assassination. In doing so, what Bugliosi did was to become, along with Gerald Posner, an arch debunker and that meant falling back on the palpable nonsense of the findings of the Warren Commission, set up in 1963 by Lyndon Johnson to investigate the assassination. *Reclaiming History*, as we shall see, has been torn to shreds by reputable critics.

There are deep and complicated reasons for conspiracy theories, but the overriding basis of them all, which the debunkers refute, is that conspiracies *do* happen; and they happen all the time. Of the four American presidents assassinated in the line of duty, three were killed as part of a conspiracy; only James Garfield in September 1881 can be deemed to have been killed by the stereotypical 'lone nut' so beloved by debunkers and the Warren Commission. But even Garfield's killer, Charles J. Guiteau, claimed to represent a political organization, the Stalwarts, who were pushing for the election of Chester Arthur as president.

The dictionary definition of conspiracy is a secret plan or agreement between people for unlawful or harmful purposes. Inevitably, this is often associated, as in the murder of John Kennedy, with political motivation. Historically, we can point to examples such as the assassination of Gaius Julius Caesar in March 44 BCE, the attempted destruction of James I and most of his parliament in November 1605, and the planned attack on Prime Minister Lord Liverpool and his cabinet in February 1820.

Recently, thanks largely to the gross intrusion of social media and ready access to information via the Internet, conspiracy obsession has grown out of hand, to the extent that some commentators have referred to our own time, sixty years after Kennedy's death, as the age of conspiracy. Authors Tom Phillips and John Elledge in their 2022 book *Conspiracy: A History of Bollocks Theories and How Not to Fall for Them* highlight the silliest of these but acknowledge that they have uncovered merely the tip of the iceberg.

Among other pieces of nonsense covered by Phillips and Elledge is the 'fact' that Beatle Paul McCartney, still alive at 81, as I write, 'died' in 1966 and that there is ample evidence for this, theorists contend, in various lyrics of the later Beatles songs and in the artwork of certain album sleeves.

Celebrities have an extraordinary knack of dying or surviving, even as doppelgangers. Marianne Faithfull, the girlfriend of Mick Jagger from The Rolling Stones was an early example. Sheryl Crow was killed in April 1996. Charlie Sheen is no more. Miley Cyrus died of an overdose in 2010 and has appeared ever since as a body double. Rapper Eminem was killed in a car crash and whoever is pretending to be Taylor Swift *definitely* is not her!

Part of this, even before the Internet age, is that we cannot accept the loss of our heroes. According to Celtic folklore, the legendary King Arthur still sleeps under a hill somewhere in Wales to gallop to our rescue if times get tough. Francis Drake will do likewise if Spain threatens to invade us again – all we have to do is beat a drum. Fans all over the world mourned the death of actor James Dean, singer Jim Reeves, and rock star Marc Bolan, many refusing to believe that they had actually died at all. We have all seen Elvis! In the case of John

Kennedy, the world, and America in particular, found it very difficult to accept that such a bright and important light could be extinguished by a deranged misfit and loser like Lee Harvey Oswald.

But conspiracy theories do not just swirl unchecked around celebrities, dead or alive. For millions of people around the world, that world is run by sinister organizations who live under the radar and manipulate people in a thousand malevolent ways. In the more simplistic age when religion dominated every aspect of life, the malevolent force was the Devil. But Satan was not a lone figure; he had people. His minions were legion; the armies of Hell, and the forces of good, defined by God and his angels (another conspiracy from the Devil's viewpoint) had to be on their guard constantly.

Sometimes, these shadowy evil-doers emerge into the light. In late seventeenth-century England, Charles II's court was dominated by five politicians: Thomas Clifford; Lord Arlington; the Duke of Buckingham; Lord Ashley and Lord Lauderdale. Their initials spelt CABAL and the term became associated with a sinister power complex now applied throughout the Western world. The fact that *Kabbalah* is a much older Hebrew word meaning acceptance and associated with secrecy, is another possible etymological origin – and we have yet another conspiracy theory.

One of the most successful novels and films of recent years is Dan Brown's *The Da Vinci Code*, linking the family of Christ through the Medieval Knights Templar to the Rosicrucians of the eighteenth century and to a sneaky, all-powerful group, the Illuminati. Brown pinched most of these ideas from the pseudo-historians Henry Lincoln, Michael Baigent and Richard Leigh, who promptly sued Brown for plagiarism. There is no copyright on ideas, of course, and the trio lost. Their work, *The Holy Blood and the Holy Grail*, is a fascinating, if specious, attempt to imply that Christ did not die on the cross, but reappeared and went to live in France! Cue resonance with Arthur, Drake, Reeves, Bolan, Dean and Presley.

But the Illuminati of the conspiracy theorists are as nothing to the ever-more-deranged notions of today. Flat earthers have been around for centuries, because that was once the scholars' view of the world. The concept of an inverted shallow bowl (the earth) supported by four elephants standing on the back of a turtle flapping through eternity, lit by the stars of heaven through holes in God's canopy, was not something invented by Terry Pratchett in his *Discworld* series but the outcome of careful research by generations of scholars in the fourteenth century, anywhere from Oxford University to Krakow. The flat-earth myth has been given a new lease of life by the Internet.

The ordinary ebb and flow of life is so incomprehensible to some people that they have to mould it into a shape that makes sense to them. Surely, it was not scientifically possible for the Americans to put a man on the moon in the summer of 1969, so a conspiracy was woven around it; the whole thing was set up in a film studio. The entirely fictional movie *Capricorn One* (1977) in which just such a scenario unfolded, was hailed by theorists as 'proof' of the plot. When 52 per cent of the British public voted to leave the European Union in 2016, Remainers were appalled and outraged; there had to be something sinister about it. At very least, the ballot was rigged. In the same year, Donald Trump was elected president of the United States and liberal America could not believe it; the Republicans had gone mad and the United States was going to hell in a handcart, driven by some (probably drug-induced) conspiracy.

Thousands of people all over the world refused to accept the vaccines rolled out to stop COVID in 2020 on the grounds that their government was using it as a way to contaminate them and control their minds. China is spying on the West via street lighting, CCTV cameras, access to university courses and electric cars. Princess Diana was murdered in the Pont de l'Alma tunnel in Paris in 1997 on the orders of the Duke of Edinburgh. According to the ex-footballer David Icke, the British royal family are all lizards and he is the son of God.

In a sane world, of course, I would not be writing any of this, but we do not live in a sane world. Icke, instead of being sectioned and treated for whatever his condition is, sells books by the thousand, leads rallies and has an army of acolytes. People died because they refused to be vaccinated; the anti-vaxxers are guilty of negligent homicide, but none of them will ever face trial, because of the Western world's obsession with the notion of free speech.

And the assassination of John Fitzgerald Kennedy on 22 November 1963 is the granddaddy of all conspiracies, because it is the first to have captured the public imagination. We all remember, the cliché runs, where we were and what we were doing at the time. For the record, I had recently turned 14 and was annoyed, that Friday evening (remembering the time difference between Britain and Texas), that my favourite Western, *Bonanza,* was not being shown on the television. In fact, nothing was being shown. There were then only two channels available (as opposed to the dozens already set up in the States) and on both, the screen was filled with static. Only later did we learn of the horrific events in Dealey Plaza and it would be fifty-eight years before all the relevant documentation was released by the United States government – and if you believe that that is true, you are probably a flat-earther or an anti-vaxxer or a lizard!

It is intriguing that the Kennedy assassination comes closest of all to accepted norms of reality. The inverted pyramid of Abbie Richards's Conspiracy Chart (2021) went viral on the Internet. Richards, in her twenties, has a different take on life from me and is described as a 'misinformation educator', which in itself can be misconstrued. A stand-up comedian and graduate from Colorado College, her research, originally for comic purposes, has become serious. I might not agree with her approach, but the Conspiracy Chart makes a certain amount of sense.

At the apex of the inverted pyramid is 'Grounded in Reality', events that actually happened. Because Ms Richards is (a) American,

(b) young and (c) not an historian, there is no mention of the three examples I have already given of actual conspiracies – the murder of Caesar, the Gunpowder Plot and the Cato Street Conspiracy. Above these certainties, proved by verifiable fact, we have a Speculation Line, unfolding a group of conspiracies about which 'we have questions'. It is depressing that within this group is: the death of actress Marilyn Monroe (linked with JFK and his brother Robert); the existence of Area 51 (the secret American base in Nevada with alien links); the whole world of ufology; the death of Princess Diana; and the concept that the millionaire paedophile Jeffrey Epstein did not commit suicide. Here too is the assassination of John Kennedy. Oh, and Free Britney.

Richards' next phase, as the pyramid widens, is 'Leaving Reality', which includes: the living Elvis; crop circles; various theories about the stone circle at Stonehenge; Scotland's Loch Ness monster and America's Big Foot. We then reach 'Science Denial', which includes: the 5G scare; the anti-vaxxers; chemtrails; and the fact that COVID-19 was deliberately manufactured in a laboratory. Then comes the inexplicable 'Anti-Semitic Point of No Return' which contains: the moon landing; the theory of a hollow earth; a new world order (which may or may not be organized by the Illuminati); Bill Gates' attempts to microchip us all; the QAnon assertion that governments are composed of raving child molesters; flat earth; and David Icke's reptilian overlords. This last group, unsurprisingly, is 'Detached from Reality'.

Conspiracy theories are all things to all men and we could all bicker for ever about which theory belongs where in the scheme of things. In my own take on the chart, I would move the JFK assassination firmly down to the lowest level – 'events that actually happened', for which the evidence is overwhelming, and is very definitely 'grounded in reality'.

With a subject as vast and controversial as the assassination of John Kennedy, it is perhaps inevitable – and equally annoying – that it has established its own foaflore or urban legend. Wikipedia has a very long alphabetical list of these worldwide, all of which are nonsense and impede genuine historical research. One of those listed is the ridiculously exaggerated coincidences between the assassinations of Kennedy and Abraham Lincoln. It is worth discussing this because the human brain has a natural inclination to repetitive patterns and it is a good example of how foaflore differs from reality. In the order in which they are usually listed:

'Lincoln' and 'Kennedy' both have seven letters.
Both men were elected to Congress in '46 and to the presidency in '60.
Both assassins (assuming for the moment that Oswald was an assassin), Lee Harvey Oswald and John Wilkes Booth were born in '39 and had three names.
Booth ran a theatre and was caught in a warehouse.
Oswald worked in a warehouse and was caught in a theatre.
Both assassins were Southerners.
Both presidents' successors were called Johnson and they were both born in '08.
Both presidents were defenders of civil rights.
Both presidents were shot in the head on a Friday.
Lincoln had a secretary called Kennedy who warned him not to go to Ford's Theatre; Kennedy had a secretary called Lincoln who warned him against the trip to Dallas.
Both assassins were killed before they could be brought to trial.

All very tantalizing – conspiracy theorists might say 'spooky' – but a considerable amount of it is untrue. And the rest is coincidence. Lincoln did not have a secretary called Kennedy. One was John M. Hay and the other John G. Nicolay. John Wilkes Booth certainly espoused the cause of the South, but since he was born in Maryland, he was technically a Northerner. He was not caught in a warehouse, but a barn in Virginia. And he was born in 1838, not 1839. As for the number of letters in surnames, this is an example of a psychological condition, apophenia, which has 'the tendency to precise order in random configurations'. Most of us prefer order to chaos, because we are more comfortable in a world we can understand. In terms of assassination controversy, however, the Lincoln/Kennedy connection is yet another instance of water-muddying.

A casual acquaintanceship with the Kennedy assassination immediately brings up a range of characters who are on the edge of reality. As the president's motorcade travelled through Dallas that Friday in November, thousands of people turned out to line the streets. Inevitably, the focus on these people was concentrated on Dealey Plaza, as the last leg of the journey, where the shots rang out. In alphabetical order, we have first the Babushka Lady. Clearly seen in a number of photographs taken that day, the Babushka Lady was standing on the grassy area to the south of Elm and Main (see plan). The name comes from the headscarf she wore which was associated with the headgear traditionally worn by Russian women (literally, the word means 'grandmother'). She was carrying a camera and taking photographs of the motorcade as the shooting started. Along with at least forty other members of the public and several motorcycle policemen, she is seen running up the grassy knoll to the north of Elm because that is where shots were heard to come from and gun smoke seen.

Confusingly, she (or perhaps another woman in a headscarf) was seen on the pavement in front of the Dallas County Court Building, placing her on Kennedy's right. Later photographs show her on his left. Are we talking about one woman who crossed the street or two different people? Six years later, Beverley Oliver told assassination researcher Gary Shaw that she was the Babushka Lady and had been filming with a Yashica camera using Super 8 film, which she handed over to two FBI agents. They promised to return the film but she never saw it again. She repeated this assertion on the influential British television documentary series *The Men Who Killed Kennedy* in 1988.

Unfortunately for conspiracy buffs, the Yashica model was not on the market until 1969. Oliver countered this with the story that hers was a prototype given to her by a friend. She further complicated matters by telling the Assassination Records Review Board in 1994 that she was only 17 at the time and complied with the FBI because of her marijuana possession. Such people do not make good witnesses.

Like the Babushka Lady, Badge Man appears on film too, but his image is far less helpful. One of the bystanders south of Elm Street, not far from the Babushka Lady was Mary Moorman. Using a Polaroid Highlander 80A camera, she photographed the presidential limousine and its police outriders as well as movie-cameraman Abraham Zapruder (see Chapter 3) and the grassy knoll area to his right (see plan). The fifth photograph she took, which coincides with a bullet hitting Kennedy's head and jolting it backwards, showed, on development and analysis, a human figure half crouching behind the fence on the top of the grassy knoll with a background of trees. Moorman saw nothing out of the ordinary in this position and never believed that her chance photograph had captured anything of significance. She did not give evidence to the Warren Commission in 1964, but the House Select Committee on Assassinations (HSCA), which had come to the conclusion that there was a second gunman on the grassy knoll (in addition to Lee Oswald in the Texas School Book Depository), had the Moorman photograph enhanced and tested. By 1978, when the HSCA met, the photograph had degraded badly.

Researcher Gary Mack, who once ran the Sixth Floor Museum in Dealey Plaza (supposedly Oswald's 'sniper's nest' in the Book Depository) tested the photograph further with professional help and concluded that the blurred image was actually of a Dallas police officer firing a gun, his face blurred by the rifle's flash. The sharp white image at the bottom right of the photograph was a badge on the policeman's chest. Jack White, a photographic technical expert, claimed in 1988 that a second figure can be discerned to Badge Man's left, wearing a white shirt and hard hat – 'Back Up Man'.

The Men Who Killed Kennedy concluded that Badge Man was Lucien Sarti, a French drug-trafficker and alleged contract killer. Others have claimed that Badge Man is J.D. Tippit, himself killed in Dallas some forty-five minutes after the Kennedy shooting (see Chapter 5). No one else admits to having seen a policeman in that particular position. Experts have measured the height of the grassy knoll fence and have concluded that Badge Man would have been impossibly tall for a human being. It may be that Kennedy's policeman assassin is nothing more than the sunlight flashing on a Coca-Cola bottle that we now know was left on the grassy knoll at the time.

Marilyn Sitzman was standing on a concrete plinth in Dealey Plaza on 22 November alongside her boss, Abraham Zapruder, who was filming the motorcade with his movie camera. She saw a young black couple having lunch and drinking Coke on a bench behind a wall to her right. This *could* be the Coke bottle referred to above. In a photograph taken seconds earlier by Major Phillip Willis, an Air France veteran watching the motorcade that day, a blurred image appears over the wall near the couple (who are not actually visible in the photograph). Willis was standing on the corner of Elm and Houston using an Argus Autronic 1 Model 35156M camera. He appears filming on the Zapruder movie, viewed from across Elm Street as the motorcade briefly disappears beyond the Stemmons Freeway road sign.

Willis appeared before the Warren Commission to testify that he heard three gunshots in the Plaza and took his fifth photograph simultaneously with the shock of one of them. The fifth image shows a dark shape between the 3ft wall and the 5ft fence which looks oddly like a black Labrador sitting down – hence 'Black Dog Man', another foaflore character to litter the scene. Willis is convinced that the fatal head shot came from the grassy knoll, not the Book Depository.

Photographic expert Robert Groden, one of the most erudite and persuasive of conspiracy theorists, believes that Black Dog Man could be seen in a pyracantha bush in frame 413 of the Zapruder film (see Chapter 3). The HSCA agreed, but concluded that Black Dog Man was standing in front of the bushes, in other words, in full view of eyewitnesses, which makes him an unlikely assassin.

Sitting on the grass verge below the grassy knoll and Abraham Zapruder's position, was the 'dark complected man'. While it may seem odd that someone should be sitting as the motorcade passed him, there is nothing particularly sinister in that. In fact, in the seconds after the head shot, there are five men on the knoll, one of whom is potentially the most outlandish of them (see below). Conspiracy theorists convinced that there was a Cuban connection in the Kennedy killing have assumed that he was a Cuban exile (see Chapter 12) intent on seeing that the assassination was carried out, at close quarters.

Jerry Boyd Belknap was one of thousands watching the motorcade that morning. He worked for the *Dallas Morning News* and was standing in his army fatigues in front of the Book Depository. Fifteen minutes before the cars arrived, Belknap had an epileptic fit; he had often had them before. Dallas police sergeant D.V. Harkness called an ambulance. Aubrey Rike drove Belknap to the nearest hospital, Parkland. In the hysteria that followed when Kennedy's entourage arrived, everybody forgot about Belknap and, having recovered, he walked out of Parkland and caught a bus back to downtown Dallas. In the conspiratorial hysteria that followed the shooting, Belknap's seizure was believed by some to be a diversion or signal of some kind. Of course, it was no such thing.

James 'Ike' Altgens was a wirephoto editor for the Associated Press in Dallas and was photographing the motorcade in Dealey Plaza that Friday. In one of the first of the sequence he took (which forms the cover of this book), he captured the presidential limousine with its outriders having turned on to Elm from Houston. Police Chief Jesse Curry's car was in front, but Altgens avoided that so that Kennedy's Lincoln convertible appears in the lead. Secret Servicemen in the car close behind are standing on the running rail on both sides of the vehicles and some of them are turning to their right and slightly behind, looking in the direction of either the Book Depository or the Dal-Tex building as they hear the first of the shots.

Clearly shown behind the car is the entrance to the Depository and, lounging against the wall, stands Lee Harvey Oswald. If this were so, the 'lone nut' still regarded by many as Kennedy's killer, would be spectacularly off the hook and would be merely a very small footnote in accounts of the murder. When the Altgens' photograph was printed (as it was worldwide) the Oswald lookalike was identified as Billy Nolan Lovelady, another employee at the Depository. The FBI were satisfied that this was correct and most researchers have accepted Lovelady's own evidence of exactly where he was as the motorcade drove past. There is no doubt, however, that Lovelady (at least in the photograph) did look very like Oswald and this led to speculation that there were several Oswald clones wandering around Dealey Plaza and Dallas generally which would account for the shooting of officer Tippit as well as other sightings of Oswald earlier in his life (see Chapter 7).

It had been raining in Dallas that morning, but by the time the president arrived at Love Field airport, the sun was shining and the temperature rising at midday. All the more odd then that a man was seen standing near the Stemmons Freeway sign on the north side of Elm Street, opening and closing an umbrella. Investigators examining various photographs and talking to eyewitnesses found that the man raised and lowered the umbrella and twirled it clockwise as Kennedy's car passed him. He then sat down next to 'dark complected man' (see above) apparently unaware that anything had happened.

Speculation, of course, raged. Some theorists believed that the umbrella was a signal to fire (wherever the gunman or gunmen were positioned) and one of them, Robert B. Cutler who later founded the Conspiracy Museum in Dallas, went so far as to suggest that the umbrella fired a dart which paralysed Kennedy's muscles making him immobile in his seat and a sitting duck for his assassin. Astonishingly, this idea was backed by Colonel Leroy Fletcher Prouty (see Chapter 13), Chief of Special Operations for the Joint Chiefs of Staff in the Kennedy administration.

Journalists eventually tracked down Umbrella Man. He was Louie Steven Witt, an insurance salesman from Rockwall, Texas and he gave evidence to the HSCA in 1978. He told the Committee, 'I think if the Guinness Book of World Records had a category for people who were at the wrong place at the wrong time, doing the wrong thing, I would be No. 1 in that position, without even a close runner-up.'

Over recent months, we have all become used to bizarre protests from fringe groups like Extinction Rebellion and Just Stop Oil, but Witt's protest takes on a new dimension in obscurity. As we shall see in Chapter 2, Kennedy's father, Joseph, was American ambassador to Britain in the 1930s and backed the appeasement of the prime minister, Neville Chamberlain, in the context of the rise of Hitler's Nazis. Chamberlain's trade mark was the carrying of an umbrella. JFK himself was acutely aware of this situation, having written an undergraduate thesis at Harvard – *Why England Slept*. At the time of the building of the Berlin Wall (1961) protestors in Germany sent a black umbrella to the White House, labelled 'Chamberlain'. Witt appears to have had no complaint against JFK himself, so the whole episode seems bizarre in the extreme. He never explained why he casually sat down at the roadside having seen the president's head destroyed by a bullet. Was it shock? We will never know because Umbrella Man died in 2014.

Herrings do not come any redder than the case of the three hoboes near Dealey Plaza on 22 November. At any crime scene there will be objects and people who have no link to the crime itself and which can lead law enforcement agencies in a completely wrong direction. A classic case would be 'Leather Apron'. 'Dark Annie' Chapman was the second victim of the Whitechapel murderer (later known to the press as Jack the Ripper) in the autumn of 1888. A leather apron was found near her body at the back of 29 Hanbury Street which was assumed to belong to the murderer. A local man, John Pizer, whose nickname was Leather Apron because he wore one, was all but lynched by the mob before the police rescued him. In fact, the apron belonged to a resident of No. 29 and it had nothing to do with the murder at all. In Dallas seventy-five years later, a crucial witness to the events of the day was Lee E. Bowers, working for the Union Terminal railroad company and sitting in a 14ft high tower overlooking the railway terminal and Dealey Plaza itself. We shall look at his testimony relating to the shooting later, but in the immediate aftermath, he saw an unscheduled train pulling out in the maze of tracks below him and ordered it stopped. He called the police who searched the freight cars and found three tramps hiding there. Photographs taken at the time clearly show the trio, escorted by Dallas police being taken into custody. There they were fingerprinted and photographed. So far, so procedural. The Dallas Police Department were leaving no stone unturned in their enquiries, but then it went pear-shaped. The mug shots and the fingerprints vanished and it took researchers twenty-seven years to find even the records of the arrest.

Inevitably, this smacked of corruption. Who were these men, so close to the shooting and why were they, for supposed tramps, so well dressed, with particularly good shoes? Conspiracy theorists have had a field day. The oldest of the three appears to have a listening device in his right ear; so has one of the arresting policemen. That is because the cop is equipped, as many officers were, with walkie-talkies. The old man is probably wearing a hearing aid. Nothing to see here, as the police would say.

But it is the identity of these men that has ruffled most feathers. The murder of John Kennedy has to be the most photographed assassination in history and yet much photographic evidence is in the eye of the beholder. One of the men looked like the hitman Charles Voyde Harrelson, father of Woody, of NBC-TV's *Cheers* fame and various movies. Another bore an uncanny resemblance to CIA agent E. Howard Hunt and a third to another shady CIA man, Frank Sturgis.

The oldest of the three, with or without his hearing aid, was actually Gus Abrams. The photographs make him look older than his 53 years and, despite speculation, he really was a vagrant. FBI agents verified that he was dead by 1993. The others were then very much alive. John Forrester Gedney was 38 at the time of the shooting, another genuine tramp. He and the others were charged with vagrancy and detained for four days before release. The FBI found him, years later, living in Melbourne, Florida and he was cleared of any involvement in the Kennedy killing. Harold Doyle was the youngest at 32 and, like the others, was hitching an illegal ride to Fort Worth. He remembers seeing Lee Oswald briefly in the Dallas police station. Doyle made no secret of his being one of the three, but was not proud of it either. When the FBI and the media tracked him down in 1992, he was working in a pool hall in Klamath Falls, Oregon. As television journalist Steve Dunleavy said, 'The tale of these three reveals what appears to be shocking laxity on the part of assassination investigators ... Why police or anyone else couldn't locate this man [Doyle] is a mystery.'

As for Charles Harrelson, he was having lunch in Houston, Texas, at the time of the shooting. He told the makers of *The Men Who Killed Kennedy* – 'I did not kill John Kennedy.' Police forensic artist Lois Gibson was still disagreeing in 1991. Harrelson was certainly a bad boy. Once an honest encyclopaedia salesman, he robbed a bank in 1960 and was convicted of contract killing eight years later. On the run, he shot out his own car tyres with a .44 Magnum and held off the police for six hours in a stand-off. During this time, high on cocaine, he held his gun to his head and confessed to the killing of Kennedy. Found guilty of the murder of Judge Wood, he served time in the United States Penitentiary, Marion, Illinois.

Yet conspiracy theorists will not leave the tramps alone. Respected photographic expert Robert Groden asks 'When did Dallas policemen carry rifles?' as they are in the arrest photograph. In fact, there are dozens of photographs that Friday of cops with rifles. The All Points Bulletin (APB) had gone out that the 'assassin' was carrying a Winchester.

As I was writing this book, one of the last survivors of that fateful day in Dallas emerged into the media spotlight. He is Paul Landis Jr., and he was riding in the motorcade directly behind the president's limousine. Landis's book, published in 2023 and appropriately titled *The Final Witness*, does not add a great deal to the critical (and well-established) viewpoint that there was more than one assassin in Dealey Plaza; it serves only to muddy the waters.

It is also at odds to both the statements Landis made at the time. It was his twenty-eighth birthday on 22 November 1963. To reflect the fact that he was the rookie of the White House Secret Service detail, his codename was Debut. He had first been appointed to protect President Eisenhower's grandchildren when he joined the Service and by 1963 had specific responsibility for the First Lady, Jacqueline Kennedy. He had already accompanied her on visits to Italy and Greece.

In the motorcade, Landis stood with another agent on the right running board of the Secret Service follow-up car and remembered:

I heard what sounded like a report of a high-powered rifle from behind me … [I drew my gun and] I heard a second report and saw the president's head split open and pieces of flesh and blood flying through the air. My reaction at the time was that the [fatal] shot came from somewhere toward the front … and [I] looked along the right side of the road.

In a sloppy piece of reporting by *MailOnline* (September 2023) Landis is referred to as standing on the *left* of the Secret Service car, a continuation of so much misinformation about the Kennedy murder. But it gets worse; the *MailOnline* refers to a 'massive, jagged exit wound in the right front [*sic*] of his skull'. This is in direct contradiction of every piece of forensic evidence, both at Parkland Hospital where doctors and nurses tried to save Kennedy's life and at Bethesda Naval Hospital where his autopsy was performed. The massive wound was at the *rear* of his skull, not the front.

So what is new about Landis's book and why has he waited sixty years (he is now 88) to produce it? In the chaos after the shooting, Landis now claims (which he had not previously) that he saw a pristine bullet lying on the top of the back seat where Kennedy had been sitting. He picked this up and placed it on the president's stretcher where he assumed it would be picked up by another Secret Service agent, the Dallas police or the Federal Bureau of Investigation. He then went about his business.

The huge significance of this bullet will be discussed later. It is the so-called 'magic' bullet which, according to the Warren Commission in 1964, smashed its way through Kennedy and Governor John Connally causing seven wounds, to end up on Connally's stretcher. According to Landis, the bullet did not fall out of Connally's thigh wound as the Warren Commission surmised, but was an undamaged round which dropped out of the shallow wound it caused in Kennedy's head or back.

As we shall see, there is considerable disagreement as to exactly where the bullet was found, but if Landis's new assertion is true, then he broke every rule in the Secret Service handbook by, effectively, tampering with evidence. He should have left the bullet in the limo where he saw it, so that scenes of crime officers and/or forensic experts could have evaluated it properly. By removing it from the scene and placing it on a stretcher (which may or may not have been Kennedy's) he unwittingly consigned Lee Harvey Oswald to the ignominy of history, that he was the lone gunman who shot the president from behind.

Landis was, understandably, haunted by the shooting which had taken place so close to him and he left the Service six months later. Like most people in the world, he accepted the Warren Commission's whitewash 'investigation' and it was not until 2014 that he read Josiah Thompson's *Six Seconds in Dallas* (1967) which poured doubt on the single bullet and single assassin theory. Landis contacted a Secret Service friend, Clint Hill, who warned him about going public with his new information. But this was fifty years after the Warren Commission and nearly thirty years after the House Select Committee on Assassinations had decided that there was indeed more than one shooter in Dealey Plaza. And by 2014 the vast majority of Americans *knew* that the Warren Commission had been a botched cover-up and that there had indeed been a conspiracy to kill the president. Why should Hill and Landis be so concerned after all that time and why did it take Landis a further nine years to decide to tell the world what he knew?

If you thought that the revelations of Paul Landis were all that there is to throw the murder of John Kennedy investigation into confusion, think again. Beverley Oliver, who claimed to have been the Babushka Lady, was a stripper in the Colony Club in Dallas. In 1970, shortly before she admitted to being in Dealey Plaza on the day of the shooting, she married a Mobster, George McCann. He was murdered, gangster-style, months later. Many people now doubt the veracity of Oliver and her claim that her film of the motorcade was confiscated by anonymous federal agents. Likewise, the testimony of Louie Witt, 'Umbrella Man', does not accord with what he is doing in film footage taken that day. Can we, therefore, trust anybody? Welcome to the topsy-turvy world of the Kennedy assassination. To try to make some sense of it, we have to make sense of that mercurial, compartmentalized man, John Fitzgerald Kennedy.

Chapter 2

Camelot?

On St Valentine's Day 1962, American television station CBS produced a first. It showed a tour of the White House and the guide was the First Lady, Jacqueline Kennedy. The president's official residence had been expensively refurbished and Jackie herself, with a university degree in Fine Arts, had requisitioned period furniture to create a living history of the White House's past. Some of this was actually from the White House originally, including wallpaper from the Franklin D. Roosevelt administration in the 1930s which was traced to a shop in downtown Washington. Millions of Americans watched spellbound as JFK himself explained the history behind the various rooms. The only period not covered, unsurprisingly, was that of the British Empire, nor was there any mention of the White House being burned down by the Redcoats in 1812!

The Kennedys had it all. John himself was the second youngest man, at 43, to win the presidency. Like his brothers Bobby and Ted, he was all hair and teeth and like them, charming, funny and good company. He was also a war hero, his torpedo boat PT109 having been sliced in half by a Japanese cruiser in the Pacific in 1943. His elder brother, Joe, had been killed in that war, flying suicidal missions with the USAAF. Jacqueline Bouvier was attractive – dark-haired, beautiful, wealthy (but not as wealthy as the Kennedys), she was the perfect wife for the president and an excellent mother to their bright, adorable children Caroline, John Jr and Patrick.

That was the veneer. It was *so* gilded, so perfect that the media equated it with Camelot, the fairy-tale castle of the legendary King

Arthur. And that analogy has never been more apt, because in Thomas Malory's fifteenth-century version of the Arthurian legend, Arthur's court was a sham. It was riddled with intrigue and malevolence, one of the king's apparently most loyal knights (Lancelot) having an affair with Arthur's wife, Guinevere, behind his back. The Knights of the Round Table themselves squabbled and bickered, some disappearing on a pointless quest for Christ's Holy Grail and others backing Mordred, Arthur's nemesis, against their king. Allowing for an American and twentieth-century slant, the Kennedy administration was much the same.

One of Kennedy's biographers, Richard Reeve, wrote, 'He was a compartmentalized man with much to hide, comfortable with secrets and lies. He needed them because that was part of the stimulation; things were rarely what they seemed.'

In police circles, there is an old adage: if you want to know why a man died, look at his life. In the case of the President of the United States, that presents vast problems. Opposition and hatred went with the territory. Kennedy was a Democrat, so Republicans loathed him anyway. He was the first Catholic to be elected to the White House and that ruffled a few feathers. Then there was the politics of envy – the Kennedys were rich, good looking and smart; an awful lot of life's losers resented all that. And this was before we look at his policies – moral and right to many; anathema to just as many.

John (or Jack as family and friends called him) Fitzgerald Kennedy was born in Brookline, Massachusetts in May 1917. The Kennedy clan was vast and it had arrived at Noddle Island, Boston, in April 1849 in the wake of the disastrous Irish potato famine which claimed a million lives and saw another million emigrate to all parts of the globe. The Kennedy men worked as stevedores, gravitating to running a bar and by the 1880s had become 'lace Irish', with an air of gentility. The paterfamilias Patrick Joseph, known as P.J., was elected to the Massachusetts House of Representatives in the first step into politics that never went away. His son, Joseph Patrick (not very adventurous with names, were the Kennedys!) was born in 1888. He inherited his father's knack of making money and his political ambitions. In America, as much as in Europe, the two went hand in hand. As George Reedy wrote of Irish Americans, 'Those who survived were lean and mean. They were quick of wit and masters of dissembling. They understood political leverage and knew when to attack, when to retreat and when to hide.'

Joe Kennedy's father was a rich banker by the time he was born. The family had horse-teams, carriages and servants. They were living the American dream. The boy grew into a bully with a raging temper and ice-cold grey eyes. Academically, he was a failure (we still have his school grades; they were never above a D), but his school year book when he graduated in June 1908 predicted that he would do well 'in a very roundabout way'. That way began when he won a place at Harvard, almost certainly because strings were pulled by the former mayor of Boston, John Fitzgerald. Kennedy married the man's daughter Rose in October 1914.

Two things mattered to Joe Kennedy above all else – winning and money. Family came third, but he expected his own children to excel at everything and making money was in his blood. He was president of the Columbia Trust bank at 25, where he was so devious that he had a silencing machine fitted to his telephone so that no one could eavesdrop.

The couple's first child, Joseph Patrick, was born in July 1915 and as time went on, Rose was relegated to professional mother, often going on walks and even holidays without her pushy, domineering husband. As author Ronald Kessler writes in *The Sins of the Father*, 'Joe ran the family like a football team. He was the coach, the manager and the referee. Rose was the water boy, constantly filling the children's minds with trivia. The aim was to win at everything, no matter what.' As John remembered from his earliest days, 'We didn't have opinions in those days. They were mostly monologues by my father.' At the time of John Fitzgerald's birth, Joe senior was up to his neck in insider trading (not then technically illegal) and other dubious financial practices. When the Volstead Act was brought in three years later, Joe Kennedy made nearly as much money as any of the hoodlums of the Prohibition era.

In the 1930s, Joe moved in on the media, buying shares in radio companies and flirting with Hollywood. He had an on-off affair with Gloria Swanson, *the* star of the day and set up a swanky apartment in New York as well as keeping the summer home at Hyannis Port near Boston. When the Wall Street Crash hit in 1929, Joe sold short and pulled out just in time, avoiding the chaos that affected many others.

In that decade, too, he backed Franklin D. Roosevelt, whose New Deal promised hope in the wake of the Wall Street Crash and the reduction of poverty for millions. He went on the campaign trail with Roosevelt in September 1932. He was buying property all over the place and took expensive holidays in Palm Beach, still making a fortune out of the (now legal again) liquor trade.

As his father courted politicians and lined his pockets, John was frequently seriously ill. Never the robust athlete his father wanted him to be, he was twice given the last rites as his mother wept by his bedside. Illness dogged him throughout his life. An attack of jaundice made him pull out of a place at London's School of Economics in 1935 and he left Princeton soon afterwards having completed only one term.

Joe became a most unlikely American ambassador to the Court of St James. There were jokes with Roosevelt as to how dreadful he would look in knee-breeches and a deep irony that an Irishman would now be hob-nobbing with English nobility and royalty in London. There is no doubt that Joe had set his heart on the White House – five previous incumbents had been ambassadors to Britain first. But Joe's time in London was not happy. He was there when the Germans marched into Poland and immediately stood behind the appeasement of Prime Minister Neville Chamberlain, believing that nothing could stop Hitler. His strong and well-known anti-Semitism did not go down well either. One British MP said, 'We have a rich man, untrained in diplomacy, unlearned in history or politics, who is a great publicity seeker and who apparently is ambitious to be the first Catholic president of the US.'

As war progressed, Joe wanted to go home, far out of the range of Hitler's bombers. At one point, he suggested to Roosevelt over the phone that America should keep out of European affairs and let Hitler take over because 'we could not possibly do business with the Russians but could always assassinate Hitler'. How ironic that two of his sons should die the same way.

Like father, like son. Gloria Swanson was only one of Joe's lovers. Another was Clare Boothe Luce, a playwright and politician who would still be making a nuisance of herself in the context of John's murder forty years later (see Chapter 10). Secretaries, researchers, even casual acquaintances – they were all within Joe's orbit and habits like that he passed on to all his sons, sometimes with dangerous or even deadly risks. Under him, at least in the 1940s, there was no sign that John could ever become his own man. He was an officer in the navy, but Joe had mapped out his boys' careers for them. By now he had given up his own White House ambitions but passed them on to Joe Jr, with John as a kind of 'spare'. John had gone to Harvard, as his father ordered, rather than stay at Princeton. When the boy wrote a thesis there – 'Why England Slept' – Joe had it turned into a 252-page book and had 80,000 copies printed. He and his employees bought most of them, making the younger Kennedy a best-selling author.

Joe had gone from the ambassadorship by early November 1940, resigned, some said, others, that he was fired by Roosevelt. A.J. Cummings wrote in the *New Chronicle*, 'While he was here, his suave monotonous smile, his nine over-photographed children and his hail-fellow-well-met manner concealed a hard-boiled businessman's eagerness to do a profitable deal with the dictators, and he deceived many decent English people.'

Back home, Joe moved his principal home to Florida which had no income or inheritance tax. When his daughter Rosemary did not shine academically, he and his wife decided she had a learning disability and sent her to a specialist who carried out (even then not standard practice) a lobotomy. Before this, she had been able to read, write and was a whizz at mathematics. Afterwards, she was a reclusive with a severe mental disability, sidelined in a family where only excellence was recognized. In fact, Joe should have been a little worried about Jack; even when he left Harvard, his spelling was appalling. Later, of course, he had people for things like that ... His back too was a problem, which is why, on the day he died, John Kennedy was wearing a brace. If the subject cropped up, Joe put it down to a sports injury, whereas in fact it was due to multiple issues including osteoporosis which have never been agreed on by medical writers.

In July 1941, John had joined the US Navy Reserve. The Japanese had not yet bombed Pearl Harbor and Roosevelt was resisting Winston Churchill's constant pressure to bring the United States into the war against Germany. His health was not really up to it, but, as ever, Kennedy gall and Kennedy money won the day. He was soon having an affair with Inga Arvad – 'Inga Binga' as he called her – who was a dazzling journalist but also an anti-Semitic supporter of Hitler. She was the first of a long line of unsuitable women who would get the second Kennedy boy into trouble. There were rumours that she was a live-and-kicking Nazi spy and the FBI probed her activities. She wanted the Bureau's Director, J. Edgar Hoover, to clear her name officially but that never happened and she got no higher than Hoover's number two, Clyde Tolson. What was alarming – and what Kennedy did not know – was that the FBI was recording the trysts of the lovers, details that would start to fill the pages of Hoover's notorious 'black book' of celebrities' indiscretions.

Articles began to appear in Washington along the lines of 'the beautiful blonde spy and the ambassador's son'. When his father tore into him, Jack dropped Inga like a hot potato. The PT109 incident, later made into a movie starring Cliff Robertson as Jack, took place on 2 August 1943. There was no doubting his heroism or that he saved the life of at least one crew member. The exploit went down well at home, *Reader's Digest* printing an article that Joe would have reprinted in vast quantities when Jack first ran for Congress. Just over a year later, Joe Jr was killed when his PB-24 Liberator blew up over England. Joe Sr and Rose were devastated, but in reality, all the senior Kennedy's ambitions now focused on Jack. With his usual warped bitterness, Joe once said to Harry S. Truman, then still a senator who was backing Roosevelt, 'Harry, what are you doing campaigning for that crippled son of a bitch who killed my son?' Truman threatened to throw Joe out of the window.

It is by no means certain that Jack wanted to become a politician, still less president. He was bullied into it by his father. And he needed his father's cash. As Joe himself said, 'It takes three things to win. The first is money and the second is money and the third is money.' Everything was done under the counter so that there could be no finger-pointing at the never-popular elder Kennedy. Like all the children, except poor Rosemary, the boys developed a swagger and a recklessness backed by their father's wealth. If they got into trouble, they could always buy their way out. Only in the context of anti-Semitism did Jack refuse to sing from his daddy's hymn sheet. Joe Jr had been anti-Semitic too but there was none of this in Jack. Even so, the family cash poured in – $300,000 on Jack's first campaign – at a time when Jack himself carried no money with him at all and somebody else was buying drinks. By September 1948, Jack was in his second term as a Congressman.

In April 1952, he ran for the Senate, glad-handing and using the toothy charm offensive at which he was so good. He had thousands of women eating out of the palm of his hand and although Joe was still pulling strings, Bobby was now Jack's official campaign manager. In November 1954, Jack beat Henry Cabot Lodge for the Senate seat. The official cost of the campaign was $349,646; in practice, it probably ran into more than a million.

Two years earlier, John had met Jacqueline Lee Bouvier. She had 'First Lady' written all over her – looks, poise, articulacy. She had attended the Sorbonne in Paris and was Debutante of the Year. And if the family was broke, no one knew that at the time. She smarmed around Joe as much as she did around Jack and the pair were officially engaged in June 1953, the wedding following in September. 'They were both actors,' their friend Lem Billings said, 'and I think they appreciated each other's performances.'

Just as Joe had bank-rolled John's university thesis and his book *PT109*, he did the same with *Profiles in Courage*, a compendium of mini-biographies of great Americans. Jack wrote long-hand and was disorganized as a writer; his work was almost all from secondary sources and he lacked the patience for primary material. Much of the hard work seems to have been done by Joe and others. Columnist Drew Pearson wrote, 'Jack Kennedy … is the only man in history that I know who won a Pulitzer prize on a book that was ghost-written for him, which indicates the kind of public relations set-up he had.' Joe screamed that there was a plot against his family. It would not be the last. The old man allegedly paid *Time* magazine $75,000 to put John's face on its front cover in December 1957.

But tragedy struck too, one of many such incidents which gave rise to the 'curse of the Kennedys' which, some say, still continues. Jackie's pregnancy resulted in a still birth, Arabella, in Newport, Rhode Island.

By the late 1950s, John probably realized that he could not hide behind his father's money and his father's ideas for ever. He quietly brought in new aides, like the 'jester' Dave Powers, men of his own age rather than his father's dinosaurs from the 1930s. He had been diagnosed with Addison's disease in 1947, which is a failure of the adrenal glands and led to occasional weight loss. He joked that this was due to Jackie's cooking and, like a number of leaders of men before and since, did not want the press to know the truth. In the eyes of Joe, of course, it was a sign of weakness and failure.

The younger Kennedy announced his intention to run for president in January 1960. There was a rich irony, bearing in mind later White House shenanigans, that he said that the place must be 'the center of moral leadership'. A month later he met Judith Exner – the White House telephone system logged seventy calls between them. Exner was also the mistress of Sam 'the Man' Giancana (see Chapter 12) the Mafia boss with whom Joe had often done business. How much money Giancana 'donated' to Jack's presidential campaign is anybody's guess. As is the extent of the Mob's strong arm help in the campaign itself. Giancana expected reciprocity – 'one of these days, the guy will do me a favor'. But another Mob leader, Johnny Roselli, was more realistic – 'If I ever get a speeding ticket, not one of those fuckers [the Kennedys and their entourage] would know me.'

Joe telegraphed his son. 'Dear Jack. Don't buy a single vote more than is necessary. I'll help you win this election, but I'll be damned if I'm going to pay for a landslide!'

American politics is a messy business. It was – and is – all about money and the Kennedys shamelessly enlisted the aid of the Catholic Church to help fundraising. None of this was illegal, but it left a nasty taste in the mouth and tarnished what Jack had hoped would be a squeaky-clean presidency. From time to time on the campaign trail, he was ill. Addison's caused complications, his back troubled him and the gonorrhoea he had contracted at Harvard would not go away. It is by no means clear how rampant Jack's philandering was. He had already made one rash and quickly dissolved marriage (see Chapter 13) and allegedly could not keep it in his trousers any more than could his predecessor

Warren Harding in the 1920s. White House staff turned blind eyes and covered tracks, but Jackie knew about most of her husband's flings and for his sake dutifully kept quiet. She protected him fiercely, even after his death, demanding passages be cut from Paul B. Fay's biography *The Pleasure of his Company* and taking William Manchester to court over *The Death of a President*. She only gave one interview to the press in the thirty years after the assassination.

John's major opponent in the 1960 election was Richard Nixon. Today, the man who gave us the Watergate scandal could not get elected to a parish council, but all that was in the future. He was already far more devious than the Kennedys, but few people were aware of that. It was television that stopped him in his tracks. Aired to the 90 per cent of Americans who now owned a set, the debates showed Nixon at his worst. His five o'clock shadow looked dreadful under studio lights and he was running with sweat. Jack, by contrast, was cool and relaxed, all teeth and hair. Such things, of course, should be irrelevant in politics, but they are not. Kennedy was the first president to embrace the television era and the public fell for it.

His inaugural address was the second most quoted in American history – 'Ask not what your country can do for you. Ask what you can do for your country.' Incidentally, he nearly blew the whole thing by wearing a top hat and tails for the ceremony – it did nothing for him at all.

In *The Dark Side of Camelot* (1998), Seymour Hersh admits that his book is about the negatives. He consciously ignores the positives: Kennedy's will to descale Vietnam; his standing up to the USSR over the Cuban Missile Crisis; his tentative steps in the direction of Civil Rights, and looks at the murky side. Hersh contends that in the days after Jack's assassination, his brother Bobby, made Attorney General at the insistence of Joe, was frantically busy burning papers and otherwise destroying evidence of the ex-president's indiscretions. The problem was that too many people knew about them: J. Edgar Hoover at the

FBI; Allen Dulles, fired by Kennedy from the CIA; Lyndon Johnson, now in the White House himself. It would be impossible to cover it all up and because of that, the Kennedy reputation, the shining glory of Camelot, was doomed to be dragged through the mud.

And it all came crashing down in a little over six seconds that day in Dealey Plaza, Dallas, on Friday, 22 November 1963.

Chapter 3

Nightmare on Elm Street: Six Seconds in Dallas

The president was late. The city had turned out in their thousands for the visit of John Fitzgerald Kennedy. The rain of that Friday morning had gone and the sun was getting fiercer as midday neared. It had been a short flight from Fort Worth, where the president had made a speech. Air Force One, the presidential jet partly designed by Kennedy himself and piloted by Colonel Jim Swindal, made it in thirteen minutes.

The president himself had decided on the flight and the motorcade that was to follow. A drive would have been 'good logistics', he said, 'but poor politics' because Dallas, in a way, the whole state of Texas, was another world.

'I crossed the American border by jet yesterday,' Henry Brandon of *The Times* wrote, 'into hostile Texas with a small guerrilla band of White House officials, led by President Kennedy. As his secret weapon and perhaps also with his security in mind, he had brought Mrs Kennedy along.' At Love Field airport, Jackie's bright pink Chanel suit and hat shone in the sun. What Nellie Connally, the wife of Texas's governor, thought we do not know. She was wearing pink too, a PR woman's nightmare.

The president had summed up the impact of his 'secret weapon' in an impromptu speech at Fort Worth's Hotel Texas earlier in the day – 'Two years ago, I introduced myself in Paris by saying that I was the man who had accompanied Mrs Kennedy to Paris. I am getting somewhat that same sensation as I travel around Texas. Nobody wonders what Lyndon and I wear ...'

For the record, JFK was wearing a lightweight grey and blue suit with a blue striped shirt and blue silk tie. Vice President Lyndon Baines Johnson, aboard Air Force Two as they reached Love Field, also wore a dark suit and tie. Texas was Johnson's state, but unlike Governor John Connally, who met the president's party at the airport, he did not wear a Stetson to make the point. They gave Jackie a bouquet of red roses; Nellie Connally, the governor's wife had yellow, as did Johnson's wife, Lady Bird.

The motorcade through downtown Dallas was planned to last about eleven minutes and the last leg would be through the triangular park space of Dealey Plaza before the entourage sped up under the triple underpass of the railway bridge and on to the Stemmons Freeway en route to Kennedy's lunch destination at the Dallas Trade Mart. With the best laid plans that almost always go wrong behind the scenes, two men were temporarily left behind at Love Field. One was Major General Chester 'Ted' Clifton, Kennedy's military aide, and the other was the 'bag-man' carrying the notorious briefcase with which the president, as commander-in-chief could, at least in theory, start World War Three.

The Kennedys stopped to wave to crowds outside the airport mesh fence. Then, a Secret Service nightmare, they crossed to the fence to shake hands. As we shall see, there is considerable dispute as to whether the exact protocol and route of the motorcade were ignored. Kennedy, it was said, had wanted the blue Lincoln's bubbletop removed so that he could see the crowds and they could see him. His Press Secretary, Bill Moyers, told officials, 'Get that god-damned bubbletop off unless it's pouring rain.' The order was actually given by Secret Service agent Forrest Sorrels who, with colleague Winston G. Lawson, had planned the route. Lawson rode in the white Sedan of Police Chief Jesse Curry, in the motorcade's lead car ahead of the president's limousine. Sorrels was in the passenger seat behind him.

A glance at the route across Dealey Plaza (see plan) immediately raises a problem. From Main Street, it made sense to continue straight on along the centre of the three streets that converge under the triple underpass. The route was changed at the last minute (why and by whom has never been fully explained) so that the motorcade turned a dog-leg sharp right on to Houston Street and then left on to Elm. This was contrary to Secret Service regulations which stipulated that no turn sharper than 90 degrees should be made. The turn on to Elm was 120 degrees. The motorcade would have to slow to 5 miles an hour to negotiate this turn and the new route was widely publicized in both Dallas newspapers prior to Kennedy's arrival.

Responsibility for security along the route rested with Chief Curry and his deputy Charles Batchelor who worked with the Secret Service in this context. Dallas policemen were to be stationed on foot at every intersection, but in Dealey Plaza itself there were no extra police and no Secret Service agents at all.

The protocol of cars in the motorcade was not observed (see Chapter 12). A police car went ahead, a quarter of a mile distant from Curry's. Behind the chief were three motorcycle cops. Then came the blue Lincoln, gleaming chrome, glass and bodywork, with the presidential flag flapping. It should have been the seventh in the usual order of things. There were no Secret Servicemen directly with Kennedy in Dealey Plaza. One of them, Clint Hill, had clung on to the Lincoln along Main but was ordered back to the Secret Service car behind. The Press bus, bristling with state-of-the-art cameras to record the day, was eight cars back, almost useless in any attempt to film what was happening.

There were, of course, crowds all the way. Most were smiling and waving, carrying little Stars and Stripes flags and keen to see the president and the First Lady. Most, but not all. Various still and cine-film of the motorcade show scowls and empty, vacant stares. In the car, Nellie Connally turned to Kennedy. 'Mr President, you can't say that Dallas doesn't love you.' But, actually, he could.

One man who was definitely not smiling that day was Joseph Milteer. One of the many photographs taken of the motorcade shows Milteer standing outside the Dallas County Records Building on Houston Street. His horn-rimmed glasses and shock of white hair are unmistakeable. He has his shirt sleeves rolled and his arms folded, with a look of grim determination on his face. It cannot have pleased him that a black woman is standing next to him. This was because Milteer was an avowed racist who deeply resented the rise of the Civil Rights movement and may well have already done something about that. The Right had held sway in America in one way or another since before the United States existed, personified by its persecution of Blacks, its espousal of slavery and the 'Jim Crow' laws that followed the American Civil War. It was white supremacy that Kennedy was talking about when he referred to Dallas as 'nut country'. Milteer came from Georgia, more conventionally 'Deep South' than Texas and he was rich. Author Carl Oglesby, founder member of the Washington Assassination Information Bureau, claimed in his 1992 book *Who Killed JFK?* that Milteer had been involved in the bombing of a church in Alabama months before the assassination in which four black schoolgirls were killed.

On 9 November 1963, Milteer was in Miami talking to another right-winger, union fixer Willie Somersett. What Milteer didn't know was that Somersett was a police informant and he taped the conversation. Milteer can be heard predicting that Kennedy's assassination was 'in the works', that he would be shot with a 'high-powered rifle from an office building and that someone would be arrested within an hour of the shooting to distract the public from the truth'. Kennedy had been due to visit Miami on 18 November, but once the FBI received Somersett's tape, he travelled by helicopter rather than motorcade and Milteer was interviewed. Astonishingly, he was released without charge and at liberty to be standing on Houston Street scowling at the would-be target.

Somewhere near him, as the motorcade passed at perhaps 11 miles an hour, stood Arnold and Barbara Rowland at the entrance to the Dallas County Records Building. Barbara was near-sighted and not wearing her glasses and anyway, the sun was in the eyes of all the watchers on the east side of Houston. Arnold, however, clearly saw, shortly before the motorcade arrived, two men in the window of the sixth floor of the Texas Schoolbook Depository, 150 feet away to his right (see plan). This was the south-west window, the nearest to the corner, and what caught Rowland's attention was the fact that one of the men was carrying a rifle. He told authorities later that the rifleman was white, with short-cropped dark hair and weighed between 140 and 150lb (10–11 stone). He was wearing a light-coloured shirt open over a T-shirt, and dark trousers. The second man was black, almost bald and very thin. He appeared to be about 55 years old. Rowland assumed the pair were Secret Servicemen.

Richard Carr saw men on this floor too, although it was later unclear which window he was talking about. As a builder, he had climbed the scaffolding on the Courts Building at the north-east corner of Houston and Main, then undergoing reconstruction. One of the men he saw was thick set with a hat (de rigueur in 1963), a tan-coloured sportscoat and horn-rimmed glasses. At the time, he thought nothing of it. There were people hanging out of other windows in the Depository, as well as the various buildings along Houston.

Howard Brennan was standing on the south-west corner of Houston and Elm with the Depository directly ahead of him. The window that came to be known as the 'sniper's nest' was on the sixth floor, 120 feet away. He saw what police later described as a 'slender white male, 5ft 10in, early thirties', which is odd for two reasons. From the ground, it was impossible to tell how tall a man was six floors up. And Howard Brennan, like Barbara Rowland, had poor eyesight.

Photographs taken as the motorcade swung left on to Elm show the pavement outside the Book Depository swarming with people.

Joe Molina was the Depository's credit manager, a Dallas-born navy veteran who had worked at the Depository since 1947. He belonged to a veterans' club called the American GI Forum which the Dallas Police Department believed was 'possibly subversive'. The early 1960s were still riven with the anti-Communist hysteria personified by the Wisconsin senator Joe McCarthy. The senator had gone too far in his violent attacks on politicians, film stars and armed forces personnel in his fanatical hunt for 'reds under the beds' and had been dismissed. There were plenty in America, however, who shared his views. Two years before the Kennedy shooting, Kirk Douglas had hired the black-listed Communist scriptwriter Dalton Trumbo to write *Spartacus*, the story of the gladiator-slave who took on Rome. The script was based on a novel by Howard Fast. Hedda Hopper, the waspiest of Hollywood critics, wrote, 'It's a movie written by a Commie based on a book written by another Commie, so don't go see it.' Whatever Joe Molina's political views, much of Texas backed Hopper.

While he was standing on his front steps, Victoria Adams was looking out of the window four floors above, with her co-workers Sandra Styles, Elsie Dorman and Dorothy Garner. They saw the floating flags and the sun dazzling on the polished chrome of the president's Lincoln. The headlights on the cycles of the flanking policemen dazzled too and the noise of engines and the cheering crowd was momentarily deafening.

Steven Wilson was watching the whole thing from the floor below the women. He saw the First Lady's pink outfit and the white Stetson of Governor Connally raised in the air in acknowledgement of the crowd's cheering. He saw the president flick back his thick head of hair as the wind caught it on the car's turn. Somebody behind the car caught the same second on their Polaroid.

Chief Curry's white lead car, slowly picking up speed as it took the slope down to the triple underpass, flashed across the vision of Charles and Beatrice Hester. They had been waiting on the grass on the north side of Elm for a while and they were sitting down. The president would soon pass right by them, slightly below and he was on their side of the limo. This was something to tell their friends and neighbours in the days and weeks ahead.

The Newmans, William and Gayle, were slightly further along Elm, to the west. He was a young design engineer and they had their two little children with them, trying to explain to them who the president was and what all the fuss was about. The Stemmons Freeway sign was a little in their way, but by sitting or crouching, their view would be unimpeded. Newman noticed a man behind him standing on a low wall, supported by a woman who was holding his legs. The man had a movie camera in his hand.

That man was Abraham Zapruder and he would become the most famous eyewitness to events in Dealey Plaza that day. The dressmaker was 58 and had forgotten to pack his camera when he set off for work that morning. His secretary, Marilyn Sitzman, had urged him to go back and get it – 'How many times will you have a crack at colour movies of the president?' It was exactly 12.30 when he pointed his 8mm Bell and Howell camera at the motorcade and started filming, Sitzman steadying him from the ground.

To Zapruder's right, Emmett Hudson may have been the proudest man in Dallas that day. He was standing on the steps that led up to what William Newman called 'the grassy knoll' and would become the most infamous piece of real estate in the world according to author Michael Benson in *Who's Who in the JFK Assassination* (1993). Hudson would have been proud because he was the groundskeeper at the Plaza. The fountains, the water-course, the trimmed hedges and grass, all of it was down to him. And clicking cameras caught it all as the president passed by. Sitting next to Hudson was a man he did not know who told him that he had not been able to find anywhere to park, but had eventually found a place in the car park behind them, beyond a wooden fence and a line of trees. What Hudson did not know is that that car park had officially been sealed off by the police. The man told the groundskeeper that he worked on Industrial Boulevard, a few blocks away. When they saw the motorcade turn on to Elm, they both stood up ...

To the west of the steps, army cadet Gary Arnold had been trying to film the motorcade with his movie camera from a spot behind the wooden fence, using the crosspiece to steady his arm. But a man in a suit had moved him on, flashing Secret Service identification. Arnold was in the military, already used to taking orders and he moved accordingly.

Maggie Brown and her co-workers were nearby. They all worked for the *Dallas Morning News* and were determined not to miss the show. Ann Donaldson was alongside her and Mary Woodward was nearest to the fence, anxious to record what happened for the paper's readers.

Across Elm, to the east of the journalist's position, James Altgens, known as 'Ike', was a photographer for the Associated Press. Many of the photographs taken by him that day form a brilliant and detailed account of what happened and form the wraparound of this book's jacket. Further along from him, another cameraman stood ready, Orville Nix. He was an amateur with a camera, an air-conditioning repairman from the General Service Administration in the Dallas Secret Service building. Near him stood Mary Moorman with her Polaroid. She was standing with her friend Jean Hill directly opposite the grassy knoll. Hill was a teacher from Oklahoma City and did not know Dallas very well, so Moorman offered to show her around. Since she knew one of the motorcycle cops in the parade, she had a double reason for being in Dealey Plaza and admitted later that she was indeed playing hooky. Friday was just another school day.

The women had been waiting in the Plaza for about an hour, mostly in front of the Book Depository. The crowds there were getting too much for the narrow pavement and Moorman and Hill wanted to make sure their policeman friend could see them. They crossed Elm to the south side but were turned back by a cop. After a little flirting he waved them through and they took up a position so that the rather short Moorman could get a clear picture of Kennedy's outriders as they passed. The pair had planned everything carefully. Polaroids are tricky to use if more than one exposure is required. Moorman could take the photo. Hill would pull it out of the camera, coat it with fixative and keep it in her pocket. That way, they could take several shots. What they did not know was that at least three other people in Dealey Plaza that day were planning to take several shots too ...

The first shot sounded to many like a firecracker, but Jean Hill was not fooled. 'I know the difference between firecrackers, echoes and gunshots,' she told a symposium in Dallas in November 1991. 'I'm the daughter of a game ranger and my father took me shooting all my life.'

This shot, according to the Warren Commission, missed the car but we can see people's reactions to it from a frame-by-frame analysis of the Zapruder film, the most detailed depiction of an assassination in history. Kennedy had been looking to his left, beyond Jackie to the grassland south of Elm. At the sound of the shot, he turned to his right, looking at the grassy knoll. His waving hand came down. John Connally turned to his right too, checking on the president. 'Oh, no, no, no,' he called out, bringing Jackie's attention to her right.

Firing started at Zapruder frame 155, when there is a blurring of the film caused by Zapruder's shock. Although several witnesses claimed that the shots came from the Book Depository, an oak tree obscured the Elm Street view, at least from the soon-to-be-notorious sixth-floor window, the sniper's nest. A more practical trajectory would have been from the Dal-Tex building to the south-west of the Depository or the Court building next to it. Just after this first shot, the president's limousine disappeared behind the Stemmons Freeway sign from Zapruder's point of view and there is an infuriating split-second interlude.

It was then that the second shot exploded – another firecracker to some people in the crowd. Joe Molina, on the Depository front steps, thought that the shots came from the western end of the Depository, above and to his right. Victoria Adams and her co-workers all believed the second shot came from their right, in the direction of the grassy knoll. This shot hit Kennedy in the throat from the front; his hands come up instinctively in the Zapruder film. Next to him, Jackie recalled, 'All I remember is seeing my husband; he had a sort of quizzical look on his face and his hand was up ... I remember thinking he just looked as if he had a slight headache. No blood or anything.' Secret Service driver Will Greer was still looking at the road ahead. There was no attempt to hit the gas and speed up. The car was travelling at an excruciating 11 miles an hour.

This was Zapruder frame 188. What appeared in the film to be Kennedy's head jerking forward was actually his body jerking backward as the bullet hit him just above the tie knot. The brace he wore to counteract chronic back pain held him upright.

On top of the triple underpass, where they were not supposed to be according to the Dallas police, a number of witnesses saw smoke drifting from the fence area on top of the grassy knoll. In Mark Lane's *Rush to Judgement* in 1966, James Simmons told the author, '[The shot] sounded like it came from ... toward the wooden fence. And there was a puff of smoke that came from underneath the trees on the embankment directly in front of the ... fence.' At this point, the oak tree still blocked the view from the sniper's nest. Zapruder's film blurred again at this stage (frames 188–191). Governor Connally turned again in reaction to this second shot, which had actually whistled past him. By Zapruder frame 238, Kennedy's hands are raised as if to grip his throat. Connally was caught in the half turn. Jackie was looking with concern at her husband. The crowd, generally oblivious, were still waving. It was now that the Stemmons Freeway sign got in Zapruder's line of vision, but others, on the south side of Elm, were still filming. Phillip Willis caught the sign itself at the exact moment of the second shot. He also caught Umbrella Man, standing on the pavement opening and closing his black umbrella above his head (see Chapter 1) and the enigmatic images of Black Dog Man at the south-eastern end of the wall that ran on to the grassy knoll from the pergola. From Willis's perspective, the motorcycle outriders who were the objects of interest of Jean Hill and Mary Moorman, were still in position, showing no awareness of what was happening. On the car behind the Lincoln, the Secret Service were still in place, some of them standing on the running boards on both sides of their car, Paul Landis among them.

Governor Connally, along with many witnesses, heard the first shot. He did not hear the second, almost certainly because it came from a relatively open space ahead and not from the echo chamber of the Dealey Plaza buildings behind. He had just turned back to the front from checking on Kennedy where he felt the impact of the third bullet. This one hit the governor in the back, blowing out the front of his jacket (visible on the Zapruder film) before exiting his chest below his right nipple. The impact drove his right shoulder down and he folded to his left, towards Nellie. For a moment, he almost lost his grip on his Stetson, but managed to hold on to it with his right hand. 'I felt the blow from something,' he said later, 'which was obviously a bullet ... and ... I didn't hear but the two shots. I think I heard the first and the third shot.'

The fourth shot came from behind, either from the Book Depository or the Dal-Tex building, hitting Kennedy 6 inches below the shoulders and slightly to the right of his spinal column. On the Zapruder film, his body slumps forward and downward. His fists were still raised in response to the second shot throat wound. Charles and Beatrice Hester, north of Elm, only heard two shots. They came, they were certain, from the Book Depository. The Newmans nearby told Dallas reporter Jim Marrs, 'As [JFK] was coming towards us there was a boom, boom, real close together. I thought someone was throwing firecrackers. He got this bewildered look on his face ... then he got nearer to us ...'

The first two shots or at least the reaction to them, was captured by Ike Altgens who was clearly on the south side of Elm, leaning out into the street once Chief Curry's lead car had passed. Of the four Secret Servicemen on their car's running boards, three are half turning to the sound from behind, the Book Depository or Dal-Tex. Oswald lookalike Billy Nolan Lovelady is clearly in the Depository entranceway, as (presumably) is Joe Molina, although his body is obscured by a Secret Serviceman. The two visible police outriders to Kennedy's left were also half turning their heads. So were Lyndon Johnson and his wife Lady Bird in the car behind the Secret Service vehicle. Interestingly, Johnson's own Secret Service car, a white limo behind him, had its doors open, as though the occupants were pre-judging the moment. This was Zapruder frame 255.

The fifth, fatal, shot hit the president in the head. When the Zapruder film was finally shown to the public, years later, it caused understandable outrage and shock. Orville Nix captured the moment on his still camera too, as did Ike Altgens. Kennedy's body lurched *backwards* with the bullet's impact, clearly fired from the front and a cloud of blood and brain matter shot skyward. Union Terminal Company employee Sam Holland saw it all clearly from the top of the triple underpass. He distinctly heard four shots, one of which hit JFK on 'part of his face' (in fact his forehead, just below the hairline) and saw a 'puff of smoke [from] 6 or 8 feet above the ground right out from under those trees' by the fence on the grassy knoll.

At this point, as a number of witnesses pointed out, the president's Lincoln was virtually stationary, its brake lights on. 'There were flesh particles,' Altgens told the press, 'that flew out of the side of his head

in my direction where I was standing [on the south side of Elm].'
One of Mary Moorman's beaux, Bobby Hargis of the Dallas police,
literally felt the impact of this shot. Riding behind the limo's left rear
bumper, as the president had ordered, he was hit in the face by blood
and brains. Part of Kennedy's skull was clinging to his lip and he
thought, for a split second, that *he* had been hit.

In the split seconds surrounding this shot, both driver Will Greer
and his wing-man Roy Kellerman in the passenger seat, turned to the
president. Kellerman was on the car radio and Greer took a second look.
It was only after this that the Lincoln accelerated towards the triple
underpass. In that split second, Mary Moorman clicked her shutter on
Elm's south side. In that still, Kennedy had slumped sideways again.
We cannot see Hargis's blood-spotted face, but did she catch Badge
Man beyond the grassy knoll fence, lowering his rifle?

Major Phillip Willis, his wife, Marilyn, and daughter Linda saw the
impact of this fifth shot. 'I'm very dead certain that at least one shot
came from the front.' They saw the back of Kennedy's head blown out.

Still the shooting went on. An estimated six-tenths of a second
after the fatal head shot, a sixth bullet shattered John Connally's right
wrist and embedded itself in his left thigh just above the knee. He was
already in shock and pain from the first bullet that had hit him (the
second fired) and slumped sideways to be held by an appalled Nellie.

While this was happening, Jackie Kennedy carried out the most
bizarre single act in an extraordinary event. As she put it to the Warren
Commission months later:

And just as I turned and looked at [JFK] I could see a piece of
his skull and I remember it was flesh coloured. And then he
put his hand to his forehead and fell in my lap. I cried 'They
have killed my husband, I have his brains in my hand,' and
then I remember falling on him and saying 'Oh, no, no, no.'
I mean, 'Oh, my God, they have shot my husband' and 'I love

you, Jack.' I remember I was shouting. And just being down in the car with his head in my lap. And it just seemed an eternity. And finally, I remember a voice behind me or something and I remember the people in the front seat, or somebody, finally knew something was wrong and a voice yelling, which must have been Mr Hill, 'get to the hospital' or it might have been Mr Kellerman, in the front seat. I was trying to hold his hair on. But from the front there was nothing. I suppose there must have been, but from the back you could see, you know, you were trying to hold his hair on and his skull on.

Witnesses in the Plaza saw Mrs Kennedy scrambling out of her seat and clambering across the car's trunk. This is clear in the Zapruder film. At the time, many believed she was trying to get out of the scene of horror in the Lincoln, although opening the door would have been a slightly safer option. Others, who saw Secret Serviceman Clint Hill jump down from the car behind the president's and dash forward to leap on to the Lincoln, thought she was reaching out for his hand. He told the Warren Commission:

Mrs Kennedy had jumped up from the seat and was, it appeared to me, reaching for something coming off the right rear bumper … when she noticed that I was trying to climb on the car. She turned to me and I grabbed her and put her back in the seat and she lay there. I noticed a portion on the president's head on the right rear side was missing and he was bleeding profusely. Part of his brain was gone … [it] was exposed … one large gaping wound in the right rear portion of the head.

Jackie had been trying to grab a piece of her husband's skull in a desperate, frantic attempt to keep him alive – 'I have his brains in my hand.' She later had no memory of doing this.

Far too late, Will Greer hit the accelerator and the Lincoln jolted forward, disappearing in the sharp shadows of the triple underpass. Roy Kellerman radioed Chief Curry in the car ahead, who ordered him to get to Parkland Hospital. Twenty-six-year-old Ed Hoffman, a deaf mute, was standing in a unique position on the overpass on the grassy knoll side. He saw the Lincoln overtake Curry's Sedan and stop for perhaps half a minute to exchange instructions. Greer had no idea where Parkland was and needed the local man's input on that. In the back of the Lincoln, Hoffman could see the damage done to Kennedy. The back of his head had gone and what was left looked like 'blood jello'. Just as importantly, Hoffman saw a man with a rifle running behind the fence on the knoll. He wore a suit, tie and overcoat and threw the rifle to what looked like a railway worker who crouched behind a switchbox, disassembled the gun in seconds and hid it in a soft, brown bag. For various reasons (see Chapter 10) it would be twenty years before Hoffman's testimony came to light. Nobody would believe him until he told his story to researcher Jim Marrs.

The press car, far behind the killing scene, now sped forward, keeping pace with the Lincoln at 70 miles an hour. Merriman Smith was a White House reporter in that car. He was the first to spread the news of the shooting, for which he would later win a Pulitzer Prize:

Suddenly, we heard three loud, almost painfully loud cracks ... Gunfire ... the president's car, possibly as much as 150 or 200 yards ahead, seemed to falter briefly. We saw a flurry of activity in the Secret Service follow-up car ... Our car stood still for probably only a few seconds, but it seemed like a lifetime ...

He pulled out the radio's microphone, preventing any other reporters from using it. Journalism, like politics, is a cut-throat business.

Even before the Lincoln vanished under the underpass, photographers captured the response of the crowd in Dealey Plaza.

Motorcycle cops abandoned their vehicles and drew their revolvers. They ran up the grassy knoll along with dozens of civilians, who had heard the shots and seen the smoke from there. Some accounts claim that as many as 200 people ran that way, among them Jean Hill. She testified later, 'I thought to myself, "This man [the shooter] is getting away. I've got to catch him."' A motorcycle policeman nearly ran her over in the chaos and instinctively, she ran back to Mary Moorman, still lying on the ground. Moorman couldn't move so Hill went back alone. At the top of the knoll, a man grabbed her shoulder. 'You're coming with me,' he said. Hill refused to do that. 'I'm not very good at doing what I'm told.' The man flashed what looked like Secret Service credentials and was joined by a second man. They held her while rummaging through her pockets and fished out the photograph that Moorman had taken. 'Smile,' one of them said, 'Act like you're with your boyfriends.' She was frog-marched to the Records Building.

Today, the flurry of photographs taken in the sun of Dealey Plaza look surreal. Most people are running, either towards the grassy knoll or the Book Depository. Others, like the Newmans, are lying on the ground, in their case shielding their children. One man stands, carrying a home-made placard with the words 'S.O.B. Jack Kennedy' written on it. The first man to reach the top of the grassy knoll, who may well have seen the 'second gunman' running away, appears in a photograph, but never came forward and has never been identified.

Somewhere behind him ran Malcolm Summers. He was running up the grassy knoll when:

> I was stopped by a guy, a well-dressed person – he had a topcoat on his shoulder – he said 'Y'all better not come up here or else you could get shot.' He had a gun under that raincoat. All I could see was the barrel of it … I didn't argue with the man because there wasn't any reason to argue with him. He seemed in authority and was stopping people there …

James Tague had an altogether more unnerving experience. Standing on the south side of Elm near the triple underpass, he was hit in the left jaw by flying shrapnel fragments caused by a bullet coming from the grassy knoll (as he believed) and hitting the pavement nearby. The trajectory marks found later on the pavement were inconclusive; they could indicate a shot from the Book Depository. Tague's wound would later cause all kinds of problems for the investigators.

Thousands of people came to downtown Dallas and Dealey Plaza on Friday, 22 November 1963 to see President Jack Kennedy. And at least three of them had come to kill him.

Chapter 4

Trauma Room

Parkland Hospital had not, in 1963, won the national plaudits it has received today, but it was highly regarded and, most importantly, only four minutes away by car from Dealey Plaza, especially when that car was travelling at 70 miles an hour. Technically, however, it was not the nearest – Zale Lipshy was – and that decision in itself gave rise to a conspiracy theory. In various photographs, as the entourage arrived by 12.35, the building gleams cream in the autumn sunlight in that day's film footage. Parkland had moved to Harry Hines Boulevard, a mile from its original site, in 1954. A year later, a renal dialysis department was set up and in 1961 a state-of-the-art burns unit.

The scene was chaotic. A mass of people, police, Secret Servicemen, the FBI and the president's staff all jostling with medical staff trying to do their job. Jackie Kennedy sat in the Lincoln, which Will Greer had driven under cover off the hospital forecourt, refusing point blank to leave her husband who was still lying across her lap. Somebody, probably Clint Hill, threw a jacket over the shattered head to keep the press ghouls away.

In the front seat, John Connally had regained consciousness and tried to stand, bleeding as he was from chest, wrist and leg. He collapsed and was lifted on to a gurney to be rushed to Trauma Room 2. Nellie was holding his hand and whispering, 'It's going to be alright. Be still.' While somebody gently coaxed Jackie to one side, Secret Service agents Greer and Kellerman manhandled JFK on to another gurney. 'He's dead,' she was mumbling. The man who had helped them probably felt worse than anybody else except the

Connallys and Jackie; he was Secret Servicemen Winston G. Lawson, who had planned the motorcycle route in the first place.

Most of the press and many officials were kept out of the way once the gurneys were through the doors. Senator Ralph Yarborough, who had been riding in Lyndon Johnson's car despite loathing the man, had smelt gunpowder as his car went through the triple underpass. Shocked and helpless like everyone else, he wandered aimlessly around the parking lot waiting for news.

One man who was late to the horror show at Parkland was Admiral George Burkley, the president's doctor. He had ridden in one of the last cars of the motorcade and his driver, unbelievably, took him to the Trade Mart rather than the hospital. He was the only one who knew what medication Kennedy needed.

Five minutes earlier, at 12.33, Anne Ferguson had taken an emergency call on hospital switchboard #2: '601 Coming in on code 3; stand by.' 601 was the president's motorcycle escort; code 3 was an extreme emergency. The Secret Service code for Kennedy was Lancer; Jackie was Lace.

Lyndon Johnson's car arrived. He and Lady Bird were still lying on the floor where the bodyguard, Rufus Wayne Youngblood, had shoved them. 'I want you and Mrs Johnson to stick with me and the other agents as close as you can. We're going into the hospital and we aren't gonna stop for anything or anybody. Do you understand?' A shocked LBJ answered, 'Okay, partner, I understand.' The vice president would be surrounded by agents for the next hour. There may have been a coup underway – nobody was safe.

Dave Powers, Kennedy's aide, had been with the Secret Service in the follow-up car. He had known the president for twenty years and had fallen on his prone body crying like a baby. He had blood and brain matter all over him. Kenny O'Donnell, also from the White House, could not bring himself to look and watched as Connally was lifted on to the gurney.

It was now that the world heard the shattering news for the first time. On ABC Radio, the nation's sweetheart Doris Day was singing *Hooray for Hollywood* when Dan Gardner broke in with Merriman Smith's news. 'We interrupt this program to bring you a special bulletin from ABC Radio. Here is a special bulletin from Dallas, Texas. Three shots were fired at President Kennedy's motorcade today in downtown Dallas. Stay tuned to your ABC station for further details.'

Three shots. That was all Merriman Smith had heard. Now it was presented as fact on the radio. It would remain the central – and erroneous – fact of the Kennedy murder for years, clung to by the subsequent Warren Commission and all the conspiracy debunking whitewash that followed.

At Parkland, medical staff and patients saw the Secret Servicemen, some with submachine guns, and hit the floor, screaming in panic. Powers dashed off a note to himself (as if he needed to) in a pocketbook. 'I carried my president on stretcher, ran to Emergency Room #1. Jackie ran beside the stretcher, holding on.' Her pink suit was soaked in Jack's blood. When a nurse suggested she wiped some of this off, the First Lady remained stoical. 'Absolutely not. I want the world to see what Dallas has done to my husband.' That statement may have been extraordinarily perceptive.

Outside, as the press mob circled, desperate for any information, Senator Yarborough said, rather elegantly in the circumstances, 'Gentleman, there has been a deed of horror. Excalibur has sunk beneath the waves.' It was a poetic reference to the Kennedy administration known as Camelot (see Chapter 2); Excalibur was King Arthur's sword.

The first of a dozen doctors to attend the president was Dr Malcolm Perry, known as 'Mac'. He was 34 and was still chewing his lunch as he arrived. There was so much blood from Kennedy's head that there was a risk of slipping in it, and Perry threw his jacket over it, hauling on his white coat. There was no time for the niceties of scrubbing up, and Perry's first thought was that lying on the table in front of him was the most powerful man in the world. And his life was in Perry's hands. With as much cool efficiency as they could manage, doctors and nurses went about their business. English nurse Diana Hamilton Bowron was only 22 and had not been in Dallas, or even the United States, for very long. She cut away Kennedy's suit jacket and striped shirt, removing his back brace and slipping his watch, temporarily, into her pocket. She had helped the others bring him from the car. 'When I went round to the other side ... I saw the condition of his head ... the back of his head ... it was very bad ... I just saw one large hole.'

Kennedy was still just about alive, and Perry made the vital decision to cut a hole in the president's neck to insert a tracheotomy tube to help him breathe. The tube in his mouth he had just tried was not working. Inserting the tube, he cut through the small throat wound which had hit Kennedy from the front just above the tie. That single act of surgical necessity would confuse everybody and provide forensic ammunition for the official nonsense that followed. Dr Marion Jenkins, chief anaesthesiologist, was there when this happened. He too saw the ghastly head wound to the rear, the blueish face, and staring eyes. He had seen this before; it was a death look. It was the ridiculous little things that people remember at times of high tension like these. Dr Paul Conrad Peters was struck by the makeshift bandages holding Kennedy's back brace in place as Nurse Bowron removed them. Like the deathbed of Abraham Lincoln ninety-eight years earlier, the little trauma room was full of people: at least six doctors (more would arrive later), eight nurses and an unknown number of presidential aides and Secret Servicemen.

In the corridor outside, two traumatized women, both bloodstained, sat opposite each other. 'You always think of [Jackie],' Lady Bird Johnson remembered later, '... as being insulated, protected. She was quite alone [despite Nellie's presence]. I went up to her, put my arms around her, and said to her something like, "God help us all."'

Dallas Police Sergeant Robert Dugger had been on duty at the Trade Mart. Author William Manchester (in *The Death of a President*, 1965) describes him as 'bespectacled ... towering bullock of a cop with a beefy face and piercing eyes; To Jacqueline Kennedy, he looked rather ugly. [She wondered] whether he could be a Bircher.' The John Birch Society was a far-right extremist group, popular in Texas and among policemen. In fact, Dugger, like JFK himself, had served in the navy during the war and he was a Kennedy Democrat.

In Trauma Room 2, three doctors were working on John Connally. Ralph Patman would operate on the governor's thigh wound later that afternoon. They found a bullet wound in his back, to the right of the spine. Another (exit) wound under his right nipple and two more, one in the right wrist, the other in the left thigh. But there was too much blood, even with all of this and Dr George Shires asked 'How many times was he shot?'

'Once,' Connally said, making everybody jump because they had assumed he was unconscious! The excess blood was Kennedy's. As it transpired, the governor had been shot twice.

In the melee in the corridor, journalists Merriman Smith and Robert MacNeil of NBC were desperately looking for phones to relay updates to their station chiefs. The entire world, it seemed, was holding its breath.

And in that surreal half an hour in Parkland Hospital, health service administration ground on, unprepared to give way for anything. A receptionist asked Nellie Connally to fill out a form for her husband's admission. Nellie ignored her. In a private cubicle, the Johnsons were waiting, like everybody else, for news. Rufus Wayne Youngblood was with them, refusing to leave the vice president's side. No one was speaking.

At 12.45, Clint Hill and Roy Kellerman were on the phone to Gerald Behn, head of the White House Secret Service. Suddenly Robert Kennedy, the president's brother and Attorney General, came on the line. He had been told of the shooting, almost casually over the phone by J. Edgar Hoover, Director of the FBI. The hatred between Hoover and the Kennedys was widely known and entirely mutual (See Chapter 12). 'How bad is it?' Bobby asked Hill. 'It's as bad as it can be,' Hill told him. The Attorney General asked after Jackie and told Hill to get the president a priest. John Kennedy was the first Catholic to reach the White House. For some, that was a black mark against him.

Local television had now kicked in. WFAA-TV in Dallas was showing *The Julie Bennell Show*, discussing the coming winter's fashion, when programme director Jay Watson interrupted in person. He was out of breath because he had just run from the site of the shooting. 'Good afternoon, ladies and gentlemen; you'll excuse the fact that I'm out of breath, but about ten or fifteen minutes ago, a tragic thing by all indications has happened in the city of Dallas ...'

At Parkland, despite Nurse Doris Nelson's attempts to keep her out, Jackie walked into Trauma Room 1 with Admiral Burkley – 'I want to be there when he dies.' The nearest doctor to her was Ronald Jones. She nudged him and handed him a piece of her husband's skull, the piece she had retrieved from the back of the Lincoln. He passed it to a nurse; it would do the president no good now.

At 12.51, an English insurance salesman, John Ravenscroft, was reading a newspaper in the toilets of his office in Dallas when a report came through on the radio about the Kennedy shooting. He had met Kennedy on the campaign trail three years earlier and could not believe what he was hearing. He would go on to become something of an icon himself in the years ahead, as DJ John Peel.

The great and good of the city had congregated at Parkland. The hospital's PR man, Steve Landrigan, had just found the priest that the Attorney General had asked for and overheard the mayor, Earle Cabell, prowling the corridor, muttering, 'It didn't happen! It didn't happen!' He himself would face death threats in the days ahead and would end up under police protection. In the car park and on the grass of the hospital grounds, people were on their knees in prayer. The media were in overdrive, asking anybody if they had heard anything; Bert Shipp of WFAA asked Sheriff Bill Decker, who had ridden with Police Chief Curry in the motorcade's lead car, 'What's it look like, Sheriff?' 'Well, did you ever see a deer hit in the back of the head?' Decker asked him. 'There's nothing back there.'

Seth Kantor had been in the motorcade too. He was a reporter for the Scripps-Howard newspaper group and one man he bumped into at the hospital was Jack Ruby, owner of a Dallas strip club, the Carousel. Kantor knew him well. Somebody else who saw Ruby there was Wilma Tice – 'If it wasn't him, it was his twin brother.' In the many interviews he gave to the police in the days and weeks ahead, Ruby denied being anywhere near Parkland.

Dr William Kemp Clark, the hospital's chief neurosurgeon, had arrived by 1 p.m. Dr Jenkins called his attention to the president's head wound – 'My God, the whole back of his head is shot off.' Mac Perry was kneeling on a stool, pounding on Kennedy's chest to get his heart going again. It was Clark who said, 'It's too late, Mac. No, Malcolm, we're through.'

They pulled a sheet over the president and Charles Baxter, the trauma room chief, turned to Jackie. 'Mrs Kennedy, your husband is dead. We will not pronounce him dead until he's had the last rites.' They pulled out the tubes and the monitors and the First Lady kissed her husband goodbye. 'There were probably more tears shed in that room,' Baxter said later, 'than in the surrounding hundred miles.' But no one in the Republic National Life Insurance Company in Dallas was crying. When news of the shooting was announced, John Ravenscroft was horrified that most of his colleagues cheered and clapped. Dave Powers wrote in his notebook, 'My president is dead.'

Father Oscar Huber had arrived and pulled back the sheet from Kennedy's face. '*Si capax, ego te absolve a peccatis tuis, in nomine Patris, et Fili, et Spiritus Sancti. Amen.*' (If possible, I absolve you from your sins in the name of the Father and of the Son and of the Holy Ghost.) He made a cross on the president's forehead with holy oil.

Jackie thanked the priest for his words, but as he left the hospital, a sudden reality crept in. A Secret Serviceman said to him, 'Father, you don't know anything about this.' It was a pointless thing to say, because Huber, like the rest of the world, would talk about it for years and I have just written it, sixty years later. But it all adds to the almost childish need for officialdom to cover things up, which lies at the heart of the Kennedy assassination.

Clint Hill telephoned O'Neal's Funeral Home, ordering the best casket they had. It was the $4,000 'Britannia' bronze model.

Malcolm (Mac) Kilduff was the White House Assistant Press Secretary and he had the unenviable task of breaking the news to the press milling outside the trauma rooms. In a breaking voice he told them that Kennedy was dead. When asked, in a barrage of hysterical questions about the wounds, he pointed to his right temple where he had seen a bullet entry wound. This was the same bullet which took out the back of the president's head, a wound that umpteen people over the years, including gunshot experts, physicists and the Warren Commission, said did not exist.

To deter ghouls taking photographs of the Lincoln, still spattered with blood, the Secret Service first threw a bucket of water over it, then covered it in a sheet. Both actions destroyed vital forensic evidence. It was the new president, Lyndon Johnson, who ordered the car to be stripped and rebuilt. Today, debunkers deny this, claiming that these acts were invented by conspiracy theorists. What followed at Parkland was perhaps the most shameful incident in an appalling day. While a trio of nurses cleaned Kennedy up as best they could, replacing the blood-soaked sheets under his head, Roy Kellerman was already on the phone to the White House. A man tapped him on the shoulder. 'I am the Dallas County Medical Examiner, Earl Rose. There's been a homicide here; you won't be able to remove the body. We will take it down to the mortuary and have an autopsy.'

Kellerman refused.

With right and justice on his side, Rose persisted. 'Well, we have a law here whereby you have to comply with it …'

At that point, Admiral Burkley walked in and Kellerman explained the situation. 'We *are* removing the body,' Burkley shouted. 'This is the president of the United States and there should be some consideration in an event like this.'

Kellerman weighed in, 'You're going to have to come up with someone a little stronger than you, to give me the law that this body can't be moved.' That someone was the state's governor, John Connally, but John Connally, at that moment, was fighting for his life in Trauma Room 2.

Tempers were frayed and fists raised. Some accounts say that guns were drawn. All of this was because 182 years earlier, the bickering Founding Fathers created a weak and complex political system in which federal and state rights were allowed to exist side by side. Rose was right. A murder in Dallas should have been investigated, including an autopsy, by Dallas officials. Instead, White House staff bullied everybody. Kellerman had already failed to keep his president safe. Burkley would go on to throw his (unauthorized) weight around at the autopsy of a man he no longer served at Bethesda Hospital (see Chapter 6). In this author's opinion, both men were guilty of a cover-up.

In those chaotic corridors, as the powers that be squabbled over Kennedy's body and John Connally was being prepared for operation, hospital senior engineer Darrell Tomlinson was moving a gurney, not the one that took Connally to the operating theatre or the one used by Kennedy. On it, he found a used bullet lying. He showed it to O.P. Wright, a personnel officer formerly with the Dallas police. He tried to find an FBI agent, could not and put the bullet in his pocket. When Tomlinson gave this testimony to the Warren Commission, he was told he was mistaken. Was this the bullet that agent Landis now claims he placed there, the almost pristine bullet that would become the 'magic' one, WC Exhibit 399? Or was it another bullet altogether, that no one ever officially recognized?

The vice president, his wife and Jackie Kennedy were taken to Love Field airport in unmarked cars, at speed but without fuss. According to the Constitution, in the event of a president's death, his vice president would take over for the duration of his term of office. The fact that Kennedy and Johnson were about as far as it was possible to be and still remain in the same political party was an unfortunate wrinkle in the messy game of American politics.

Johnson went to Air Force One, not Two, with his wife, staff and the already ex-First Lady, still in her bloody suit. Agent Youngblood demanded that the plane's blinds be drawn, in case of snipers. As we have seen, a number of people that day feared that the death of Kennedy was part of a much wider coup (as was supposed to happen in the murder of Abraham Lincoln in 1865) and Youngblood was taking no chances. With this in mind, Johnson decided to take the oath of office now, on board the plane, so that the United States had a bona fide leader. In 1963 it was the height of the Cold War; Russia was the enemy and Russian-backed Cuba was only 90 miles away from the American mainland.

At 2.12 p.m., the president's casket was loaded on to the plane. It was too large and the Secret Service agents had to break off the handles. James Darrell, who had been in the press bus in the motorcade, tried to film this, but the camera was taken off him by a Dallas policeman. 'Let me have that! That's sacrilegious!' Darrell never saw the film again.

The transition of power from the Kennedy administration to that of Johnson was not all that easy. Youngblood was pushing his weight around, ahead of Kellerman. Malcolm Kilduff was anxious to wait until Johnson was sworn in. General Godfrey McHugh, JFK's military aide, who would be accused of being a conspirator later, snapped at him, 'I have only one president and he's lying back in that cabin.' Kennedy's body had been placed in the plane's bedroom, according to one report; in a corridor space in another. According to theorist David S. Lifton, while there, gruesome head surgery was performed to tamper with forensic evidence. According to Kilduff, McHugh and several others, the body was never left unwatched throughout its time on board.

The undertaker, Vernon O'Neal, arrived to take his white hearse back from the airfield. Over the next year, he sent several bills to Jackie for the casket. The White House eventually paid him $3,400.

Johnson's secretary scribbled down the words of the oath of office during dictation over the phone from Nicholas deBelleville Katzenbach, Assistant Attorney General. Johnson made sure the press were present for the hurried ceremony which meant that twenty-six people were crammed into the plane's stateroom. The air conditioning was not on. Sarah T. Hughes, an old friend of Johnson's and a High Court judge, was whisked from the Trade Mart to officiate. Jackie stood alongside LBJ as he intoned the words, the whole thing lasting half a minute. The new president was holding a missal, not a Bible in his hand, which some Catholics in the months ahead found ominous. Mac Kilduff recorded the whole thing and no one could have missed Johnson turning to Representative Albert Thomas, grinning and winking. To many, it was at best incongruous. To some, it was evidence of guilt.

'Now,' Johnson said in the Texas drawl many of Kennedy's staff had learned to loathe, 'let's get airborne.'

It was the start of a brave new world and the beginning of questions for which we still have no answers.

Chapter 5

Officer Down

Forty-five minutes after Kennedy was shot, another man died in Dallas. He was Dallas policeman J.D. Tippit and his links with the man accused of shooting him (if there were any) have still not been explained today.

The whole thing started immediately after the shots had been fired in Dealey Plaza. Police Dictabelt recordings clearly show that both Chief Curry and Sheriff Bill Decker gave orders over their phones to their men to investigate the grassy knoll area. Both men had heard shots from there, had seen smoke, and narrowly missed watching dozens of civilians swarming up to the fence at the top. One of the motorcycle cops – almost certainly H.B. McLain – had left his microphone stuck on channel 1, which was hindering effective communication between officers and the central dispatcher. This meant that his Dictabelt recorded the *actual* number of shots fired, not shocked witnesses' recollection.

At 12.30, Curry called the dispatcher. 'Get a man on top of that triple underpass and see what happened up there. Have Parkland stand by.' The technology was not good. Decker could not catch all that was being said to him. The dispatcher, as calmly as he could, relayed, 'Dallas. [Decker] I repeat. I didn't get all of it...' Decker ordered every available man to the railway yards behind the grassy knoll. Patrolman L.L. Hill reported over his radio, 'I have one guy [this was James Tague] that was probably hit by a ricochet from the bullet off the concrete ...'

Patrolman 137 Ed Brewer had been riding his motorcycle half a block ahead of the motorcade. Zapruder's film shows him clearly. He radioed, 'We have a man here who says he saw him pull the weapon back through the window from the south-east corner of the Depository building.' Later, Brewer could not remember who had told him this, but it might have been Howard Brennan. Within less than a minute, Patrolman 142 Clyde Haygood radioed, 'I just talked to a guy here who was standing close to [the Depository] and the best he could tell, [the shots] came from [the Depository] with that Hertz renting sign on top … If you're facing it on Elm Street, looking towards the building, it would be the upper right-hand window, the second window from the end.' His source is again likely to have been Brennan and it changed the police investigation direction at once. Haygood himself had dashed up the grassy knoll, so why he crossed to the Depository is unclear. In those crucial minutes, a potential killer was making his escape beyond the railway tracks, while dozens of policemen had their attention diverted to the Depository.

Sergeant D.V. Harkness, who had called the ambulance for Jerry Belknap who had had a fit outside the Depository a quarter of an hour earlier, was told by another witness of a shooter on the fifth floor. The witness was probably Amos Euins, a 'little Black boy' of 15 who actually saw *two* men in the window, one of whom was black. Harkness ordered his men, arriving fast, to seal off the building. In fact, that never happened. He dashed inside and at the back where there was a loading bay and exit not visible from the front, he saw two men who claimed to be Secret Service. Harkness did not ask for ID and probably did not realize that all Secret Servicemen, at least according to the official line, were with the motorcade. Harkness was a busy man that day. Under orders from Inspector Herbert Sawyer of the Dallas police, he arrested the three hobos found in the railway car trucks (see Chapter 1), which gave rise to all kinds of misinformation. In fact, misinformation seems to have been Sawyer's stock in trade. At 12.44, he told the dispatcher, 'The wanted person in this is a slender white male, about 30, five feet ten, 165 pounds, carrying what looks to be a 30-30 or some type of Winchester.' Sawyer later could not remember who gave him this information – 'He was a white man [80 per cent of Dallas inhabitants were] and he was there,' was all he could say. Half an hour later, Sawyer was talking nonsense again. What kind of idiot, having shot the president, would walk about Dallas carrying his rifle? Sawyer had no answer for that.

Captain Cecil E. Talbert had an altogether better grip on things, telling his men via the dispatcher to search other buildings, too. A brief look up Elm Street must have convinced him that both the Dal-Tex Building and the County Records Office could have provided a shooting platform. With the shots ringing out as the motorcade turned on to Elm, all eyes followed the cars. No one was looking at either of these buildings.

The dispatcher then broadcast to all units a message that would have been relayed instantly to every officer in the city – 'Attention all squads. The suspect in the shooting at Elm and Houston is supposed to be an unknown white male, approximately 30, 165 pounds. Slender build, armed with what is thought to be a 30-30 rifle – repeat – no further description at this time.'

As things turned out, no further description was needed. That dispatch was probably enough to get Officer J.D. Tippit killed.

One of the many men in Dallas answering the dispatcher's description was Lee Harvey Oswald (see Chapter 7) who had been working for a few weeks as a stockman in the Texas School Book Depository. Mrs Carolyn Arnold, a co-worker, had seen Oswald about a quarter of an hour before the assassination in the lunchroom on the building's second floor. He was eating his lunch alone on the right-hand side of the room. This was 12.15 when Arnold Rowland, outside the County Records Building on Houston Street saw a man with a high-powered rifle in the south-west corner of the Depository. If Arnold and Rowland are right about the time (and why should they not be?) the sniper on the sixth floor could not have been Oswald.

At an estimated 75–90 seconds after the shooting, the first policeman in the Depository was Motorcycle Patrolman Marrion L. Baker. He had been behind JFK's car in the motorcade and had seen pigeons flying up from the Depository's roof as the shots rang out. He swung his bike back and rode up Elm, drawing his revolver and bumping into Roy Truly, the Depository's manager and the two of them ran to the elevators, both of which were stuck on the upper floors. They dashed up the stairs and on the second floor, Baker caught sight of a man in the lunchroom. Baker beckoned him over. 'Do you know this man?' the cop asked Truly. 'Does he work here?' 'Yes,' Truly told him. 'He works for me.' The pair continued up the stairs. In the report Baker wrote the next day for the FBI, he said that Oswald was drinking a Coke from the vending machine. These words were crossed through, although Mrs Elizabeth Reid saw Oswald with the Coke two minutes later, by which time he was making his way towards the main entrance.

The official version, which has been challenged many times, is that Oswald left the Depository by the front door (despite there being a virtually invisible rear exit which would have been more sensible for a fleeing assassin). Henry Wade, the decidedly average – and some said shady – District Attorney of Dallas, muddied the waters considerably the next day. His statement read:

A police officer [Baker] immediately after the assassination, ran in the building and saw this man [Oswald] in a corner and started to arrest him, but the manager of the building [Truly] said that he was an employee and was alright. Every other employee was located but this defendant, of the company. A description and name of him went out by police to look for him.

The second half of this is riddled with errors. Baker was not about to arrest Oswald – on what charge? He was by no means the only employee of the Depository to leave the building; in fact, including those who did not turn up for work that day at all, twenty-three were missing from Truly's later roll call if one was actually held. And other companies used the building too. The police did not know Oswald's name until they arrested him later in the day.

Officially, Oswald walked along Elm Street, where it ran east into the grid of the city and caught a bus at the corner of Murphy Street (see map) which took him back along Elm in the direction from which he had come. Needless to say, he was not carrying a rifle or anything that could have been mistaken for one. Sitting on the bus was Mary E. Bledsoe, who knew Oswald because she had rented a room to him the previous month. 'He looked like a maniac,' she told the Warren Commission, 'and his face was so distorted.' This is undoubtedly taken from memories of television photographs after Oswald's arrest, when he had been beaten up by the police. And it is likely that she knew Oswald for another reason, not discovered until her death six years later which we will discuss below.

Oswald, realizing that the bus was caught in gridlock traffic chaos, got off at Lamar Street and walked towards the Greyhound bus station. Here he saw a cab but courteously let someone else arriving at the same time get on it. William Whaley was just about to leave his cab to buy some cigarettes when he saw a fare flagging him down. 'May I have a cab, sir?' he asked. He got in next to Whaley and the driver made small talk about the police sirens, wondering what was happening. Oswald did not say a word other than the destination he wanted – 500 North Beckley. Whaley commented later on how casual Oswald was, but he must have got his timings wrong because he claimed that he picked him up at 12.30. In fact, Oswald was still in the Depository dining room at that time and no shots had been fired, let alone police sirens sounded.

Whaley's route took them along Houston Street to the viaduct that crosses the Trinity River and on to Zayn Boulevard. According to the cabman, he dropped Oswald along Beckley at 12.45. Oswald paid the $1 fare for the 95-cent ride. He then doubled back to his boarding house at 1026 North Beckley, a red-roofed bungalow owned by Mrs Earline Roberts. According to her testimony, Oswald arrived about 1 p.m., clearly in a hurry, and was in his shirt sleeves. He stayed for a few minutes in his room, during which Roberts saw a police car with the number 107 on the side waiting outside. It had two men in it, and the car sounded its horn twice – 'ti-tit' as she described it – and left. Oswald put on a grey zipped jacket and left the house. According to various reports that followed, he had a snub-nosed .38 Smith and Wesson stuffed into his waistband. She saw him briefly standing by a bus stop on the east side of the street, but when she looked again, moments later, he had gone. Mrs Roberts, like much of Dallas, had been watching television coverage of the assassination when Oswald arrived – 'Isn't it terrible about the president?' All she got from Oswald was a grunt.

According to the official version (made so by the Warren Commission), Oswald walked down Crawford Street and turned left on to 10th Street. From there, he may have seen a patrol car, the typical dark Sedan, numbered 10, with Patrolman Tippit sitting in it. He may or may not have seen Helen Markham at the corner of 10th and Patton Avenue. She was on the opposite side of the road from him, a waitress waiting to cross the road. Markham's evidence to the Warren Commission has Oswald walking past her and Tippit's car approaching from his rear and pulling up alongside him. Had Tippit heard the dispatcher's generic description of the Elm Street shooter and was he being ultra-diligent? To be the cop who caught the man who killed the president would be a huge feather in his cap.

Oswald leaned into Tippit's car and chatted to him. Then he pulled back as the officer opened his door. Tippit walked slowly towards the front of the car, at which point Oswald pulled a gun and fired three times. Tippit collapsed in the road near the car's front left wheel and his killer 'in a kind of a little trot' headed down Patton towards Jefferson Boulevard.

Virtually opposite Tippit's parked car was Domingo Benavides, a car mechanic. He was driving past when he heard shots and pulled up about 25 feet away. The gunman was walking towards Patton, apparently removing cartridge cases as he went. Revolvers do not eject cartridges – the whole bullet leaves the chamber of a .38 revolver. What Benavides may have seen was Oswald reloading, in that five slugs were found in the gun's chamber when he was arrested. Benavides dashed to Tippit. The officer was lying on his side, his gun already drawn, and he appeared to be dead. What is odd about this is that according to her, Helen Markham was there too and that Tippit tried to talk to her. In fact, he had a fourth bullet in his head and would not have been able to do this.

Benavides tried to use Tippit' s car radio, which at first he could not work and the call came through a little after 1.16 p.m. Along from him, eyewitness William Smith saw no such thing. He heard shots up the road and saw a man running west. It was not until several days later he told his story to the FBI, by which time Oswald's photograph had been all over the media and any possible identification by Smith would have been worthless.

William Scoggins was also nearer than Smith. He was a cab driver, parked on the east side of Patton facing north, near the corner of 10th Street. Shrubs got in the way of seeing the shooting but he heard the shots and saw a man coming towards him – 'I could see his face, his features and everything plain … kind of loping, trotting … He had a pistol in his left hand … I heard him mutter something like "Poor damn cop" or "poor dumb cop." He said that over twice.' He later identified the man as Oswald.

Barbara and Virginia Davis were sisters-in-law who lived at No. 400 at the corner of 10th and Patton. They heard shots and ran, rather bravely, to their front door. A man was running across their lawn, dropping shells as he did so. Two of these they found later in the bushes and gave them to the police. Virginia ran to Tippit's car and remembered the passenger window, which Helen Markham had said was open, was in fact closed. Both women identified Oswald, but once again we have the palpable inconsistency of revolvers and bullets, and the fact that Oswald's face became common property within hours.

Further along Patton, in the direction that Oswald officially took, Ted Callaway claimed that he also rang in the shooting using Tippit's car radio and he did not mention Mrs Markham or Benavides. He saw a man with a gun in his hand. He was muttering 'Poor dumb cop' under his breath. Sam Guinyard was nearby. He was a porter at the local used-car sale room and saw the gunman – 'Oswald' – tuck his gun into his waistband and untuck his shirt to cover it. Across the road on Jefferson Boulevard as Oswald turned left along it, four other men, watched events unfold. Warren Reynolds certainly saw a man running, but he could not identify him as Oswald. Not, that is, until he was shot in the head in his used-car dealership (see Chapter 11), after which he changed his mind. Harold Russell was there too and, like Reynolds, could not identify Oswald. According to *Spotlight* magazine, Russell 'was beaten to death by a policeman using a revolver on July 23 1965 in Sulphur Oklahoma' (see Chapter 11). One of his co-workers was B.M. 'Pat' Patterson, with the Reynolds Motor Company. The FBI claimed that Patterson had recognized the shooter he saw as Oswald from a photograph. Patterson said he had seen no such photo. L.J. Lewis was the fourth employee. His time frame did not agree with the others, believing he saw the man 'several minutes' after the shots, but his description of the gun as an automatic makes sense in the context of ejected shells mentioned by others. Oswald did not carry one.

Along Jefferson, Mary Brock, the wife of another car mechanic, saw a white man, 5ft 10in, wearing light-coloured clothing with his hands in his pockets. He cut between two buildings opposite her viewpoint across a parking lot where a light jacket was later found. Was Oswald trying to change his appearance because too many people had seen him? Or was he afraid that he had Tippit's blood on his clothing? He was now walking south-west along West Jefferson and it was 1.40 p.m.

Johnny Brewer was the manager of Hardy's shoe shop. He had been listening to the newsflash of the shooting of a policeman nearby (as if the Dealey Plaza news was not enough) and saw a man pass his window, turning away as a police car drove past. The man dashed into a cinema, the Texas Theater, where *Cry of Battle* and *War is Hell* was the double bill, with the actor, Van Heflin as the star attraction. Brewer waited until Oswald was inside, then crossed the road and talked to Julia Postal, the cashier. Oswald had sneaked past her, not buying a ticket, and Brewer suggested she call the police. It was now 1.45 p.m. and it had taken the killer between twenty-four and twenty-nine minutes to make the short walk from the scene of the Tippit crime. No one ever explained why.

Brewer and usher Warren 'Butch' Burroughs checked the bars on the fire exits. It was too dark in the cinema to see anybody clearly; the projectionist had the same problem. The police were there in record time, dozens of armed officers bristling with determination. Nothing energises a policeman more than the death of another policeman, and they were ready for anything. Officer Jim Leavelle told researcher Joseph McBride years later, 'What some people don't realize is that when a police officer gets killed, that takes precedence over the shooting of the president, because that's close to him' – which is probably all we need to know about the Dallas police. With the cops' arrival, inevitably a crowd was forming outside the cinema. The house lights came halfway up and Brewer rattled one of the side doors, only to be dragged outside by an officer who stuck a gun in his stomach. The projectionist, shocked, shut down the film and the house lights came up fully. Brewer pointed out the man he had seen sneaking in, but officers cleverly approached two men sitting nearby and Officer

Nick McDonald told them to stand and frisked them for weapons. 'A moon-faced man with dark skin and a high forehead,' according to author Jim Bishop, McDonald was in fact bald. He turned his attention to Oswald, who said, 'Well, it's all over now.' He raised his hands and punched the cop between the eyes and pulled his gun. McDonald had the speed and instinct to stick his thumb and forefinger between the hammer and primer. Somebody hit Oswald from behind with a shotgun butt and he was handcuffed for what turned out to be the rest of his life. He carried the marks of this scuffle – a gash to his right temple and a swollen and bruised left eye – until he died. 'Kill the president, will you?' somebody shouted in what sounded like a bad line from a B movie. 'Don't hit me any more,' Oswald shouted. 'I am not resisting arrest. I know my rights. I want a lawyer.' In fact, he never got one.

Assistant District Attorney William Alexander was the kind of man who found it hard to keep out of the limelight. Often wearing a Texas Stetson and with a .30 automatic at his hip, he looked more like a Western stuntman than a serious prosecuting attorney. He certainly had no definite right to be at the scene of the Tippit shooting, the Texas School Book Depository or arrest of Oswald in the cinema, all of which he was. A crony attorney, Elmer Gertz, claimed that Alexander carried a gun because it was, 'A symbol to him of the strength of the law'. If American law derives its strength from the barrel of a gun, then the country was in a worse state than anyone realized. He once described his politics as being 'just to the left of Little Orphan Annie and just to the right of the John Birchers'. As much as Alexander might have like to use that gun on Oswald if he tried to break his way out of the cinema, he did not get a chance. 'Let's have him!' the crowd roared. 'We'll kill him!' An old lady hit Oswald with her umbrella.

In the car between two officers racing for Dallas police station, Oswald said again, 'I know my rights. What is this all about?' They told him of the murder of Tippit. 'Police officer being killed?' Oswald said. 'I hear they burn for murder.' C.T. Walker, riding with him, replied, 'You may find out.'

But there were two eyewitnesses who never gave their full testimony to either the Dallas police or the Warren Commission. Acquilla Clemons lived in a house four along from the corner of 10th and Patton and saw the whole thing. There were *two* men talking to the officer, and one of them shot him, before they fled in opposite directions. The shooter was 'kind of a short guy and kind of heavy' which of course ruled out Oswald. The other man could have been him – tall and thin, in khaki trousers and a white shirt (although allegedly he was wearing a pale jacket by this time). When Dallas police finally found her, they told her to keep her mouth shut because she 'might get hurt'.

Another witness who managed to stay under the radar was the occupant of a red Ford Falcon parked six cars away from Tippit. On the day in question, he was seen by both Domingo Benavides and Acquilla Clemons, and was known to live nearby at Sunset Manor in Oak Cliff. He was Igor Vaganov, known as 'Turk' who had a number of aliases and was a Latvian from Philadelphia who had moved to Dallas two weeks earlier. He had applied three times to be moved by his company, the General Electric Credit Corporation, and when all requests were turned down, he resigned and moved anyway. Every day, Vaganov dressed as for the office and spent the day doing ... who knew what. He had married a shop girl, Anne Dubin, after a whirlwind romance and told her that he was looking for a job. A committed racist, he hated 'n*ggers and Jews'. On the morning of the assassination, Vaganov changed his usual routine and slept in until midday. His landlady remembered that when he went out, he was wearing a white shirt and khaki trousers. He left the house at 12.45, delighted to hear of Kennedy's death and watched television. At 12.50 he suddenly went out, ostensibly to the bank. He never arrived.

Of such are conspiracy theories made. Vaganov was certainly odd and deeply unpleasant, and he owned guns, one of them a .38.

Inquiries by the FBI and the investigative journalists of *Esquire* magazine, however, turned up the fact that Vaganov was a con man with a history of theft and embezzlement in Philadelphia and had 'acute fuzz paranoia' (a fear of police). He did not object to having his photograph taken and was prepared to confront Dallas witnesses who might recognize him. It may simply be that his shady lifestyle (he was a bigamist, too) may have precluded him from going to the police with whatever he might have seen on 10th Street.

J.D. Tippit's body was taken to the nearby Methodist Hospital. All the many photographs of the crime scene, with his car still parked, were taken afterwards. Conspiracy theorists have found it odd that he was not in Dealey Plaza with nearly all his fellow officers that day, but a city the size of Dallas has to be policed in totality. As Michael Benson, the author of *Who's Who in the JFK Assassination*, says, 'Tippit's death may be the least-investigated homicide of a police officer in history. It was just assumed that Oswald shot him.'

Inevitably, Tippit himself came under scrutiny. It did not help that there were *two* officers with the same surname in the police department, and the J.D. did not stand for Jefferson Davis (the president of the 1861–5 Confederacy) as many have claimed, but were simply initials in their own right, rather like the S in President Harry S. Truman. Neither did it help that nightclub owner Jack Ruby, who would kill Oswald two days later, lived nearby – although Warren Commission apologist Gerald Posner, of course, claims that it was the *other* Tippit who was known to Ruby – and that both Tippit and Oswald were said to have drunk coffee at the local Dobbs House restaurant. The Warren Commission discovered that Tippit worked part-time at Austin's BBQ (many police officers did similar work to augment their limited salary; Tippit was on a pitiful $480 a month) and his boss was a member of the John Birch Society. There is no doubt that the average white cop in Dallas in 1963 was, to say the least, conservative. Their attitudes had virtually no links with the liberal America of, say, John Kennedy.

Jack Tatum came rather late to the story of the Tippit shooting. He told the House Select Committee on Assassinations in 1977 that Helen Markham was anxious to catch the 1.12 bus to take her to work. If she was confused about the time (and Helen Markham was an hysterical and unreliable witness) then she could not possibly have seen Oswald shoot the officer. What Tatum saw was a young white male walking near a squad car, both pointing east along 10th Street. He saw the male lean over the passenger side (à la Markham) with his hands in his pockets. As Tatum drove past, he heard three shots in quick succession and saw the officer lying on the ground. The gunman stopped, went back and fired a fourth time. Tatum's version actually supports Markham's. According to him, there was no second short shooter and the gunman could have been Oswald.

Tippit was born in Annona, Texas in September 1924 of English ancestry. He was raised a Baptist and served in the Second World War in the 17th Airborne Division, seeing action as he crossed the Rhine in March 1945. He won the Bronze Star. Trying his hand at ranching in Texas did not work, and he joined the Dallas police in July 1952. He was cited twice for bravery.

The autopsy report, under the jurisdiction of the Honourable Joe B. Brown, Justice of the Peace, was carried out by Medical Examiner Earl Rose, presumably still seething over his rough handling by Secret Servicemen at Parkland earlier in the day. The cause of death, unsurprisingly, was gunshot trauma to the head and chest, with bullet penetrations of lungs and liver, and extensive brain damage. The autopsy paperwork shows that copies were sent to District Attorney Henry Wade, Sheriff Bill Decker, Capital John 'Will' Fritz of the Dallas police and, oddly, Fire Chief C.N. Penn. All this was sanctioned at 3 p.m. and the body was to be released to the Dudley Hughes Funeral Home. Tippit was still warm when the medical examiner went to work, and rigor mortis had not set in. There were four bullet entry wounds, all measured vertically from the top of the head, with careful evaluation of wound size and position.

The head wound was tracked using a probe, and the likelihood was that it was fired downwards while Tippit lay on the ground. This was probably the last shot fired, for which the gunman specifically returned to the body. The toxicology report showed no abnormalities, and Tippit's blood type was A. The body diagram showed the position of the bullet wounds together with measurements. The head diagram showed the same, but confusingly it was referred to as 'Wound #1'.

This simple report, running to some fourteen pages, two of which are diagrams, is precisely what would have been written by Rose on Kennedy's body had he been allowed to carry out an autopsy on the president. Instead, as we shall see in Chapter 6, we have the nightmare confusion of Bethesda Naval Hospital, where a mixture of incompetence and egotism led to the most abject failure in modern forensic science.

What caused controversy in the murder of J.D. Tippit was the bullets. Rose's autopsy was clear enough, but the ballistics were a different story. Sergeant Gerald Hill of the Dallas police was in the thick of things. He had been present at the Book Depository shortly before 1 p.m. and was on the sixth floor when the sniper's nest was found behind packing cases. He left the building and on his way out met Assistant District Attorney Bill Alexander. The call came through over the police radio that there was an officer down in Oak Cliff. Hill, Alexander and Tippit's immediate boss, Sergeant Calvin 'Bud' Owens drove to the scene. Tippit's body had already been removed, so Hill and the others roamed the area looking for a potential suspect and Hill was handed an empty package of Winston cigarettes by Officer J.M. Poe. The carton contained three shells given to him by the shooting witness, Domingo Benavides. Like all policemen, Hill knew that revolvers do not eject shells. So, if the Benavides/Poe shells came from the shooting, the killer was using an automatic. It was standard practice for a middle-ranking officer like Hill to mark evidence with his initials, as would be evident later; Benavides had found two shells but Poe's cigarette packet contains three. Hill was clearly making it up later that afternoon when, in a taped radio interview, he said that the murder weapon was 'a .38 snub-nose that was fired twice and both shots hit the officer in the head'. By this time, of course, Oswald had been arrested with just such a gun. The murder weapon had been fired five times, not twice, and there was only one shot to the head. In the Texas Theater, Oswald's revolver was fully loaded.

Hill's volte-face in the question of guns and bullets has raised huge questions and is bread and butter to conspiracy theorists, as was the behaviour of Tippit himself. Even for an 'officer at large', he was out of his area in North Oak Cliff, as opposed to Oak Cliff nearly a mile away. He did not respond to calls from the dispatcher in the minutes before his death and was seen waiting (for what purpose?) in the car park of a gas station for nearly ten minutes. He drove off at high speed and lied to his dispatcher about his position at 12.45. 'I'm about Keist and Bonine View.' No, he was not. At 1 p.m., Tippit left his car and went into a record store, Top Ten Records, and made a phone call. Apparently, no one answered and he left in a hurry.

According to eyewitness testimony, Tippit pulled over a car along 10th Street, not in the usual way of sounding his siren, but cutting across the car's front, stopping his own vehicle at an oblique angle. The driver was an insurance salesman, James Andrews, but Tippit merely checked the interior of the car and drove off. There was no record of this incident, largely because Tippit was dead six minutes later. He stopped his car so abruptly that a driver behind collided with him, yet Tippit did nothing about this and drove to the kerb at 10th and Patton.

The timing of the shooting was crucial. Oswald had been seen by his landlady, Earline Roberts, standing at the bus stop near her house at 1.04 p.m. T.F. Bowley, driving past Tippit's parked car at 1.10, saw the body and a crowd around it, the shooter having gone. Earl Rose's estimate pinpointed the murder at between 1.00 and 1.15 and the call from Benavides over Tippit's radio was timed three minutes after that. If Mrs Roberts' timing was right – and Bowley's – Oswald could not possibly have shot Tippit; the bus stop was a mile away from the shooting. There would have been no time for him to have had a casual chat with the officer before killing him.

In its own way, the murder of J.D. Tippit was as convoluted and suspicious as that of Kennedy. We shall look at it in more detail later.

Chapter 6

Bethesda

The scenes at Parkland Hospital in Dallas as medical professionals rushed around trying to save John Kennedy's life and then trying to explain to a shocked and bewildered world why they had failed, were chaotic enough. But they were as nothing to what happened at Bethesda Naval Hospital in Maryland during the autopsy on the president of the United States.

Bethesda, of course, should never have happened. Technically and legally, Kennedy should have been autopsied by Dallas Medical Examiner Dr Earl Rose. Because of the illegal actions of the Secret Service, backed by the FBI, matters were taken out of Rose's hands and placed in those of a relative amateur – Dr James Humes – whose professionalism, on that terrible night, has to be called into question.

Kennedy's body was flown in a casket aboard Air Force One and routed to Bethesda at the request of Jackie Kennedy. JFK had served in the navy during the Second World War and his own personal physician, George Burkley, was an admiral. In fact, he was the *only* doctor to be present at both Parkland and Bethesda. His role was pivotal, but he signally failed to provide the integrity and expertise which should have been routinely expected of him. It was Burkley who signed the death certificate with the infuriatingly vague phrase 'the president was struck in the head'.

At one point in the assassination of Abraham Lincoln, there were at least seventeen people crowded into the small room where the president's autopsy was carried out in April 1865. At Bethesda, there were nearly thirty. Three doctors were ultimately responsible for carrying out a forensic investigation, but who was actually in charge is very much open to dispute. Some of the most crucial evidence of what happened at Bethesda comes not from medical personnel but from two FBI agents, James W. Sibert and Francis X. O'Neill. Although it can be argued that neither man should have been there, their presence turned out to be vital because their report did not square with the official version of the autopsy as reported by the three wise monkeys, doctors James J. Humes, J. Thornton Boswell and Pierre A. Finck. All three men held naval or army rank which in itself has raised issues. In the medical fraternity, forces doctors are not held in the highest esteem and Humes was not a forensic pathologist; neither had he any experience with an autopsy involving gunshot wounds.

Continually interrupted and pressured by high-ranking navy and army officials, as well as CIA and NSA agents, Humes panicked and made mistakes. He made no attempt to contact the Dallas doctors to find out what they had observed when Kennedy was wheeled in to Parkland. He assumed that the tracheotomy site in the throat was just that, rather than an enlargement of a bullet entry wound from the front. When it came to the wound in Kennedy's back, he failed to track the bullet's path using probes (a basic procedure carried out on Lincoln a century earlier) and claimed that he had been told not to by an unnamed general who might actually have been Admiral Burkley!

J. Thornton Boswell remembered Humes exploring Kennedy's back wound with his finger, giving a penetration of 1 or 2 inches. Miraculously, this bullet entry lined up with the 'exit wound' in the president's throat, giving rise in part to the nonsensical 'magic bullet' hypothesis of the Warren Commission (see Chapter 10).

Of the three doctors, only Finck was experienced in gunshot wounds. He was chief of the Wound Ballistics Pathology Branch and was called in to the autopsy room as a consultant. He remembered Humes asking who was in charge and an army general told him, 'I am.' Finck seems to have been as easily cowed by the flash of the top brass as Humes – 'You have to coordinate the operation according to directions.' He admitted that his focus was the president's body and he did not pay much attention to who else was there or in what capacity. This is, to say the least, a pity, because the presence of anonymous officials screams conspiracy and plays into the hands of the obsessionists who see skulduggery in the most random and innocent cloud patterns. Finck remembered being told by Admiral Kinney that no one was to discuss the case under threat of court martial. Someone else told the doctors not to dissect the neck (why is not recorded) which of course left open the dichotomy of the throat wound/tracheotomy site for all eternity.

Finck's testimony revealed everything that was wrong with a military autopsy – non-medical personnel making arbitrary decisions over the heads of scientific experts. 'When you are a lieutenant in the army,' Finck wrote, 'you just follow orders.'

None of this would have mattered quite so much had Humes not personally burned the autopsy notes he made at the time. Contrary to all protocol, he destroyed documents concerning the murder of the president of the United States, specifically, he said, because Kennedy's blood stains were on the pages. He was told to do so by Admiral Burkley. Conspiracy theorists had a field day; who *really* told Humes to do that and what were they hiding?

A series of photographs was taken as the autopsy was performed, which ought to have been an accurate recording of what went on, but, as with the Zapruder cine-film of the assassination, the camera can (surprisingly easily) be made to lie. A cine-film was made by Lieutenant Commander William B. Pitzer of the navy, which is odd because his name does not feature in the official list of those present. Pitzer was found dead in his office at Bethesda on 29 October 1966 with a .45 calibre pistol beside him. This is one of several suspicious deaths in the context of the Kennedy killing which we will discuss in Chapter 11.

Humes explained that (as was usual in head shot cases) the president's brain was removed and placed in a container with a formalin solution. What *should* have happened is that the brain should have been dissected to track bullet trajectories, but there is no record of this happening. Is that because the actual trajectories would not be in line with shots from the rear (the Book Depository) which would eventually become the Warren Commission's conclusion?

Forensic photographer Robert Groden testified before the House Select Committee on Assassinations in 1976 and in his book *The Killing of a President* (1993) discusses each of Kennedy's wounds in detail. The throat wound, described as 3–5mm in size by Dr Malcolm Perry at Parkland, had been enlarged by the tracheotomy incision to help the president breathe. If that was a bullet exit wound, Nurse Margaret Hinchcliffe of Parkland said she had never seen another like it (and she had seen many). She stoically maintained this even when bullied by Arlen Specter, the rottweiler attorney of the Warren Commission who invented the magic bullet theory. It is reaction to this wound (from the front) that we see in Zapruder's film. Just before the Lincoln disappears momentarily behind the Stemmons Freeway sign, Kennedy's hands come up to his throat.

The back wounds were vital if it was to be maintained (as it was by the Warren Commission) that the president was hit from behind by a lone gunman. Autopsy photographs and the testimony of Admiral Burkley show a bullet wound 5 or 6 inches below the neck, between the shoulder blades and to the right of the spine. Humes's autopsy drawing (see plates) shows the same. This is consistent with a bullet hole in both Kennedy's jacket and shirt. For this back wound to match the 'exit wound' to the throat, however, it had to be placed higher by at least 4 inches. Various artists' diagrams made for the Warren Commission show these false wound positions (see diagrams in this book).

Nothing was more contentious, however, than the head shot. Part of the problem is that layman's and doctors' language is significantly different (see diagram). Occipital and parietal merely become the back and top of the head in layman's terms. Groden assembled the evidence from a number of medical professionals and eyewitnesses to the shooting and its aftermath which is so universally similar that it cannot be ignored (except, of course, by the Warren Commission). In Dealey Plaza, Beverley Oliver, the 'Babushka Lady', told reporters, 'The whole of the back of his head went flying out of the back of the car.' Husband and wife Phillip and Marilyn Willis were standing on the north side of Elm Street (Phillip took twelve photographs as the motorcade passed). He said, '[The shot] took the back of his head off.' Marilyn saw 'a red halo. Matter [was] coming out of the back of his head.' Ed Hoffman, who saw what were almost certainly assassins on the grassy knoll, told reporters, 'The rear of his head was gone, blasted outward.'

At Parkland, there was universal agreement. Doctors and nurses in Trauma Room 1 had at least twenty minutes with the dying president during which time they saw the extent of the head damage. Dr Charles Crenshaw described the rear exit wound as the size of a baseball. Dr Robert McClelland – 'It was in the right back part of the head – very large ... a portion of the cerebellum fell out on the table as we were doing the tracheotomy.' 'Right there,' reported Dr Peters, pointing to his own head, 'occipital parietal.'

Adding in the testimony of others, we have clear evidence (as per the Zapruder film) of a fatal head shot from the front which blew out the back of Kennedy's head. That was why Jackie was crawling back over the limousine's trunk to grab a piece of her husband's skull. It was also why Dallas police outriders, on either side and slightly to the rear of the car, were hit with blood and brain tissue. And it was why teenager Billy Harper was able to pick up a piece of the president's skull 25 feet from the position of the Lincoln. For reasons that are unclear, the 'Harper fragment' was handed over to the chief pathologist at Methodist Hospital, not Parkland. It was clear evidence of the damage done because it came from the occipital part of the skull (an area completely undamaged according to the official Warren Commission photographs).

The existing photographs of Kennedy's body show ample evidence of falsification. The body is held upright by gloved hands (presumably Humes's, Thornton's or Finck's) and not, as might be expected, with the president lying face down. This distorts the back wound position. The back of Kennedy's head shows a small entry wound, near what is usually referred to (annoyingly and unmedically) as the 'cow lick area', rather than the gaping hole testified to by *all* Parkland personnel. Robert Groden, with his photographic expertise, has identified how this was done. The lower portion of Kennedy's hair, between the ears and down to the neck, is dark auburn and dry. Above that, it is wet and virtually black. This is evidence of a matte insert having been substituted. While the photograph taken from the top of the head, with the camera in line with the morgue table shows a tangle of hair and brain tissue, the photograph of the *back* of the same skull shows a head intact except for the entry wound (placed there artificially by tampering) and a flap of skull out of place above the right ear.

In the world of forensics and bullet trajectories, a missile travelling *downwards* (as it would have done from the Book Depository's sixth floor) would have exited Kennedy's face and left considerable evidence from an exit wound. No such wound was commented on at Parkland, nor is it apparent in the autopsy photographs.

But perhaps the most bizarre point about the autopsy is Dr Humes's comment that it looked as though surgery had been performed on the top of the president's skull and fairly recently. It has never been adequately explained what Humes saw and what he was talking about, but it led David S. Lifton, one of the most respected of conspiracy theorists, into an unlikely and convoluted cover-up which has all the hallmarks of a crime thriller. In *Best Evidence* (1980), a mighty tome that runs to over 700 pages, Lifton outlines a scenario to explain the dichotomy between various autopsy photographs, drawings and X-ray photographs and the reality of events in Dealey Plaza. The bombshell comment by Humes is referred to by FBI agent James W. Sibert, present at the autopsy that 'a missle [sic]' had been removed from JFK's body. Lifton's theory has not been accepted by medical experts.

Because the FBI agents were outside the White House 'inner sanctum', it has been assumed that they were conscientious observers of events; we have no idea whether this was so. They watched in the autopsy room on Bethesda's seventeenth floor as the president's body was taken from the casket and placed on the table. His naked body was wrapped in a sheet with additional wrapping around the head, which was how it left Parkland. It was Sibert who wrote, 'it was also apparent that a tracheotomy had been performed as well as surgery of the head area, in the top of the skull.' This, Lifton contends, is evidence that a bullet was removed from the president's head before Humes saw it. Perhaps, but why? To cover up the fact that this bullet, which blew out the back of Kennedy's head, had been fired from the front. But the colossal damage to the back of the skull could only have been caused by a fragmentary or 'dum-dum' bullet which shatters on impact. There would have been no 'missile' to remove, merely fragments of lead.

How could such surgery have taken place? Where did it happen? And who carried it out? Kennedy's body was placed in a casket and manhandled on to Air Force One where it was placed in the president's bedroom (or elsewhere). The flight time from Dallas to Bethesda was about four hours (long enough for surgery to take place) but a number of people, including Jackie Kennedy and the president's friend David Powers, were in and out of the bedroom throughout the flight. The only person on board remotely qualified to remove a bullet or attempt head surgery was Admiral Burkley, but are we seriously expected to believe that he had all the equipment necessary to carry out such an operation and that no one saw him do it?

One alternative theory is that the body was taken to Andrews Air Force Base and smuggled (avoiding the ever-intrusive Press Corps of course) on to a helicopter and taken to a more suitable space than Air Force One and the operation carried out. The whole thing is so far-fetched to the extent that Lifton and others have done nothing but muddy the waters in the Kennedy case. There would simply not have been time to 'doctor' the president's wounds before the autopsy. Manipulating photographs and X-rays however is another matter and there is compelling evidence that was exactly what was done.

When Malcolm Kilduff, the president's acting Press Secretary on the trip, told reporters what he had just seen in Parkland, he pointed to an entry wound to the right temple. This was described by various doctors as 'just below the hairline'. A frangible bullet fired from the front would enter at this point and explode in Kennedy's brain, causing the huge wound at the back of the head. But none of the photographs of the president's face show any damage to the forehead. The X-ray photographs, however, do, with a section of the skull in that area badly damaged. Jerrol Custer took the X-rays himself and did not recognize the versions he was shown five weeks later by the Ramsey Clark Panel which was investigating the forensic evidence. By that time, of course, the president's brain was missing and has never been found.

There were so many anomalies in the Bethesda autopsy that only a Congressional enquiry had the clout to set up an investigation. This became one of the worst-managed and most blatant cover-ups in American history – the Warren Commission.

Chapter 7

'Oh Ruby, for God's sakes, turn around'*

The Bethesda autopsy took place that night, but to return to Dealey Plaza earlier in the day, the police focus had shifted from the grassy knoll to the Book Depository. The original building, erected in 1899, had three storeys and was built by the Southern Rock Island Phone Company when Dallas was still essentially cattle country. Struck by lightning two years later, it was rebuilt in Romanesque period style with an extra few floors, and from 1940 it had been used by property developer D. Harold Byrd and was the headquarters of Sexton Tools.

It was only in 1963 that the School Book Depository had moved in from the Dal-Tex building across the corner of the Plaza. The upper floors had sustained damage from oil seeping from storage in the years before this and at the time of Kennedy's assassination, workmen were operating all over the sixth floor, laying new floorboards and 'leaving the scene in disarray, with stock shifted as far as the east wall and stacks in between piled unusually high'. There is no mention of construction workers being in the building on the day in question.

For those (like the Warren Commission) who believed that this was the site of the 'sniper's nest' it made an inconvenient and surprisingly public setting for slaughter. It should be pointed out that the sixth floor was one large open space running the length of the building. It was not subdivided into separate rooms (see diagram). A number of DPD officers, Secret Service and FBI combed each floor

---

* Chorus from *Ruby*, Waylon Jennings, 1966.

of the Depository and three of them found a rifle on the ground between packing cases. This was on the west side of the sixth floor, almost the entire length of the building from the alleged shooting position. Dallas County Deputy Sheriff Roger Craig testified that the weapon was a 7.65 Mauser; apart from anything else (like years of experience with firearms) it had 'Mauser' stamped on the butt. His colleague Eugene Boone saw the same weapon, as did Seymore Weitzman, who was not only a deputy constable, but owned a gun shop! Yet another police report stated that the gun found was a .303 of the type issued to the British Army. The final report, issued by the Warren Commission, as the definitive version, was that it was a 6.5 Mannlicher-Carcano bolt action with an unfired slug still in the breech. Are we talking about three different guns on the sixth floor and if so, how was a lone gunman supposed to fire them? The only other explanation, if there was only one rifle, is that Craig, Boone and Weitzman all got it wrong or somebody switched guns. At the time, a photograph was taken of two police officers handing a gun down from the roof to the seventh-floor fire escape. It was examined in the street and was not a Carcano.

There was a sweep of the Plaza by the police, who talked to the still-shocked eyewitnesses and even made one or two arrests. But there was no search of the vehicles in the car park beyond the grassy knoll, even though it had been supposedly sealed off by police, and was actually owned by the Dallas Police Department!

It must have occurred to some that the Dal–Tex building was just as likely a 'sniper's nest' as the Depository and two men were arrested there in the aftermath of the shooting. One was 23-year-old Larry Florer coming out of the County Records Building, another likely shooting platform. He was photographed being searched by police and was allegedly drunk. He said that he had been on the third floor looking for a pay phone and had been at a BBQ diner on Pacific Street and had heard about the shooting on the radio. Pacific Street is just under a mile from Dealey Plaza. Inexplicably, Florer was released after questioning.

Altogether more suspicious was Eugene Brading who usually went by the name of Jim Braden. He was found in the Dal-Tex Building with no good reason to be there. Like Florer, he claimed to be trying to find a phone and like him, was released. No checks were made on him by the police or they would have discovered that he was on parole at the time with a rap sheet of thirty-five arrests for burglary, embezzlement and bank robbery. His driving licence, newly issued in September, was a fake. *So* crooked was Brading that some have claimed that he was an assassin. He certainly had unfortunate connections, both with the underworld and Texas oil.

Various photographs taken in the Plaza show enforcement officers searching for forensic clues. Bullet marks on tarmac and kerbstones and in one case, a bullet, were all examined. Deputy Sheriff 'Buddy' Walthers had spoken to James Tague hit by flying concrete from a shot near the triple underpass. He found the bullet mark that had caused the wound and was photographed ten minutes after the shooting on the south side of Elm. He is with two men in suits, one of whom bends down to retrieve what was almost certainly a bullet. Either way, the assumed FBI agent pocketed the evidence and it was never seen again. In the days ahead, the kerbstone with its bullet mark was removed and replaced.

By mid-afternoon, an increasing number of law enforcement officers had been told and even came to believe, that they had their man. Officially, Lee Oswald was charged with the murder of Patrolman Tippit, but the evidence was stacking up against him for the killing of the president too. The buzz of media activity around Dealey Plaza, Parkland Hospital, the Tippit murder scene, the Texas Theater and Dallas police station was extraordinary. Everybody, from newspapers, magazines, radio and television were all over the police, jostling for position, pestering anybody they thought might know something. By the evening, most of American media had sent or were sending reporters. By the next day, the rest of the world had arrived.

In 1965, the results of an extraordinary sociology survey on the Kennedy assassination were published. Stanford University experts quizzed a large cross-section of American society to ask, among other things, how people heard the news in the first place. Mostly, it was word of mouth, although the constant stream of television and radio coverage provided much more detail, with newspapers coming a poor fourth. With what we now know, this survey seems extraordinarily naïve. Harrison E. Salisbury, the editor of the *New York Times*, congratulated himself glibly by concluding '... in any event, the editors had achieved their purpose; to provide a detailed, objective [*sic!*] and inclusive record against which all future official versions and unofficial rumors might be evaluated and confirmed or disproved.' In 1965, *all* major American media outlets sang from the Warren Commission's hymn sheet. We shall see why in Chapter 14.

One of the best-known conspiracy books on the case is *Oswald Talked* by Ray and Mary La Fontaine (Pelican 1996), but did he? For a suspect supposedly accused of killing the most powerful man in the world, we have no idea what Oswald told his interrogators, which is itself, bizarre. At first, there was no repetition of the deplorable bickering over jurisdiction we have seen at Parkland. Oswald was interviewed by John 'Will' Fritz, the Dallas police captain, an experienced and qualified cop with thousands of interrogations to his credit. He had already seen the Carcano at the Depository and now proceeded to grill Oswald.

Jonathan Mayo, in his book *The Assassination of JFK: Minute by Minute* (2013) reports dialogue between Fritz and Oswald which is odd, because (incredibly) Fritz made no tape recording of the conversation and based his later written reports on rough notes (which was hardly police procedure and does not square with someone of

Fritz's experience). Those notes were never made available to the public. The interrogation took place in Room 317 in City Hall (which housed the DPD). Fritz had been in the job so long that he was part of the posse that hunted down and killed the tearaway gangsters Bonnie and Clyde in 1934. He was softly spoken and habitually wore, as did nearly all his detectives, a white Stetson.

The captain took a number of phone calls during this interview. One was from Guy F. Rose who had questioned Oswald before Fritz took over. Oswald had given the name 'Alek Hidell'. Rose made the call from Ruth Paine's house in Irving. Paine was a friend of the Oswalds, particularly his wife, Marina, and she had arranged for the TSBD job to become available to Oswald. Marina was staying with Ruth Paine at the time and Fritz wanted to know if Oswald owned a rifle. Paine's answer was 'No', but Marina (speaking in Russian to Paine), said that he did.

It was now that the FBI intervened, unable to keep their noses out. Oddly, the murder of a president was not a federal offence, so technically, the FBI had no right to intrude. Probably, Fritz needed all the help he could get and agent James Hosty muscled his way into Room 317. He introduced himself to Oswald who accused him of harassing his wife (which, in a way, he had). On 12 November, Oswald had left Hosty a note at the Dallas FBI office – 'cease bothering my wife. If you have anything you want to learn about me, come talk to me directly.'

Fritz was asking questions about Oswald's career in the Marines and was especially interested in his shooting ability. Oswald told him he was a marksman, which meant something very specific in the military and had a different connotation for civilians. A marksman was the lowest level of shooter in the Marines. When Oswald's service record was checked later, his success rate on the range was below average. Fritz asked him why he carried a gun into the Texas Theater. This was a redundant question in a state like Texas, where men took the Second Amendment – the right to bear arms – very seriously. He denied shooting Tippit; his only crime, he said, was hitting Officer McDonald during the scuffle.

By 4.10 p.m., Fritz had gone as far as he could at that point. Oswald was taken by the detectives for an ID parade, inching their way through a mob of reporters, all of them hoping for a scoop and shoving their microphones up Oswald's nose. He was wearing a white T-shirt and dark trousers, his bruises obvious. He had not seen a doctor or a lawyer.

'Did you kill the president?' someone asked him, proving, not for the first or last time, the idiocy of the press. 'No sir,' Oswald said, 'I have not been charged with that.' He said that the first he had heard of it was on his way down the corridor, from a journalist. Five .38 calibre bullets had been found in Oswald's pocket, as well as the full chamber in his revolver. At that stage, the police were probably confident that slugs in Tippit's body would match that weapon.

The prime witness for the line-up was Helen Markham, who, as it turned out, was a spectacularly poor observer of homicide. She would later tell the Warren Commission that she saw the shooting at 1.15 but she had caught her bus at 1.12; the times clearly did not match. From the time the Dallas police took her to the station, she was initially hysterical, convinced that the killer would see her and could exact vengeance. Officers assured her that it would all happen behind glass and she would not be visible. Markham's testimony to the Warren Commission indicates her – continued – confusion. She told counsel questioning her that she did not recognize anybody in the line-up. Her answers implied that she was of very limited intelligence and her evidence did not square with other eyewitness accounts. Nevertheless, in common with other police forces who have already made up their minds about a suspect, this was called a 'positive identification' (the Warren Commission's words). The actual line-up was borderline illegal. Four men were selected, two in suits and ties, two in casual clothes. From their photographs, they are all older than Oswald and one of them is blond. Above all, only Oswald had a battered face. He was number two of the five and Markham hesitantly picked him out. That could be because Oswald lost his composure and ranted at the unfairness of it all. Even so, his claim that 'They've had me in this [T-shirt] for days' was nonsense; at this stage he had only been in police custody for three hours. This was the only time that Oswald lost it; otherwise, he was rational, calm and polite. Helen Markham, by comparison, had been lying down in a darkened room, sobbing, having fainted after identifying Tippit's killer.

By the early evening, Captain Fritz had brought Marina Oswald to the station to identify the Mannlicher-Carcano found at the Depository. Reporters filmed Lieutenant Carl Day of the DPD carrying the weapon high over his head, complete with its serial number C-2766. He had scratched his initials on the stock, as Patrolman Poe claimed to have done with the shells found near the Tippit shooting scene (see Chapter 5). We will look in detail at Marina Oswald later, but for now, she merely told Fritz that it looked like it, with dark wood and a telescopic sight, but was not sure.

Shortly after 7 p.m., Judge David L. Johnston was brought to the station to charge Oswald, that he 'unlawfully, voluntarily and with malice aforethought killed J.D. Tippit by shooting him with a gun'.

'This isn't an arraignment,' Oswald said. 'This isn't a court. How do I know this is a judge?'

Assistant District Attorney Bill Alexander, the gun-toting cop wannabe told him to shut up and listen. Nowhere is the lack of integrity of law enforcement more obvious than in Bill Alexander. At 7.50, Oswald went through a second line-up. This time his accuser was construction worker Howard Brennan and the identification centred on the Book Depository and the shooting of Kennedy. Brennan was more concerned that he and his family might be targeted and clearly did not buy the 'lone nut' philosophy to which the Warren Commission later proscribed. Nobody at this stage knew about Brennan's poor long sight and nobody seems to have questioned how he knew that the man he saw six floors above him was 5ft 10in. Brennan was not sure when he saw Oswald that he was, in fact, the man in the window. Police assured him that they had Oswald for the Tippit murder anyway, so his testimony did not matter much. The Warren Commission used it anyway.

After this, Oswald was led back through reporters on the third floor and came out with the most famous single line in the whole story of the Kennedy killing – 'they're taking me in because of the fact I visited the Soviet Union. I'm just a patsy!' Shortly after 9 p.m., Sergeant Peter Barnes of the DPD tested Oswald by making a paraffin cast of his hands to determine whether he had fired the Carcano. Nitrate tests to hands and cheek were negative, although his hands showed a slight residue, possibly caused by handling newspapers or other objects from the Depository. Unaware of this and for reasons of his own that we will look at later, the new president, Lyndon Johnson, rang Captain Fritz – 'You've got your man. The investigation is over.' With all the anomalies in this case, there are still, astonishingly, some people who still say that today.

Bill Alexander cranked up the right-wing Texas rhetoric in a meeting with *Dallas Times Herald* newsman, George Carter. The wording the DA would have liked to put in the newspaper was 'Did then and there voluntarily and with malice aforethought, kill John F. Kennedy by shooting him with a gun in furtherance of a communist conspiracy'. Alexander had personally searched Oswald's room in North Beckley (once again exceeding his authority) and had found copies of *The Worker* and other Communist literature. He had no evidence of a Communist plot and his case against Oswald, even as a 'lone nut', was extremely weak, but that did not stop him from telling reporter Joe Groulden of the *Philadelphia Inquirer*, 'Yeah, we're getting ready to file on the communist son of a bitch.' In Texas, in 1963, the spirit of Joe McCarthy was still very much alive.

At 11.50, the police arranged a press conference at the station in City Hall. Reporters had been there since lunchtime and it was time to establish some parameters. Alexander mouthing off about a conspiracy, especially indicating communists, could have serious international repercussions at the height of the Cold War. 'Was there any indication,' somebody asked, 'that this was an organized plot or was there just one man?' Henry Wade, the District Attorney, replied, 'There's no one else but him,' which gave the Warren Commission its raison d'être and shut down forever notions of justice, common sense and free speech in the United States of America. One man at the press conference was John Ravenscroft, the future DJ John Peel. He posed as a reporter from the *Liverpool Echo* and claimed that his friend was a cameraman. There was no camera, not even a journalist's notebook, but Dallas police had been told to accommodate the press. Ravenscroft was just being nosey. But no one checked IDs; so much for the security on that maddest of days in Dallas. They brought Oswald up into the room and let the press question him. It was very brief and the suspect was in maximum security cell F-2 by 12.20, with guards on his door. By now he had been photographed and finger printed. The press conference continued with Henry Wade taking most of the media flak. 'Any organizations that [Oswald] belongs to that you know of?' 'The only one mention was the Free Cuba movement or whatever.'

Someone from the back called 'That's Fair Play for Cuba, Henry.'

That someone should not have been there, any more than Ravenscroft should. He was a nightclub owner called Jack Ruby. And he was carrying a .38 Colt Cobra revolver under his jacket.

Other than Oswald himself, no one is more controversial and convoluted than the man who killed him. That said, conspiracy theorists have almost certainly read far more into Jack Ruby than there actually was and we have to try to untangle it all.

Jacob (Jack) Leon Rubenstein, known as 'Sparky', was born in March 1911 in Chicago and, still a child, became included in the Mob that dominated the city (and several others) in the 'Roaring Twenties'. This was the age of the bootleggers and the speakeasies, with prostitution, illegal alcohol and protection rackets a way of life for many people. Hollywood cashed in on it a decade later with anti-heroes like Jimmy Cagney, George Raft, Edward G. Robinson and Humphrey Bogart swaggering across the big screen in their 'tough-guy' personas. Ruby ran numbers for Frank 'The Enforcer' Nitti, Al Capone's right-hand accountant, and many years later moved to Dallas where he opened a strip club called the Carousel, employing girls known as 'dancers' who were actually part-time prostitutes. Volatile and prone to bursting into tears, Ruby was also a tough nut. He did his own 'bouncing' at the club, throwing out undesirables and reminding them that he ran a 'classy establishment'.

With dysfunctional parents (his father was a drunk and his mother was eventually incarcerated believing she had a fish bone permanently stuck in her gullet), it was probably inevitable that Ruby would end up in a life of crime. He was popular, gregarious and could be generous to those whose friendship he needed. He certainly knew scores of Dallas policemen who were regulars at the Carousel and he was a regular visitor at their headquarters, with gifts of sandwiches and doughnuts. He may have been homosexual, although in 1963, the 'Sixties' (especially in Texas) was not yet 'swinging' and that sort of thing was kept under wraps in a way that would be unthinkable today.

We shall look in detail at Ruby's involvement in the Kennedy killing later (Chapter 9) but for now, let us take his word for what happened on Friday, 22 November. In the late morning, he visited the office of his friend Tony Zoppi of the *Dallas Morning News*. As a businessman, Ruby was constantly placing ads in local papers for his club. He was still in the newspaper office when he heard the news of Kennedy's assassination. What is not clear from Ruby's account is that the *The Dallas Morning News* office was very close to Dealey Plaza. He did not have to watch television; he could almost get a ringside view of events from Concourse Street (see map). When at least two witnesses claimed they saw Ruby in Dealey Plaza soon after midday, they almost certainly did.

Ruby rang his sister from the paper's office belonging to John Newnam. He had been complaining, according to Newnam, about the full-page advertisement in the paper that morning, accusing JFK of treason (see Chapter 12) and when news of the assassination came through, said (inexplicably to some), 'John, I will have to leave Dallas.' Eva was hysterical and Ruby put in a call to his other sister Eileen in Chicago. He then drove to the Carousel and told Andy Armstrong, his manager, that the club would not be open that night as a mark of respect. There was discussion about other clubs in the city and when the Carousel would reopen.

In the evening, Ruby went to the Shearith Israel synagogue and talked to the rabbi, Hillel Silverman, especially concerned about Eva. At 11.15, he decided that the DPD, who were clearly working flat out, needed sandwiches and ordered some. Ruby's statement, cluttered with unnecessary phone calls shortly before midnight, sounds like a man obsessed with time, or trying to establish some sort of alibi. At the station by midnight, he saw Oswald – 'that was the first time I had ever seen him' – either with Curry or Fritz. He had, however, tried to see him earlier. At 6.25, a WFAA radio reporter had seen him about to enter Captain Fritz's office while he was questioning Oswald. A police guard told him, 'You can't go in there, Jack.' Chief Curry would later deny that any of his officers knew Jack Ruby. At a little after 1 a.m. on the Saturday, Ruby had the brass neck to give one of his club cards to Judge Johnston to 'come by and see me some time…'. Soon after that, he had the temerity to correct DA Wade about the name of Oswald's niche society in support of Cuba – and this is the context of a man who claimed in his own statement, he had never seen before!

At this point, Ruby decided to give his sandwiches to the newsboys at KLIF instead of the police (so why was he in the press conference at all?). In conversation with the newsmen in the early hours, Ruby mentioned how he thought Oswald looked like the actor Paul Newman, which, to my mind, casts doubt on Ruby's sanity! So cosy was the night club owner with law enforcement in Dallas, that he effectively arranged a radio interview with Henry Wade.

A bizarre interlude followed in which Ruby, his room-mate George Senator, and an employee at the club, Larry Crafard, drove out to the expressway at 4 a.m. and took photographs of a billboard which read 'Impeach Earl Warren [the Chief Justice], Write to Beltham, Box 1757 Mass.' All three then had breakfast at Halb's Coffee Shop, and Ruby went home to bed.

For most of that Saturday morning, Ruby watched television, watching the eulogies for Kennedy mount up – 'and it just tore me apart when [Rabbi Seligman of New York] said to think that our president had untold courage to combat anything and everywhere, and then to be struck down by some enemy from behind'. Already the mystery of the 'lone nut' killer in the Texas School Book Depository was gathering ground.

At Elm Street, Ruby was moved by the flowers laid on the pavement and grass. He spoke to DPD Officer James Chaney, who had ridden just behind the president's limo. Chaney pointed out the window that the killer had used and had told reporters that the first shot missed. He also said that Kennedy had been 'struck in the face', which did not square with the trajectory comment of shots coming from behind. Ruby became very emotional and had to leave. He visited Eva and went to a club (the Pogo) before going home to bed.

At 10 a.m. on Sunday, Ruby received a phone call from one of his dancers, Karen Carlin, knows as 'Little Lynn'. She was broke and asked Ruby for a loan. Clearly, the man generous with his sandwiches was less so when it came to employees as the girls were only paid for the work they did. Reluctantly, Ruby agreed to wire Karen some money ($25) via the Western Union and on his way saw a huge crowd outside the County Jail. Intrigued and thinking that Oswald had already been moved, as was planned, to the jail for his own safety, Ruby walked down the unguarded ramp into the police station basement. 'I continued walking down the ramp and just hit the bottom part of the ramp. That is all I remember…'

At what point Ruby's reminiscences part company with the truth is anybody's guess. *He* may not have been able to remember what happened next, but dozens of eyewitnesses saw it all and live television covered it for the whole world. At 2.30 that Saturday afternoon, Ruby had rung KLIF and offered to cover Oswald's transfer for the radio station because 'I am a pretty good friend of Henry Wade.' Needless to say, this was not part of Ruby's testimony. What was – and was irrelevant to the assassination – was a row that Ruby had with his friend, jeweller Frank Bellocchio, who blamed Dallas for the murder and had plans to leave. He had rung Eva in the evening, still ranting about the offensive billboards and planning to attend Tippit's funeral on Monday. He had gone to the funerals of every police officer killed in the line of duty.

George Senator, Ruby's room-mate, became ever more concerned about him as time went on. Over breakfast he was mumbling incoherently. He was crying by the time he read the *Dallas Times Herald* article suggesting that Jackie Kennedy would have to return to Dallas for Oswald's trial. While he was sorting out the money transfer for Karen Carlin, he left his dachshund, Sheba, in his parked car. He was carrying $2,000 in notes and his revolver.

CBS News solemnly announced 'strict security measures have been experienced from the very beginning [excluding, of course, a British insurance salesman posing as a journalist and Jack Ruby carrying a concealed weapon] and have even been increased this morning, as fear arises and grows stronger that someone may attempt to take the life

of the man accused of murdering the president of the United States.'
This was based on two premises. First, this was Dallas, Kennedy's 'nut
country' and anything could happen. Second, and more importantly,
the sheriff's office and the FBI in Dallas had received anonymous
phone calls – 'I represent a committee that is neither right nor left
wing and tonight, tomorrow morning, or tomorrow night, we are
going to kill the man what [sic] killed the president. There will be no
excitement and we will kill him. We wanted to be sure to tell the FBI,
Police Department and Sheriff's Office.' One policeman who heard
the taped message thought he recognized Ruby's voice.

The plan, worked out by Chief Curry, was to bring Oswald down in
the elevator and put him in an armoured truck in the basement. From
there, he would be driven up the ramp and escorted by police cars
to the County Jail. All five doorways to the car park in the basement
(for building employees) were guarded. Assistant Police Chief Charles
Batchelor was in charge of the operation and the signal to begin was
given by Lieutenant George Butler. Butler was an odd choice to be a
policeman – or alternatively, he may have fitted right in. He was former
head of the Dallas Policemen's Union (a sort of Jimmy Hoffa in blues),
a friend of oil millionaire Haroldson Lafayette Hunt (see Chapter 13)
and a member of the illegal Ku Klux Klan. Having given the signal to
move Oswald, he stood next to a reporter, Thayer Waldo of the *Fort
Worth Star Telegram*, who knew him well. The cop's lips were trembling.
At the last minute, the armoured truck had been changed to a car and
that vehicle was not yet in position; yet Oswald was moving, with a
detective on either side of him, Jim Leavelle in his white Stetson and
L.C. Graves in rather more conventional trilby. Oswald was wearing a
dark jumper over a white shirt and had clearly been allowed to change
since his earlier appearances before the cameras.

Roy Vaughn was the officer on duty on the Main Street ramp and he
was distracted at the crucial moment by a shout from the basement as
vehicles were manoeuvring. 'Jack Ruby did not come down that ramp,'

Vaughn told the author of *The Men Who Killed Kennedy* in 1988, 'I'll go to my grave saying that…' He probably did, but Ruby had sneaked in past him anyway. Pressmen had been allowed in already, their passes checked. Once again, Ruby mingled with the crowd, next to Icarus 'Ike' Pappas, a New York City radio reporter who elbowed his way to be as close to Oswald as possible.

'Are they ready?' Captain Fritz asked Lieutenant Woodrow Wiggins.

'Security is alright,' Wiggins told him in what must be – along with Nellie Connally's comment about how much Dallas loved Kennedy – the most ironic statement of an unbelievable weekend. Ruby had elbowed forward too; he was now standing next to CBS cameraman George Phenix – he would capture the drama of the next few seconds.

Fritz was not ready for the crowd of pressman. He had given orders (to Wiggins) to move them back behind a barrier. Wiggins later denied that he had received any such order. The car that was to carry Oswald was still out of position, too far away. Cameras flashed and popped as Oswald emerged from the elevator with his escort. Pappas stepped forward, microphone in hand 'Do you have anything to say in your defence?'

A man dashed diagonally across photographer Robert Jackson of the *Times Herald*, who still managed to press his shutter, winning him a Pulitzer Prize. Leavelle recognized the figure as that of Jack Ruby, his .38 in his hand. There was an explosion as Leavelle tried to pull Oswald back by his handcuff. Oswald grimaced in agony as the bullet ripped through his body, hitting his spleen, pancreas, kidney, liver and aorta. He crumpled to the ground as Ruby raised the Colt to fire again. Graves grabbed the assassin's gun hand and wrestled him to the ground alongside Oswald, 'Turn it loose!' he yelled and five cops jumped on Ruby, hitting him in the head.

'I hope I killed the son of a bitch!'

'That's a shot!' Pappas told his disbelieving listeners, 'Oswald has been shot! Oswald has been shot! A shot rang out. Mass confusion here, all the doors have been locked.'

'Nobody out! Nobody Out!' Captain Talbert shouted up to officers at the top of the ramps.

As writer Jonathan Mayo put it 'American television has just filmed its first live murder'.

The shooter, disarmed now, was handcuffed.

'Who is this son of a bitch?' somebody asked.

'I'm Jack Ruby!' he told him, 'You all know me! I'm Jack Ruby!'

Yes, everybody knew Jack Ruby, especially the Dallas police. What they did not know was why he killed Oswald. And in pulling that trigger of his .38 the world was denied the answer to much bigger questions. Forever.

Chapter 8

The Patsy ...

As a number of researchers have noted, *nothing* about Lee Harvey Oswald makes sense. Previous assassins of American presidents – John Wilkes Booth, Charles J. Guiteau, Leon Czolgosz – all gave reasons for their actions. The two who faced a court of law – Guiteau and Czolgosz – rejected their defence counsel's plea of insanity because they knew what they were doing and why. Lee Oswald never admitted to anything and took his secrets to the grave. He was a Communist and a traitor to his country. He was an FBI informant. He was a crack shot. He was an average rifleman. He was a dimwit, overawed by others. He was part of a crack Intelligence team working with Dallas police to protect John Kennedy. He was CIA. He defected to Russia, even marrying the daughter of a government officer. He frequently visited Communist Cuba and the Russian embassy there. He used the alias Alek Hidell and under that name bought the Mannlicher-Carcano with which he killed the president. He knew Jack Ruby and J.D. Tippit, whom he shot with a .38 revolver that miraculously ejected cartridge shells. He tried to murder General Edwin A. Walker. He was a fan of John Kennedy. Above all, he was able to fire at least three bullets in a record time that could not be matched by genuine marksmen, using a clapped out, second-hand, bolt-action rifle with wonky sights. And one of those bullets was so magic that it was able to pierce Kennedy and Connally, zig-zagging in mid-air to do it before ending up, virtually undamaged, on a stretcher in Parkland Hospital.

Where do we start?

The most famous – and inept – assassin in history was born in October 1939 in a rundown suburb of New Orleans. The connections with that city never went away, leading to the attempted prosecution of Clay Shaw of New Orleans, the only man charged with conspiracy to murder John Kennedy. Oswald's father died before he was born and his mother, Marguerite, was a deeply unpleasant, domineering woman who drove all her children away from her. All told, she had three marriages and seemed to resent all her offspring. She sent two of her sons, Robert and John, to an orphanage and Lee joined them, briefly, later. She moved constantly and had innumerable jobs. Lee was difficult and short tempered. The rare photograph of him as an 8-year-old with a cowboy gun in his hand is one carefully chosen by debunker Gerald Posner in his book *Case Closed* (1993). The implication is that this is an unstable 'lone nut' interested in firearms. As an only child of the 1950s, I suppose I am too. Every boy of my generation had a six-shooter; and to date I have not consciously killed anyone.

In 1944, Marguerite took her three boys and moved to Dallas, where she married Edwin Ekdahl, whose job took him away a lot. The older boys were enrolled in a military academy and Lee got on well with his stepfather. The marriage was not happy and Marguerite continued to move, causing havoc with Lee's schooling. By 1948, Ekdahl had gone and Lee lived with his mother in Fort Worth, the boy's thirteenth move since his birth. After that, she doted on the boys, but her presence was overbearing. Lee became introverted, staying at home and reading a lot. He also, according to various neighbours and classmates, had a short temper. In various IQ tests, his results ranged from 103 to 118 which hardly fits the high-flying CIA operative and special forces unit member that some theorists will have us believe.

When Robert joined the Marines in the summer of 1952, 13-year-old Lee became fascinated with the Service, reading the handbooks his brother sent him. Debunker Posner makes much of an incident involving Lee, a knife and his sister-in-law and mother. Theorists like

Robert Groden, Jim Garrison and Harold Weisberg do not mention it at all. Now in New York, Lee felt like a fish out of water, mocked for his Southern drawl and shabby appearance. He was sent for psychiatric evaluation and came under the aegis of Dr Renatus Hartogs whose lop-sided evaluation has painted a distorted figure of Lee Oswald which fits perfectly with the 'lone nut' killer of the future – 'This child had a potential for explosive, aggressive, assaulting acting out which was rather unusual ...' His conclusion was that the boy 'has to be diagnosed as "personality pattern disturbance with schizoid features and passive-aggressive tendencies".' He was 'emotionally quite disturbed'. On the other hand, Oswald was 13, in a conflicted family dynamic and, as no doubt would have happened had Oswald ever come to trial for murder, another psychiatrist (working for the defence) would have offered a radically different viewpoint. Today, Hartogs's diagnosis is recognized as being deeply flawed. The detached and neglected boy became in Hartogs's (and therefore, the world's) eyes, a dangerous man with schizoid tendencies. The day after the assassination, Hartogs told a television reporter that the killer was 'very likely a mentally disturbed person, who has a personal grudge against persons in authority and very likely is a person who in his search to overcome his own insignificance and helplessness will try to commit an act which will make others frightened, which will shatter the world'.

While some readers will regard this as a blinding glimpse of the obvious, it does not square with the psyches of dozens of trained assassins around the world who kill for money or because it is their duty. Hartogs had no experience of such people.

In the 1970s, he paid $350,000 to a female patient he had indecently assaulted as part of her 'treatment'. Look him up online today and there are complaints from other individuals assaulted by him before the website is mysteriously cut off in mid-forum. Hartogs's incompetence has never been properly exposed.

Gerald Posner, squarely in the Warren Commission camp, goes so far as to give credence to two Soviet psychiatrists who evaluated Oswald in Moscow in 1959. Without wishing to sound *too* much like Joe McCarthy, how far can we rely on 'scientists' whose whole raison d'être was skewed by Marxist ideology? To them, Oswald was a defecting foreigner and obviously not one to be trusted. It was in their interests to rubbish him.

One minor incident stands out for me. One of the criticisms of Oswald at Public School 44 (how cold and regimented is *that*?) in New York is that he did not salute the flag during the daily pledge of allegiance. No doubt 1950s Americans found this appalling and an example of aberrant behaviour. Those outside the country take a different view; is America the land of the free? As I write, a number of players in the current US women's soccer team have also refused to salute. The logic is decidedly flawed – Lee Oswald refused to honour the flag morphs into Lee Oswald killed the president.

Gerald Posner, accusing conspiracy theorists left, right and centre of glossing over reality, does the same on page 17 of *Case Closed* (1993) by saying '[Oswald] was briefly a member of the Civil Air Patrol ...' He was indeed and it was here (there is a photograph to prove it) that he met the odd-ball pilot/gun-runner David Ferrie whom Posner first mentions on page 132 in a different context. In passing, we might note that another of the Civil Air Patrol's cadets was the son of Mary E. Bledsoe who saw Oswald on the bus soon after the assassination looking 'like a maniac'. She had rented a room to Oswald for a week in October, but did she also know him as a friend of her son?

Even before he left school, Oswald had become, according to Posner, a committed Marxist. It is difficult, from the standpoint of the twenty-first century, to understand how taboo this was. Senator Joe McCarthy had spearheaded a crusade, more properly a witch-hunt, against the 'Red peril' in all its forms, encouraging the House Un-American Activities Committee to interrogate would-be lefties live on television. He personally overstepped the mark when he went for Eisenhower and the army, but what McCarthy stood for was enshrined in the John Birch Society, prevalent and powerful in Texas, and the majority of Americans were horrified by a populist doctrine they did not understand. Given America's obsession with capitalism and the concept that 'greed is good', it was probably impossible for a Marxist revolution to succeed there. It only worked in Russia and China because society there was so impoverished. As Karl Marx had written, 'You have nothing to lose but your chains. You have a world to win.' While writing this book, I met an American whose family believe that the capitalist entrepreneur Richard Branson is a socialist! With a cock-eyed world view such as that, can we wonder at the ultra-rightism of most of America in the 1960s?

In discussing Oswald's childhood, I have followed the line taken by debunkers, specifically Posner, to paint a picture of a disturbed, spoiled young man whose oddity is fully in accord with the Marxism to which he became addicted. This ignores the fact, of course, that millions of people all over the world have espoused the same ideology and they have not all become killers. No 'assassin' in history has been more analysed than Lee Oswald so we have no yardstick by which to measure him. If we had the childhood details of Gavrilo Princip who assassinated Archduke Franz Ferdinand in 1914, or Decimus Junius Brutus, one of the killers of Julius Caesar, we might be able to get a handle on Oswald. All we can be sure of is that he was not very bright and the image of a closeted bookworm does not square with what we know of him in his adult life. Such men may or may not become assassins, but they are certainly the raw material for 'Patsies'.

Conspiracists would have us believe that Oswald was earmarked for espionage while still at school. Alex Cox in *The President and the Provocateur* (2013) talks of *two* Lee Harvey Oswalds in two schools at the same time, a shape-shifting skill which was even prevalent in Dealey Plaza. Oswald's first jobs after leaving school are equally vague – there is no paper trail which routine employment throws up. Some say he was in Texas in the late 1950s; others that he was in New Orleans. What is not in doubt is that, like his big brother, he joined the Marines. This was in October 1956 and the recruit was trained at a radar school in Biloxi, Mississippi. In September 1957, he was sent to the Naval Air Facility Atsugi in Japan and it was here that he shot himself (by accident, it must be added, which gives us some idea of his competence with firearms). The gun was a nickel–plated Derringer which he had bought by mail order. Such purchases were illegal in the Marines, but they let Oswald off lightly. In fact, such leniency would invariably be shown to him until he crossed paths with Jack Ruby in the police station basement in Dallas.

According to various reports, Oswald, with several others of course, was part of a team of technicians working on the U–2 spy planes which were monitoring Russian missile capability. This, despite the fact that two years earlier, as a 16-year-old, he had applied to join the youth league of the American Socialist Party. Posted to the Philippines, Oswald now became a mess cook. In this context, during horse–play, Oswald poured a drink over an NCO and was sent to the brig briefly – *another* lenient sentence. By the end of 1957, he was back in the States (at the naval base of El Toro in California) and started to learn Russian – as you do when you are in the United States Marines! He extolled the USSR and the new Marxist government in Cuba led by Fidel Castro who had overthrown the dictator Fulgencio Batista. Oswald's comrades called him 'Oswaldkovich'.

To reiterate what I wrote earlier, none of this makes sense. CIA agent Victor Marchetti explains it because at the time, a number of young recruits like Oswald were given a 'front' of being disenchanted with the American way of life and encouraged to be open Communists. The idea was to let them defect to the USSR to collect what intelligence data they could and feed it back to the CIA.

In March 1959, Oswald applied to the Albert Schweitzer College in Switzerland, ostensibly to learn German. He asked – and got – early release from the Marines, because his mother was ill. How Oswald was able to get to Moscow is unclear. He did not have enough money for the trip, which, at the height of the Cold War, was tortuous. He travelled via France and Britain, to Helsinki where he obtained permission to enter the Soviet Union without a visa. He got the necessary papers in two days, which, in the scheme of things, *should* have been impossible.

In Russia, like many men who defected in the 1950s, Oswald found life miserable. The Russians (not unnaturally) did not trust him and he did not like them. When his visa compromise ran out, he had to leave, so he attempted suicide. This is the moment when Gerald Posner quotes the Russian psychiatrists as, effectively, supporting Dr Hartogs's claims about Oswald's instability, but the *timing* seems highly suspicious. Was it merely a ruse to allow him to stay, his spy work unfinished? Debunkers claim that Oswald never had sufficient clearance, even at Atsugi, to be of use to the Russians had the defection been genuine. So either the espionage deception did not work or here is more evidence of the irrational behaviour of the 'lone nut'.

At the end of October, he went to the American embassy in Moscow and told them he wanted to renounce his US citizenship and defect permanently. This information was relayed to Washington, the CIA, the FBI and the ONI (Office of Naval Intelligence). If these institutions did not know about Oswald already (and the chances are that they did, especially the CIA) they certainly did now. Technically, Oswald never renounced his American citizenship because he never signed the relevant papers.

For a year, the defector effectively disappeared. The Warren Commission examined a diary purportedly written by Oswald covering 1960 but it was probably a fake. The writer Norman Mailer spoke to Igor Golubtsov, Director of Counterintelligence for the KGB in Minsk and (if the Russian 'spook' can be trusted) the authorities there were as much confused by Oswald as the rest of us. Some believed he was a straightforward spy. Others that the defection was genuine. Still others found his grasp of Marxism deficient. And a fourth group were convinced that he spoke better Russian than he let on. He was employed as a technician in a factory and was constantly under surveillance.

According to his diary, Oswald was bored with endless trades union dances and found nowhere to spend his money. The Soviet Union was not big on bowling alleys and nightclubs. Enigma kicks in again; in January 1961, Lee Harvey Oswald was in New Orleans thinking of buying a fleet of trucks to be sent to Cuba. Weeks later, he was test-driving a Chevrolet in a dealership in the same city, but Lee Harvey Oswald was not only still in Russia, he could not drive. On 17 March, the 'real' Oswald met Marina Prusakova, niece of an MVD (police) colonel at one of the ghastly dances he hated and within a month he had proposed to her. Conspiracy theorist Edward Jay Epstein believes that Marina was a spy too, finding their relationship, when Oswald was trying to leave Russia, fabricated.

In July, he visited the American embassy again, asking for assurances that, if he returned to America, he would not face a prison sentence for treason. The embassy told him he would not – more leniency. But the Marine Corps was less forgiving. They revoked his honourable discharge ranking and Oswald wrote to Texas Governor John Connally to complain. At the time, Connally was navy secretary.

By now, the Oswalds were not only married but had a daughter, June Lee. With cash lent to them by the American embassy, they travelled by train to the Netherlands, then sailed for the States, disembarking at Hoboken in New Jersey on 13 June. Here they were met by Spas Raikin of the Travellers' Aid Society Union. New Orleans DA Jim Garrison had Raikin down as the secretary-general of the American Friends of the Anti-Bolshevik Bloc of Nations, with links to the CIA and FBI. Was Raikin intent on 'turning' the Communist or had there been a similar umbrella over Oswald all along?

On the journey to Fort Worth to live temporarily with his brother Robert, Lee shed a number of suitcases. At Hoboken he had seven; in New York five and in Texas, only two. Where were the others and what was in them? At the end of June, Oswald told the Fort Worth Commercial Employment Agency that he had been working in the USSR for the State Department. He was then interviewed by FBI agents John Fain and Thomas Carter. In fact, Fain met him twice and, on both occasions, Oswald was belligerent and non-cooperative, refusing to take a polygraph test. Alex Cox believes that these meetings – or at least Fain's account of them – were bogus and the *real* contents of the discussions remain unknown. Perhaps the FBI was considering taking Oswald on as an informant. He spoke Russian and there were a surprising number of Russian emigres in Texas. Deputy Sheriff Allan Sweatt was sure that this was the case. He would be in Dealey Plaza on 22 November high-handedly taking Mary Moorman's Polaroids off her, but he also had the goods on Oswald in the investigation that followed the shooting. Oswald was paid $200 a month by the FBI and his code number was S72. Sweatt passed this information to Waggoner Carr, the Texas Attorney General who passed it to the Warren Commission, who promptly ignored it.

In the middle of July, the Oswalds moved in with Marguerite at West Seventh Street, Fort Worth. The employment agency found Lee a job at a welding company and this gave him the wherewithal to rent an apartment for himself, Marina and the baby. He also ostentatiously ordered a subscription to *The Worker* and to a Russian magazine, as well as writing to the Socialist Workers Party which was being watched by the Post Office Inspection Service as subversive.

It was in September 1961 that Oswald met one of the most enigmatic characters in this entire story – Baron George de Mohrenschildt. Perhaps unsurprisingly, given his complex lifestyle, de Mohrenschildt will appear later in this book in the context of the many suspicious deaths of assassination witnesses. He appeared before the Warren Commission in 1964 and said of Oswald, 'His mind was of a man with exceedingly poor background, who read rather advanced books and did not understand even the words in them ... how can you take seriously a person like that? You just laugh at him ...'

But in 1964 nobody was laughing at Oswald. He was dead and most of America (and certainly the Warren Commission) believed that he had killed the president. Few people have made the obvious comment that de Mohrenschildt was an inveterate snob. What makes no sense at all is why a suave, multilingual socialite with a White Russian origin should give the time of day to 'Southern trash' like Lee Oswald, still less befriend him. Unless the baron had a hankering after the very pretty Marina. Unless he was ordered to ...

De Mohrenschildt was a Russian national who had come to the States in 1938 at the height of Stalin's tyranny. He became an American citizen with surprising ease, especially since some suspected him of being a Nazi agent. He lived briefly in Moscow, then enrolled on an art course at the University of Texas. There is little doubt that the baron worked for the CIA; with his cosmopolitan background, he was an obvious asset to them. His handler was J. Walton Moore, the agency's top man in Dallas, who, true to form in the context of the organization he worked for, denied ever discussing Oswald with de Mohrenschildt.

The baron told the Commission that it was out of the question that Oswald was any kind of agent – 'I never would believe that any government would be stupid enough to trust Lee with anything important ... an unstable individual, mixed-up ... uneducated ... without background ... Even the government of Ghana would not give him any kind of job.'

Today the Ghana slur is totally unacceptable. Africa in the 1960s was experiencing the 'wind of change' (in the words of British

Prime Minister Harold Macmillan), various countries shaking off their imperial pasts and establishing their own native governments; inevitably, there were teething troubles. Bizarrely, de Mohrenschildt wrote a lengthy, rambling treatise entitled 'I am a Patsy! I am a Patsy!' in which Oswald was portrayed as a hero with convictions. Marina, however, was mousy with 'bad teeths' – presumably the baron was mocking her English here; his own was impeccable.

The relationship with de Mohrenschildt veering from contempt to a sneaking admiration only makes any kind of sense if he was a 'cut-out' for Oswald, a middle man between the ex-Marine and his ultimate CIA bosses, who either recruited him on his return from Minsk or had engineered his going there in the first place. The de Mohrenschildts and other Russian ex-pats helped Oswald out, providing clothes, toys and a cot. Marina was expecting again. The couple quarrelled with increasing frequency and even violence. Marina smoked and drank; Lee did not. Eventually, she moved out, encouraged by the de Mohrenschildts, to live with Russian-speaking friends. Oswald moved to Dallas, where the baron got him a job at a graphic arts company, Jaggars-Chiles-Stovall. Conspiracy theorists claim that this company painted classified maps of Communist areas, including Cuba, based on spy-plane evidence. Security clearance was therefore vital. Be that as it may, Jaggars also produced humdrum newspaper ads and we have no clear idea in which department Oswald worked.

In early November, the family moved into an apartment in a rough area in Elspeth Street. De Mohrenschildt thought the place depressing, but the Oswalds quarrelled after a day and Lee moved out. According to Edward Jay Epstein, Oswald was trained in photographic distortion techniques at Jaggars, which is why he could tell immediately that the infamous 'backyard' photographs of him armed to the teeth and carrying Communist literature were fakes. He now carried his own fake, a certificate of US Marine Corps service in the name of Alek James Hidell. Conspiracy theorists claim that this was a genuine

Intelligence name, like 'Elmer Fudd' that could be applied to anyone working for the government in an undercover way.

There was a big Oswald family reunion at Thanksgiving in Fort Worth. John Pic, Lee's half-brother, had not seen him for ten years. 'I would never have recognized him,' adding to the shape-shifting image that we have of the man.

On 27 January 1963, Oswald ordered a .38 Smith and Wesson revolver from a Los Angeles firm under the A.J. Hidell alias. It cost $29.95 and, in common with every other revolver in the world, did not eject cartridges. This purchase is odd. Technically, sending a firearm through the mail was illegal. In Texas, more than any other state, he could simply have walked into any gun shop, like Dave's House of Guns in Dallas and bought one over the counter without any form of ID. Hidell's Smith and Wesson was an easily traced weapon. Was he, as some conspiracy theorists have suggested, working for the Dodd Committee to control the availability of guns at a time when gun ownership and gun violence was already up for debate? There is no evidence for this and it does not actually explain his behaviour during this period – ordering guns and contacting various left-wing political groups.

It was now that Oswald met another enigmatic character in the story – the Quaker Ruth Paine and her husband, Michael. De Mohrenschildt introduced them in late February and Ruth became very 'mumsy' with Marina, eventually providing her with a home. After Ruby shot Oswald, however, Marina cut all ties with her. Ruth told the Warren Commission, 'I thought that he was not very intelligent ... he had no particular contacts. He was not a person I would have hired for a job of any sort, no more than I would let him borrow my car.' All very Quakerly, but the Paines were anything but a straightforward couple. The Warren Commission, duped by the FBI, could find no fault in them, but they reeked of duplicity. Michael was an avowed pacifist who had fought in France and worked for an arms manufacturer –

Bell Helicopter, part of the Military-Industrial Complex that would benefit hugely from Lyndon Johnson's escalation of the Vietnam War from 1969 onwards (see Chapter 13). Ruth's sister worked for the CIA. And of course, it was Ruth who got Oswald his job at the School Book Depository, despite not wanting to hire him himself. And how could he borrow her car, when he could not drive?

In early March, the couple moved again, to West Neely Street and Oswald ordered another gun to be delivered to his usual postal address, PO Box 2915, Dallas. It was from Klein's Sporting Goods in Chicago and was a cheap, second-hand Mannlicher-Carcano, a rifle of Second World War Italian manufacture. When the assassination occurred and the world was made aware of the rifle, Italians were mortified, referring to it as *la pistola maledetta*, the accursed gun. No one knows who collected the rifle or the revolver from the mail box. Other people had access to it, although the approved list of these went missing (as so much key evidence does in cases like this) so we are unable to check. The Carcano took 6.5mm cartridges, unusual in Texas, and both local gun shops denied selling anything to Oswald (although, aping the response from Mandy Rice-Davies in a very different case in Britain in 1963, 'they would, wouldn't they?').

Because of Oswald's known subscription to *The Worker*, the FBI office in Dallas reopened a file on him at the end of March. As we shall see, the Bureau, because of its rabid, possibly deranged Director, J. Edgar Hoover, was obsessed with Communism and the threat it posed to security. With the Cuban Missile Crisis of the previous year, a threat from Soviet Russia was a real possibility. The likelihood of thousands of Reds inside America joining in was negligible and probably only in the minds of three men – Joe McCarthy of Wisconsin, J. Edgar Hoover and a man who would soon feature in the Oswald story, General Edwin A. Walker. The agent who reopened the file was James Hosty.

On 31 March, according to Marina who says she took them, Oswald posed for the backyard photographs which linked him conveniently with both Communism and firearms. When the Warren Commission and eventually the public saw them, they were convinced that here was the man who tried to kill General Walker and actually did kill Kennedy and Tippit. There were the guns to prove it. And there was the motive – Communism. Some assassins have openly admitted their actions. They are proud of their efforts and simply want to be arrested or killed. Taking just the presidential examples – John Wilkes Booth leapt on to the stage having shot Lincoln with the histrionic words, *sic semper tyrannis* (so it always is with tyrants); Guiteau and Czolgosz let themselves be manhandled by bodyguards with no further attempts at violence. But according to the Warren Commission, Oswald went to great lengths *not* to be caught. He hid inside a building; he stashed the murder weapon; he skulked away and changed his clothes, presumably to avoid detection and hid in the darkness of a cinema when the police came looking for him. Did he do all this, having posed as an assassin? A number of photographic experts, including Robert Groden, have analysed these photographs and found them wanting. The rifle is indeed a Mannlicher-Carcano but the revolver could be any make, obscured by the holster on Oswald's hip as it is. The Communist literature in his hand is particularly unclear and too large, relative to the figure, to be *The Worker* as the Warren Commission claimed. The angle of the head and body are odd, and in all cases (there are a total of six photographs, although Marina says she only took one) Oswald's right leg looks far shorter than his left. Above all, the shadows are incorrect. Those on the ground do not line up with those under Oswald's chin. When Will Fritz of the Dallas police showed Oswald these, he immediately denounced them as fakes, having worked recently for a photographic company. The rifle is too long (by 6 inches) and the angle of Oswald's head is identical in all photographs. Researcher Robert Groden, among others, has decisively proved that the backyard work was fabricated.

Bizarrely, bearing in mind they had the chance to right the disgraceful misconduct of the Warren Commission, the HSCA in 1977 also declared the photographs genuine. 'There is no support for the statement [that they have been faked]', the HSCA said pompously, ignoring expert testimony left, right and centre.

Sooner or later, we have to tackle the issue of Marina Oswald. She is still alive at the time of writing, is still living in Dallas and has remarried. She very rarely gives interviews, which is a pity because her evidence damned her husband. She apparently now believes that he was innocent, but in 1963 things were different. She told the FBI that she had taken one photograph, then changed that to two. Her English was still not very good and, no doubt terrified that she would be deported and/or lose her children, she was even more of a patsy than her husband. It is only from her that we have the accusation that Oswald tried to shoot General Walker.

There have been a number of Hollywood movies, some serious, over time which deal with senior members of the American military. In many of them, there is a four-star general in the White House situation room, his chest ablaze with medals and he is demanding the immediate use of nuclear weapons. His type is perhaps best presented by Robert Duvall in *Apocalypse Now* – 'I love the smell of napalm in the morning.' Such a one was Edwin A. Walker and how he rose above the rank of lieutenant amazes me. Despite a reputable role in NATO, he was a rabid white supremacist (and therefore highly popular in Texas) and was fired by President Kennedy for distributing right-wing literature to the men under his command. Free from the restrictions (if he ever had any) of the military, he became a hero to the Fascist John Birch Society and helped orchestrate the barring of black student James Meredith from entry to the University of Mississippi.

He made a speech under the statue of a Confederate general, deploring the sending in of federal troops to quell rioting in the state.

'This is the conspiracy of the crucifixion by Antichrist conspirators of the Supreme Court,' he ranted, 'in their denial of prayer and their betrayal of a nation.' While nobody was ready with a straitjacket, Walker was delighted that racist thugs descended on the area from California to Florida. In Dallas, a right-wing activist, Ashland Burchnell, was arrested in possession of a .303 rifle, a revolver, three automatics, a switchblade and 3,000 rounds of ammunition. The army was indeed sent in, but only after Kennedy had delayed and insisted that newly integrated black soldiers should be kept out.

Furious with all this, Bobby Kennedy, the Attorney General, had Walker arrested and forced a psychiatric evaluation. According to Marina, on 10 April, Oswald decided to kill the general. Oswald had lost his job four days earlier, perhaps because of his known Marxist sympathies, perhaps for incompetence. Walker was fully aware of how unpopular he was with 'liberal' America and, according to conspiracy theorists, set up a ruse to turn himself into a victim. If a plot could be exposed whereby somebody took a shot at the general, he would win more support and besmirch the desegregationists. Accordingly, after dark on 8 April, two men, in suits and smoking, were sitting near to the general's house in a new white Ford, apparently, in police parlance 'casing the joint'. Two nights later, Walker was sitting at his desk, writing, when a shot shattered the window. Two cars were seen driving away at speed. Walker was unhurt apart from superficial cuts from flying glass and found the bullet that missed him. It was badly damaged but he recognized it at once as a .30.06 steel-jacketed type. A Mannlicher-Carcano cannot fire such a bullet. Nothing daunted, Marina told the Warren Commission that Oswald had gone out that night between 6 and 7 p.m., ostensibly to a typing course from which (unbeknownst to her) he had been dropped for non-attendance. He told her she was to ask him no questions but that he had shot at the general.

Nothing about this attempted murder fits Oswald. He could not drive and would have had to change buses to get to Walker's house, carrying, of course, a rifle. Alternatively, how likely was it that the solitary Marxist, the lone nut so beloved of the Commission, would have had not one, but two accomplices? In Oswald's possession after the assassination of Kennedy, police found a photograph of the back of Walker's house with a Chevy parked outside. Originally the licence plate was visible, but by the time it became a Warren Commission exhibit, someone had cut a hole in the photograph removing it. No one was ever charged with the attack on General Walker. Or of evidence tampering.

Gerald Posner has a very different take on the incident. Oswald had 'cased the joint' in advance and buried the rifle near the house. There is no mention of how he could have done this unnoticed. Posner says that the ballistics tests concluded that the slug *was* a 6.5mm and 'there was a good probability that it was fired from Oswald's gun'. This is patent nonsense. What does Oswald do with the weapon while, according to Walker's own testimony, two mysterious cars are driving away? He buries it again, doubling the chances of being observed. In fact, bearing in mind Posner and the Commission have the Carcano with him in the Book Depository on 22 November, he actually *trebled* the risk of discovery, by having to dig it up again. Weakly, in his discussion of the Walker shooting, Posner says that 'Marina may be mistaken'. He got that right!

Two days later, Oswald wrote to the Fair Play for Cuba Committee (FPCC). The loss of Cuba to the Communists was a blow to the United States; a potentially enemy state was only 96 miles away from Florida. It was also a blow to organized crime, because Fidel Castro closed the casinos owned by the Mob and cut them off, financially, at the knees. Many Cubans had left their island when Castro took over and had settled all over the south-west, especially in Florida and New Orleans. As an apparent good Communist, it made sense for Oswald to support the Castro regime. He may have been the unknown man handing out pro-Castro leaflets in Dallas, witnessed by two cops, Finegan and Harkness.

Perhaps to prove how 'mistaken' Marina Oswald could be, she claimed to the FBI in February 1964 that her husband had dressed in a suit and packed his revolver to attend the visit of Richard Nixon, who had lost to Kennedy in the 1960 election, in April 1963. Marina locked him in the bathroom to stop him leaving the house. All of which is very odd, because Nixon was not in Dallas in April 1963. Ironically, he *was* there on Friday, 22 November.

It was at this point that the Oswalds separated again. Ruth Paine persuaded Marina (now three months pregnant) to stay while Oswald went on alone to New Orleans. Ruth and Michael Paine had separated, so Marina and little June moved in with her. In New Orleans, Oswald stayed with his aunt and uncle, Lilian and Charles Murret. Murret, known as 'Dutz', adds a new dimension to the story of Lee Oswald. He was 63 and a surrogate father to the boy, having looked after him from time to time during his childhood. Dutz, however, was, according to the HSCA, 'a minor underworld gambling figure' and 'associate of significant organized crime figures affiliated with the Marcello organization'. In all probability, Oswald knew all about it. Conspiracy theorists who see the Mob written all over the Kennedy killing have had a field day with this. As we shall see, Carlos Marcello was the 'godfather' of New Orleans and loathed Kennedy with a passion, especially as Robert, as Attorney General, had effectively waged war on the Mafia.

Once established, Oswald moved into his own apartment and started working for the Reily Coffee Company. The company was run by brothers with CIA connections and it is uncertain whether Oswald was actually there as a barista or something altogether more political. He wrote to the FPCC, not for the first time, asking for leaflets to hand out and set out in business. He had no office and no backers, despite a mention of volunteers in his letter. He is not known to have made contact with any Marxist organization. On 16 June, he was handing out his leaflets to sailors getting off the USS *Wasp* in the harbour

– a rather unlikely group of potential converts, perhaps! He got his own box number wrong. Just over a week later, he applied for a new passport and got one in less than twenty-four hours.

On 1 July, both Oswalds applied, separately, to be allowed to return to Russia and, at some point, Lee set up an office at 544 Camp Street where the principal tenant was William Guy Banister. This man stepped right out of a film script. A hard-nosed 'G Man' before the FBI earned itself a more sinister reputation, he had been involved in the Dillinger case – 'Public Enemy Number 1' – in the 1930s, was a protégé of J. Edgar Hoover and may have worked with the ONI during the Second World War. A hard-drinking right-winger, he became Deputy Chief of Police in New Orleans but was forced into early retirement by the more relaxed attitudes of the early 1960s. He operated as a private investigator from the Camp Street address, was a member of the John Birch Society and published his own right-wing paper, *The Intelligence Digest.*

One of his operatives was David Ferrie, who had run the Civil Air Patrol that Oswald had joined as a teenager. Ferrie was a hypnotist, a self-ordained Catholic bishop and a pilot. He was also *very* distinguishable, because he suffered from alopecia and wore bright red wigs and even false eyebrows, which hardly made him blend in. Banister's secretary, Delphine Roberts, told researcher Anthony Summers that Oswald was a regular visitor, meeting behind closed doors with Ferrie and Banister. Gerald Posner, who interviewed Roberts years later, found a rather deranged racist who claimed not to have told Summers the whole truth. But the 544 Camp Street address on Oswald's first batch of leaflets will not go away. Posner 'explains' that by claiming a list of possibilities which do not make sense.

For conspiracists, the theory runs that Oswald, far from being a Communist, was actually anti-Communist and anti-Castro, adopting a front with the help of Banister et al. to out as many actual pro-Castro Cubans as possible. At 544 Camp Street, the Cuban Revolutionary

Council (anti-Castro) had its headquarters and was founded by E. Howard Hunt of the CIA. What is undoubtedly true is that the Central Intelligence Agency had become *far* too big for its boots by the early 1960s. It had nearly started World War Three with its ludicrous plan to invade Cuba via the Bay of Pigs and John Kennedy had promised to smash it 'into a thousand pieces'. Was Dealey Plaza payback time? No fewer than six people saw Oswald on the premises at various times in the summer of 1963; the debunkers have besmirched them all as liars and drunks.

Three months before he allegedly shot John Kennedy, Oswald was still the arch man of mystery. Was he: a Communist, cosying up to Banister's people to cover the fact; an agent for the FBI spying on Birchers and the equally fascistic Minutemen, even the KKK; a right-wing activist, plotting to destroy the Left in New Orleans; or a CIA courier? He cannot have been all of the above but because the institution(s) he may have worked for have refused to open their files on their own (American) people, we are none the wiser. At the end of July, Lee Harvey Oswald turned up in Scranton, Pennsylvania, several states away from Louisiana, distributing leaflets. Was that the convoluted ex-Marine from Dallas or somebody else entirely? The real Oswald gave a pro-Russian speech in Mobile, Alabama on the 27th with various family members in attendance, but other, unexplained, visits to Atlanta, Baton Rouge and Mexico City have not been substantiated.

The peculiar public punch-up with Cuban Carlos Bringuier and his friends on 7 August has still not been explained. Bringuier was rabidly anti-Castro and has claimed that he thought that Oswald was trying to infiltrate his one-man group, the DRE (*Directorio Revolucionario Estudiantil*) and that fists flew. In fact, Oswald offered no resistance but was arrested along with the others and fined $10 for disturbing the peace. He also appeared on local radio with Bringuier, discussing Russia and Marxism. Then, for nearly a month, he went under the radar and FBI surveillance lost track of him. He later claimed that, having lost his coffee shop job, he applied to seventeen companies for work. Thirteen had never heard of him and four did not exist.

Another bizarre incident occurred in September when three men, Oswald, Ferrie and New Orleans businessman Clay Shaw turned up in a Cadillac at Clinton, Louisiana. While the others waited in the car, Oswald stood in the queue to register for a vote. This was a Civil Rights move on the part of CORE, the Congress on Racial Equality; Oswald was the only white man in the line. Clinton was, at that time, right at the heart of the segregation movement. White supremacists claimed that CORE was a Communist organization – and here was Oswald, technically ineligible for a vote in the area, giving them plenty of ammunition. The link between the three men was at the heart of District Attorney Jim Garrison's decision to charge Shaw with conspiracy to murder John Kennedy. That, however morally right and well intentioned, spectacularly backfired.

On 23 September, Ruth Paine persuaded Marina to go back with her to her home in Irving, Texas to give birth to her second child. Four days later, according to the Warren Commission, Oswald took a bus, via a circuitous Texas route, to Mexico City. The same day and again two days later, he visited both the Cuban consulate and the Russian embassy. He demanded a visa to return to Russia via Cuba and ranted and raved to officials who told him he would have to wait. Such a public display, like the fight with Bringuier, would ensure that people remembered the name Lee Harvey Oswald. The problem was that security cameras outside both buildings were used as a matter of routine and whoever gave these performances at the end of September, it was not the ex–Marine who would soon get a job in the Texas School Book Depository. Several men have been suggested, but they are all too old and too heavy for Oswald, who was 24 and weighed 131lb. A number of officials, from bus drivers to hotel clerks could not equate the photographs the FBI showed them after the assassination with the man they had seen. Conspiracies, even those orchestrated by the government, can only go so far.

On 26 September, the White House announced the president's visit to Dallas and Fort Worth, scheduled for 21/22 November. While he was still, according to the Warren Commission, in Mexico, Oswald turned up with two Cuban exiles at the home of a third, Silvia Odio, in Dallas. Odio was one of the principal anti-Castro forces in Texas. She probably knew the other two men, but not the third, an American introduced to her as 'Leon Oswald', a crack shot who said that 'Kennedy should have been killed after the Bay of Pigs fiasco and that the Cubans should have done it'. Since this meeting contradicted Oswald's presence in Mexico, the Warren Commission rejected it. True to form, debunkers like Posner have found Silvia Odio to be 'unstable' – the usual description of anyone who disagrees with the biggest whitewash in American history.

Oswald was back in Texas by 3 October and hitch-hiked to Irving to find Marina. He was clearly broke and had no job. He stayed with his family for four days then went back to Dallas again, job hunting. He rented a room from Mary E. Bledsoe who seems to have taken an instant dislike to him (remember the Civil Air Patrol connection) and he stayed with her only one week. On 13 October, he moved into the bungalow belonging to Earline Roberts in North Beckley, Oak Cliff.

Exactly how Oswald got his job at the Book Depository is open to debate, like the rest of his life. Ruth Paine, who was either a good Quaker friend or a secret agent – take your pick – heard of a vacancy via Mrs Bill Randle, that superintendent Roy Truly was looking to hire. Both of them denied any such information. Nevertheless, Oswald turned up, was interviewed by Truly and offered the stock control job at $1.25 an hour, the last of a string of low-paid employment he had had since his return from Russia. He began work on 16 October.

In the world of conspiracy theorists, even the Texas School Book Depository takes on sinister properties. The building's original owner,

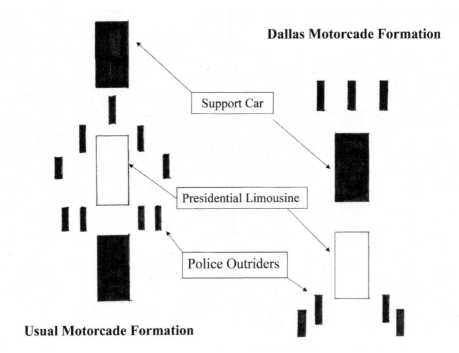

Dallas Motorcade Formation

Support Car

Presidential Limousine

Police Outriders

Usual Motorcade Formation

A comparison of the usual motorcade formation (left) and what happened in Dallas (right). Note that the presidential limousine is usually surrounded by motorcycle outriders. This was not the case in Dallas and the outriders were told to keep back from the presidential limousine. It is unclear whether this decision came from the president or the Secret Service.

The motorcade route at the end of its run through Dallas. The logical route would have been straight down Main Street (see bottom of diagram), but a decision was made, by the Secret Service and Dallas Police, to turn right onto Houston Street and then left onto Elm. This involved two tight turns which slowed the motorcade to less than 5mph.

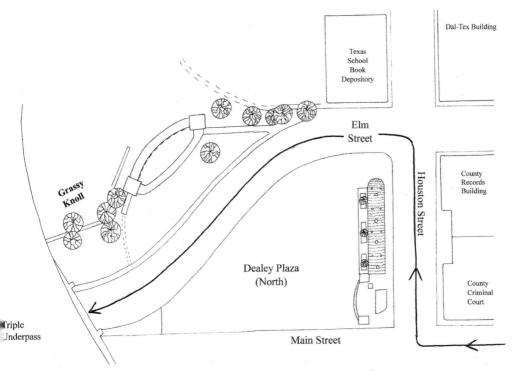

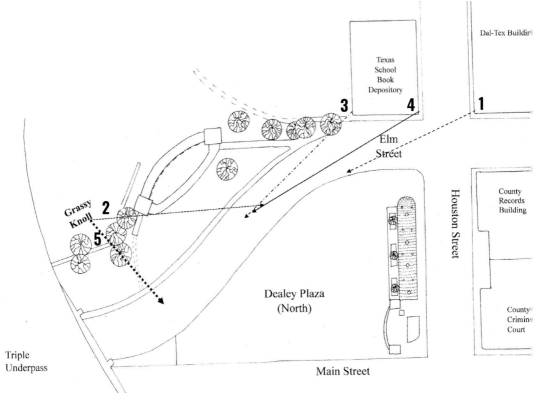

Contrary to the Warren Commission's findings, there were at least six shots fired in Dealey Plaza on 22 November. The first, probably from the Dal-Tex Building, missed. The second was fired from the grassy knoll and hit the president in the throat. The third shot probably came from the south-west corner of the Texas School Book Depository and hit Governor Connolly from behind. The fourth shot was possibly fired from the south-east corner of the Depository (the 'sniper's nest') and hit Kennedy in the back. The fifth shot was fired from the grassy knoll and hit Kennedy in the front of the head. This was, in effect, the fatal shot. The sixth shot followed the same trajectory as the third shot and hit Connolly in the wrist.

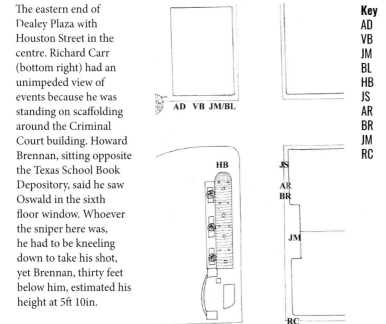

The eastern end of Dealey Plaza with Houston Street in the centre. Richard Carr (bottom right) had an unimpeded view of events because he was standing on scaffolding around the Criminal Court building. Howard Brennan, sitting opposite the Texas School Book Depository, said he saw Oswald in the sixth floor window. Whoever the sniper here was, he had to be kneeling down to take his shot, yet Brennan, thirty feet below him, estimated his height at 5ft 10in.

Key

AD	Mrs Avery Davis
VB	Virginia Baker
JM	Joe Molina
BL	Billy Lovelady
HB	Howard Brennan
JS	Officer Joe Marshall Smith
AR	Arnold Rowland
BR	Barbara Rowland
JM	Joseph Milteer
RC	Richard Carr

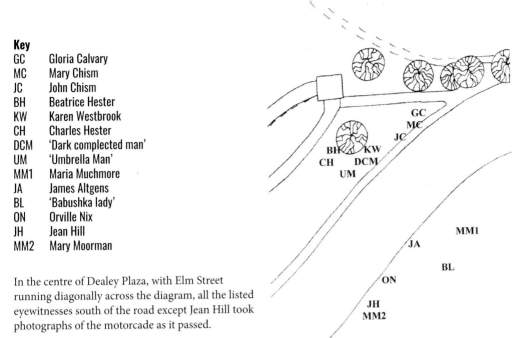

Key

GC	Gloria Calvary
MC	Mary Chism
JC	John Chism
BH	Beatrice Hester
KW	Karen Westbrook
CH	Charles Hester
DCM	'Dark complected man'
UM	'Umbrella Man'
MM1	Maria Muchmore
JA	James Altgens
BL	'Babushka lady'
ON	Orville Nix
JH	Jean Hill
MM2	Mary Moorman

In the centre of Dealey Plaza, with Elm Street running diagonally across the diagram, all the listed eyewitnesses south of the road except Jean Hill took photographs of the motorcade as it passed.

The most famous observer of the day's events was Abraham Zapruder, standing on a raised concrete block with his secretary, Marilyn Stiltzman. His cinefilm of the assassination ought to have explained what happened, but it has been interpreted in a variety of ways over the past sixty years. The only other cameraman was Gary Arnold, who tried to take photographs from behind the fence on the top of the grassy knoll but was shooed away by someone he believed was Secret Service. Sam Holland and James Simmons should not have been on top of the triple underpass because the police had cleared that area. James Tague (bottom of diagram) was hit by flying debris caused by a bullet.

Key

MS	Marilyn Stiltzman
AZ	Abraham Zapruder
WN	William Newman
GN	Gayle Newman
EH	Ed Hoffman
GA	Gary Arnold
AL	Aurelia Lorenzo
MW	Mary Woodward
AD	Ann Donaldson
MB	Maggie Brown
SH	Sam Holland
JS	James Simmons
MS	Malcolm Summers
JT	James Tague

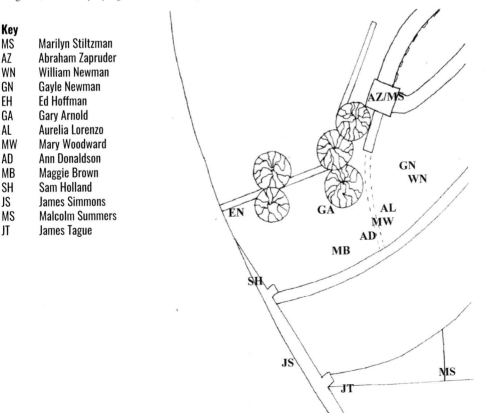

The focus of the Kennedy Assassination was the Texas School Book Depository on Elm Street. The odd shape on top of the roof is a Hertz Rentacar ad. The blacked-out window, top right, is the so-called 'sniper's nest' or 'Oswald window' on the sixth floor. British readers should note that Americans start counting at 'one', not 'ground'. Experts argue that at least two shots came from the opposite window on the left of the diagram on the sixth floor.

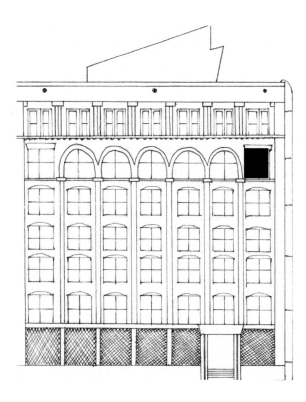

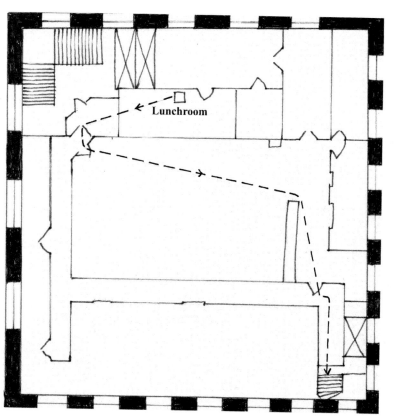

Lunchroom

Oswald was seen by two witnesses at a Coke machine in the lunchroom and by another witness on his way out (where the arrow is in the diagonal dotted line on diagram). After that, his route out of the building is merely an assumption. Would a man who had just killed the president not go out of the readily available back entrance rather than so publicly through the front?

Elm Street

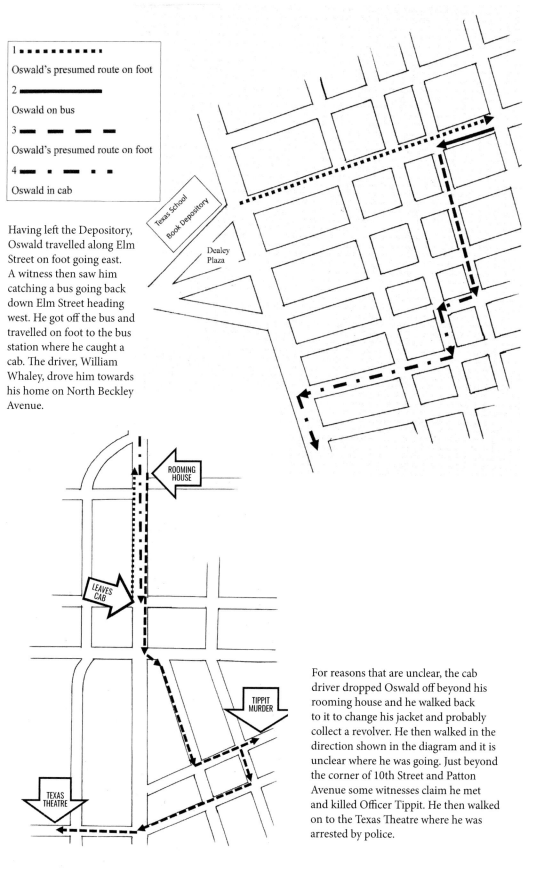

1 ▪ ▪ ▪ ▪ ▪ ▪ ▪ ▪ ▪ ▪

Oswald's presumed route on foot

2 ━━━━━━━━━

Oswald on bus

3 ━ ━ ━ ━ ━

Oswald's presumed route on foot

4 ━ ▪ ━ ▪ ━ ▪

Oswald in cab

Having left the Depository, Oswald travelled along Elm Street on foot going east. A witness then saw him catching a bus going back down Elm Street heading west. He got off the bus and travelled on foot to the bus station where he caught a cab. The driver, William Whaley, drove him towards his home on North Beckley Avenue.

Texas School Book Depository

Dealey Plaza

ROOMING HOUSE

LEAVES CAB

TIPPIT MURDER

TEXAS THEATRE

For reasons that are unclear, the cab driver dropped Oswald off beyond his rooming house and he walked back to it to change his jacket and probably collect a revolver. He then walked in the direction shown in the diagram and it is unclear where he was going. Just beyond the corner of 10th Street and Patton Avenue some witnesses claim he met and killed Officer Tippit. He then walked on to the Texas Theatre where he was arrested by police.

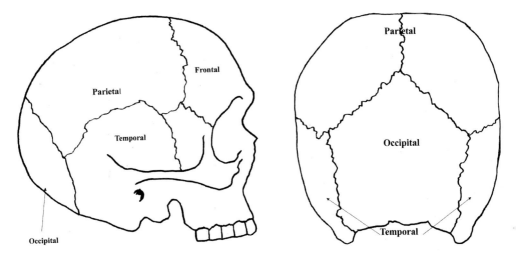

The doctors at Parkland and Bethesda Hospitals inevitably used medical jargon to describe Kennedy's head wounds. Almost all of them talk about sections of the parietal and occipital areas being affected by the wounds.

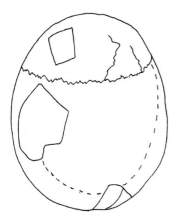

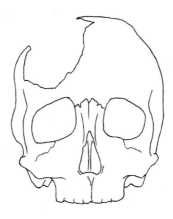

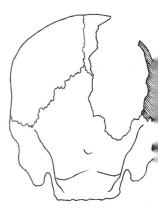

This diagram is taken from a sketch made by Dr J. Thornton Boswell during the Bethesda autopsy. The original sketch is very unclear but it is obvious that the area inside the dotted line above was the section of skull that was blown out by the impact of a bullet.

The gruesome photographs taken during the autopsy show a mass of blood and brains tangled with the hair. This diagram shows the extent of the wound had the skull been completely visible.

This diagram is taken from the sketch made during the autopsy by lab technician Paul O'Connor. The shaded area on the right was blown sideways by the bullet's impact and was almost separated from the rest of the skull.

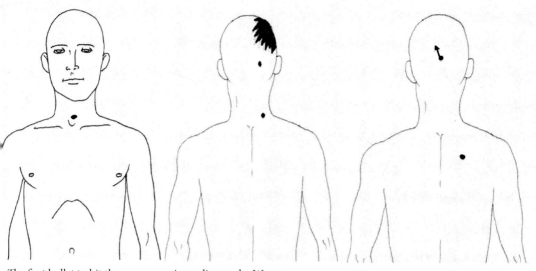

The first bullet to hit the president struck him just above the tie knot. Doctors at Parkland Hospital inserted a tracheotomy tube into this wound to help the president breathe. Doctors at the Bethesda autopsy did not know that this was an entry wound and according to the Warren Commission it was actually an exit wound from a bullet fired from behind.

According to the Warren Commission, Kennedy was hit only from behind and in this diagram the lowest wound is shown in the neck to fit what the Commission called an exit wound at the front of the throat. In fact, this wound was six inches lower down in Kennedy's back.

This diagram, taken from Dr Boswell's original at Bethesda, shows the correct position of the back wound and the arrow in the head wound is there to indicate that the shot could not have come from a steep angle above.

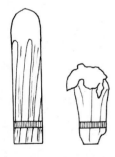

On the left, we have Warren Commission Exhibit 399. This bullet, almost pristine, was allegedly responsible for a total of seven wounds to Kennedy and Connolly. It became known as the 'magic bullet' because it had to turn in midair in order to hit both men. The bullet on the right is of the same calibre and was fired through the wrist of a cadaver as a test. It only, therefore, caused one wound and the extent of the damage to the bullet is apparent.

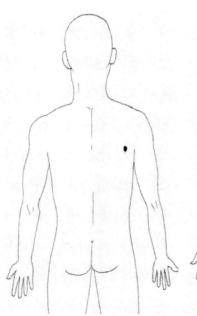

The first shot to hit Governor Connolly struck him from behind. Experts contend that this is not consistent with a shot from the 'sniper's nest'.

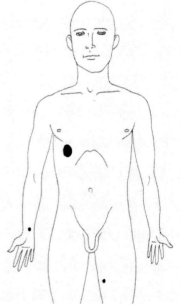

The exit wound of the bullet fired from behind is apparent below Connolly's right nipple. The wrist wound was the result of another shot, the bullet bouncing off bone and embedding itself in the Governor's left thigh.

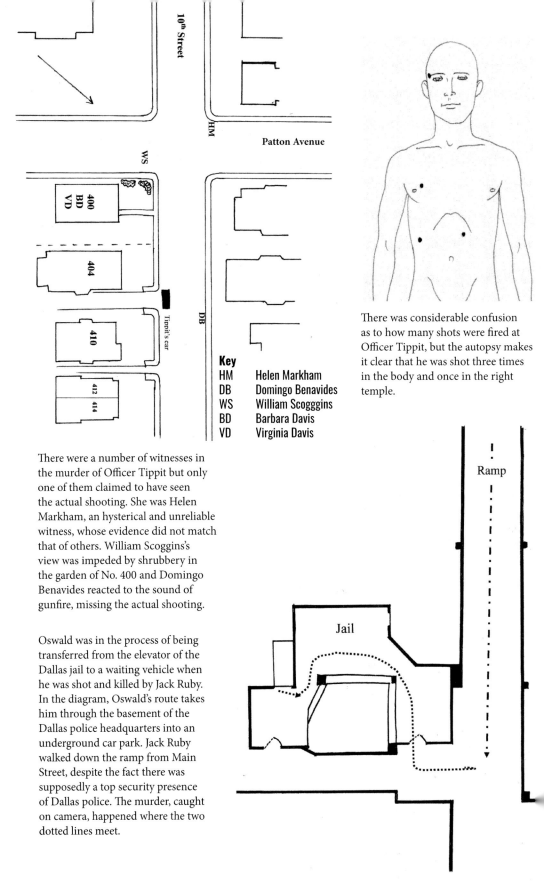

Key

HM	Helen Markham
DB	Domingo Benavides
WS	William Scogggins
BD	Barbara Davis
VD	Virginia Davis

There was considerable confusion as to how many shots were fired at Officer Tippit, but the autopsy makes it clear that he was shot three times in the body and once in the right temple.

There were a number of witnesses in the murder of Officer Tippit but only one of them claimed to have seen the actual shooting. She was Helen Markham, an hysterical and unreliable witness, whose evidence did not match that of others. William Scoggins's view was impeded by shrubbery in the garden of No. 400 and Domingo Benavides reacted to the sound of gunfire, missing the actual shooting.

Oswald was in the process of being transferred from the elevator of the Dallas jail to a waiting vehicle when he was shot and killed by Jack Ruby. In the diagram, Oswald's route takes him through the basement of the Dallas police headquarters into an underground car park. Jack Ruby walked down the ramp from Main Street, despite the fact there was supposedly a top security presence of Dallas police. The murder, caught on camera, happened where the two dotted lines meet.

David Harold Byrd, had founded the Civil Air Patrol to which both Oswald and David Ferrie belonged. The upper floors had no elevator access so that it was likely that only TSBD employees would be up there – this conveniently ignores the existence of workmen repairing the floorboards in November, of course. The building overlooked the proposed route of the presidential motorcade and even if that ran straight along Main Street rather than turning the 'dog-leg' on to Houston and Elm (see map) it would still be within range of a sniper's rifle. There is speculation that the TSBD was a front for illicit gun-running operations to Cuba. Oswald's immediate supervisor in October was William Shelley who claimed not only to have been in the Office of Strategic Services (OSS) in the war, but still had CIA contacts at the time (this has not been substantiated).

Marina's story, which appeared in *Marina and Lee* (1977) that she and Oswald watched Frank Sinatra's *Suddenly* (1954) movie on television appears to be a fabrication. The plot was about a discontented ex-serviceman who plans to shoot a president from a high window with a high-powered rifle. It was almost a perfect blueprint for Dealey Plaza, except that the film was not shown on television any time during October 1963 and in the movie, the plot is discovered and the presidential train does not stop.

On 26 October, Marina gave birth to Audrey at Parkland Hospital. Oswald stayed with Ruth Paine. Almost as soon as the hospital released her, Marina was interviewed by FBI agent Hosty, with Ruth there as an interpreter. Clearly, the surveillance of Oswald was still continuing and Hosty apparently called back, trying to find him. This makes no sense; if the FBI had talked to Marina and Ruth, they certainly knew where Oswald worked, if not where he lived.

The Depository clerk was incensed by this and stormed into the FBI office on 6 November looking for Hosty. He was not in so Oswald left a note, which Hosty later destroyed. He did so on the orders of his boss, James Gordon Shanklin in a move that is bread and butter for the conspiracy theorists. Memories of the note may vary, however. Hosty quoted it later as saying, 'Dear Mr Hasty [*sic*] If you want to talk to me, talk to me. Do not talk to my wife when I am not around. If you do not cease and desist, I will have to take the matter up with the proper authorities.' FBI receptionist Mary Fenner remembered it differently. 'Let this be a warning. I will blow up the FBI and the Dallas Police Department if you don't stop bothering my wife.' The note was not known publicly until 1971, by which time most of America still clung to the belief that Oswald had shot the president even if he did not act alone; perhaps Ms Fenner should have lain down in a darkened room!

The HSCA criticized both Hosty and Shanklin (quite rightly) for the destruction of this note. Alex Cox thinks they should have been jailed, but if Hosty's recollection of the contents is correct, how does it pertain to the assassination of the president? What is inexcusable is that various television documentaries consistently treated Hosty as a reliable witness, especially since his name and address was in Oswald's address book. If, of course, Oswald really was an FBI informant, the removal of the note and the address makes sense.

Another mysterious note, apparently written by Oswald on 8 November, was very vague and addressed to 'Mr Hunt'. That caused confusion, because the name is scattered all over the Kennedy killing; Haroldson Lafayette Hunt was the millionaire oil man and right-wing friend of Lyndon Johnson. He had two sons – Nelson and Lamar – who, unsurprisingly, shared their father's wealth and politics. Then there was E. Howard Hunt, the CIA agent later up to his neck in Richard Nixon's Watergate scandal. Author Mark Lane believes that he killed JFK but it remains unclear to whom Oswald was writing. The note asked for a meeting to make Oswald's position clear, but which of the Hunts could help him with this (or what his position was) remains a mystery. It may, of course, be a forgery.

The next day, 9 November, Oswald used Ruth Paine's typewriter (the only typed letter of his in existence) for a letter to the Russian embassy in Washington. This sounds like a forgery. Oswald could write in Russian and the Russophile Paine had a Russian typewriter. The spelling mistakes (a trademark of the dyslexic Oswald) are more numerous than usual, especially since we have the handwritten original, in which there are fewer errors. Incidentally, Ruth Paine made a copy of this letter and passed it to the FBI. It has vanished. The inference in the letter is that Oswald was in Mexico to meet KGB agents, including, possibly, 'Comrade Kostin' (Valeri Kostin) a Soviet assassin. The same day, Oswald, who could not drive, test-drove a car near Dealey Plaza, complaining to the salesman, Albert Bogard, that the price was prohibitive and compared it to the situation in Russia, to which he might return. Whoever this was, it was not Lee Harvey Oswald.

Similarly, it was not Oswald who turned up at the Sports Drome Rifle Range on 15 November, being loud and obnoxious and shooting at other people's targets. But a lone nut with a rifle in his hand – somebody knew that was too good an opportunity to pass up. Three days later, both Dallas newspapers reported the changed route for the president's motorcade, including the potentially dangerous dog-leg that would take him right under Oswald's window at a dangerously slow speed.

On Friday, 22 November, St Cecilia's Day to Catholics like Kennedy, Lee Oswald had spent the night with Marina at the Paine house and left his wedding ring on the bedside table. Some reports claimed that he left his wallet too, but he was carrying that later in the day when he was arrested and a second one, bizarrely, turned up near the Tippit murder scene where two Dallas police claimed he had dropped it. Oswald had a lift from a co-worker Buell Wesley Frazier, who was a neighbour of the Paines. This was the only time other than Mondays when Frazier took Oswald to work. He and his sister testified to the Warren Commission that Oswald carried a package in brown paper, which he said were curtain rods. Exactly why he should be taking these to the Book Depository was unknown but both Frazier and his sister denied that the bag was large enough to hold a rifle, even disassembled. They got to Dealey Plaza at 8 a.m.

From then on, presumably, Oswald went about his stock-taking business as usual. After that, he either ignored the crowds outside and sat having his lunch in the refectory at 12.15 or he made his way to the sixth floor, assembled the gun he may have had in the package after all and created the 'sniper's nest' for his shots on to Elm Street.

Then he killed John Kennedy.

Chapter 9

... and his Killer

Jack Leon Rubenstein is nearly as enigmatic and complicated as Lee Harvey Oswald. Whole books have been written about him as they have about Oswald, but Jack Ruby is the only man in Dallas that fateful November weekend who we *know* killed somebody.

The testimony that you read in Chapter 7 is taken solely from Ruby's account of his involvement in the assassination of both the president and Oswald. But we know that Ruby was Mob and to such men, lying is a way of life. When asked why he killed Oswald, Ruby told his interrogators that he felt sorry for Mrs Kennedy and did not want her to have to relive the horror of Dealey Plaza by returning to Dallas for a trial. He later admitted that that was a ruse dreamed up by his first legal counsel because it put him in a good light. Nobody believed it for a moment, any more than they believed Ruby's family and friends who all claimed that the night club owner had no links with the Mafia at all. 'Family and friends' – is that not what the Mafia is all about? At least as long as family and friends do not get in the way of profit and power. The debunkers, of course, just see Ruby as a soft-hearted patriot.

Ruby had a reputation as a hard man. He was 5ft 9in and putting on weight by 1963 but he was pugnacious and surprisingly fast on his feet. Barney Weinstein, who ran a rival club to Ruby's Carousel Club, told newsmen, 'Jack had seven fights a week. I've had three ... in thirty years.'

In Dallas, Ruby was regarded as a foreigner, with his Chicago accent and northern city suits. What made him acceptable, apart from the way he would 'flash the cash' and smarm around the police force, was his membership of the Mob, an international brotherhood best represented in the South by Carlos Marcello. The Mafioso was based in New Orleans with its convoluted links with Lee Oswald, but Dallas was part of his empire by 1960. It was not until 1978 that the HSCA established 'associations between Jack Ruby and several individuals affiliated with the underworld activities of Carlos Marcello'. Ruby's personal friend Joseph Civello was the go-between for the nightclub owner and the godfather and was one of nearly a hundred Mafiosi arrested by police in the notorious Apalachin raid in 1957. At that meeting, the hoods had simultaneously turned up to inquire after the health of their host, Joseph Barbara, apparently on a whim. One told police that he had a cracked windshield in his car and had driven 65 miles out of his way to have it fixed. Like Ruby, he was lying for America! When District Attorney Jim Garrison launched the only legal attempt to nail JFK's killers, he did not include Marcello, claiming that he found no evidence of his involvement in organized crime. This could be that Garrison was as crook-blind as J. Edgar Hoover, who said there *was* no organized crime in the United States. Or it could be (as *Life* magazine said in 1967) that Marcello's bag-man, Mario Marino, had arranged (and paid for) a number of stays for Garrison at Las Vegas hotels.

In his prolonged account of the twenty-four hours before Kennedy was killed and afterwards, Ruby gabbled out thirty-five names of people he contacted, either by phone or in person. No doubt running a seedy enterprise like the Carousel brought him into contact with a large number of people, but shooting out names as though from a scatter-gun seems like a ruse to confuse. His own lawyers and, more especially, the prosecution, would have to spend weeks chasing them all up. What he did *not* admit to, but which was uncovered by FBI phone checks, was that he made several calls to various Mob associates, especially in the run-up to the killing of Kennedy.

Ruby admitted that he was in the *Dallas Morning News* office at the time of the shooting and could have had a more or less ringside seat overlooking Dealey Plaza. Two independent witnesses place him in Parkland Hospital soon after Kennedy was brought in and there is even a photograph of a man who *may* be him standing in a crowd on the top of the grassy knoll.

One of those who saw him at the hospital was Seth Kantor, a Scripps-Howard newsman who rode in the motorcade. He wrote *Who Was Jack Ruby?* in 1978, re-released as *The Ruby Cover-Up* in 1992, in which he posed vital questions that should have been raised at Ruby's trial for Oswald's murder and by the Warren Commission. Ruby was in deep financial trouble in November 1963. This, of course, is not criminal in itself, but it was a motive for a desperate man to become somebody's patsy, just as Oswald had. That afternoon, bank employee William Cox witnessed Ruby carrying several thousand dollars in cash, which did not go into or come out of his account. Ruby's links with the DPD were well established; he got into the station basement unimpeded and sheltered behind a policeman before jumping out to shoot Oswald. That policeman was William J. 'Blackie' Harrison, who may have told the shooter the precise time at which Oswald was to be moved. Both Harrison and his fellow cop Louis D. Miller testified before the Warren Commission and Miller in particular was openly hostile. For a man who claimed only to have drunk coffee with Harrison on the morning of Oswald's murder, he seemed to have a lot of baggage he would rather the Warren Commission did not know about. Ruby's testimony of his sudden impulse to kill Oswald and his ease of access down the ramp was clearly hogwash.

On the afternoon of the Kennedy killing, Ruby met a DPD officer, Harry N. Olsen, who was living with one of Ruby's girls, a British stripper, Kay Coleman, in Eighth Street, Oak Cliff, not far from Ruby's home and the scene of J.D. Tippit's murder. Olsen had broken his kneecap earlier in the year and was now on restricted duties as a result. That day, he was on a desk job as a security guard in Oak Cliff, but, bizarrely, could not remember exactly where or for whom. As a number of people have commented, Olsen must be the only person in Dallas (perhaps the entire United States) who could not remember where he was when Kennedy was killed. It may be a stretch too far to conclude, as conspiracy theorist Penn Jones does, that, if Olsen was on Eighth Street, on high ground, he *could* have witnessed the Tippit shooting. Olsen was known, even by his own boss, Chief Curry, to be unstable. He carried an illegal gun and brass knuckles (neither of which would be allowed today) and had been at the Carousel late the previous night. Ruby told Olsen that he had seen Oswald at the police station and that he looked 'just like a little rat. He was sneaky looking, like a weasel.' Clearly, Jack Ruby had it in for rodents.

Bearing in mind Ruby's propensity for muscling in anywhere he was not wanted, it is not too surprising to find him either at the grassy knoll or Parkland. What *is* surprising is that he did not mention it. Was that because he may have had a specific purpose for the hospital visit, rather than general nosiness, and the appearance of Kantor and Wilma Tice who knew him must have thrown him into a panic.

One of the most ludicrous pieces of 'evidence' on which the Warren Commission relied was Exhibit 399, which came to be known as the 'magic bullet' (see Chapter 10). It was found on a stretcher at Parkland, is brass-jacketed and has a single twist or deformity halfway along its length. According to Arlen Specter, the lawyer who invented the theory, that bullet had already smashed through Kennedy, turned miraculously in mid-air, ploughed through Governor Connally and ended up on the stretcher, having fallen out of his thigh wound. As we have seen, the tortuous tale of this missile has recently been made even more so by Secret Serviceman Landis. Needless to say, the bullet was a match for Oswald's Carcano rifle. Was it a match because Jack Ruby had put it there? Was that what he was *really* doing at Parkland Hospital?

Ruby's counsel was the mercurial Californian attorney Melvin Belli. As one commentator wrote at the time, 'he came into town like God on a sunbeam … He's a real talking piece of furniture.' It was obvious that Belli had no affinity with Dallas or the South and had nothing but contempt for DA Wade and Bill Alexander. In the book on Ruby that Belli wrote in 1964, he cited five reasons for defending a clearly guilty man: 'to save Jack Ruby; to strengthen our law; to demonstrate the inadequacy of the archaic M'Naghten Rule on legal insanity; to wed more securely modern science to modern law; to help Dallas solve its problem.'

In pleading temporary insanity for Ruby, Belli got it spectacularly wrong. The M'Naghten Rule applied in both the United States and Britain ever since a maniac (Daniel M'Naghten) tried to assassinate Prime Minister Robert Peel in 1843 and even at the time, such a defence plea was inadequate. Belli's point was that psychiatry had moved on in the past 120 years, but to most Americans (and, one suspects, the jury) that was irrelevant. A huge number of citizens who had watched the Oswald murder on live television, actually approved of what Ruby had done and the Mobster himself clearly expected to walk from court a free man. Belli claimed that Ruby's temporary insanity (one of the most convenient excuses ever devised in a law court) was caused by the nightclub owner's psychomotor epilepsy, the result of repeated head injuries throughout his life. Incidentally, it is not likely that twelve Dallas citizens would take kindly to the attorney's assertion that their city had a 'problem' which only Belli could solve.

Not only did the jury find Ruby guilty but they demanded the death penalty. Belli was gobsmacked and furious in equal measure – 'May I thank the jury for a victory for bigotry and injustice!' he screamed in front of the cameras and even played the race card – 'I try to be clinical, but I guess I'm at my best when somebody's kicking the shit out of some poor little Jew boy.'

Looking at his behaviour and his swagger, it is *very* difficult to see Jack Ruby as a victim. Belli had not done the man any favours either by implying that Ruby was homosexual (he shared an apartment with George Senator), had gonorrhoea and was borderline village idiot.

Ruby's time in prison was cushy. At first on suicide watch (Jack was *far* too fond of Jack for that) he liked nothing better than to gossip with other inmates and even prison guards. If Ruby was paranoid, this probably worsened in jail and he was taken to Parkland from time to time for check-ups. He was deluged with mail, mostly from 'fans' applauding what he had done.

Just how paranoid Ruby was by June 1964 while he waited for his trial is uncertain, but he asked to see Earl Warren and Gerald Ford, two members of the Commission that had produced twenty-six volumes detailing Kennedy's assassination (see Chapter 10). Ruby was polite throughout, but clearly terrified. He asked Warren if he could be transferred to Washington. He was prepared to take any polygraph tests and doubted whether his counsel, Joe Tonahill, would defend him properly. 'I want to tell the truth,' he told Warren, 'and I can't tell it here … Gentlemen, my life is in danger here … my whole family is in jeopardy.' He pointed a finger at a 'certain organization', the right-wing John Birch Society, run by General Edwin A. Walker. 'Don't register with you, does it?' Warren admitted that he had no idea what Ruby was talking about; but then, the former chief justice *did* have the legal power to have the Mobster moved to Washington and refused to do it.

For two and a half years after the trial, Ruby's defence team (minus Belli, who had been fired) lodged various appeals on ever-more-spurious grounds. Tonahill, Wade, Alexander and others attached to Ruby's case in whatever capacity, argued among themselves about whether Ruby's original defence had really been in his best interests. There was talk of 'Commie lawyers' and Jack being 'railroaded' but by October 1966 Ruby's conviction was reversed. By the time he heard the news, the Mobster was already vomiting blood, a symptom of the cancer that would kill him on 3 January 1967.

Before he died, Ruby made two accusations, both of which have entered the murky world of conspiracy theories and neither of which can be validated. The first was that the man who orchestrated Kennedy's murder was the man with most to gain by it – his vice president and successor in the White House, Lyndon Johnson. In letters that Ruby wrote to family and friends from prison, he said, 'Isn't it strange that Oswald ... should be fortunate enough to get a job at the [Book Depository] two weeks before?' Technically, it was Marina Oswald's friend Ruth Paine who got Oswald the job but the building itself was owned by David Harold Byrd, a Bircher with links to most of the Dallas oil men.

Not enough research has been carried out on Ruth Paine and her husband Michael. He had worked for the Bell Helicopter company in Fort Worth, one of the defence contractors who benefited from Lyndon Johnson's upping of American involvement in Vietnam to war level (see Chapter 13), and Paine's amicable moving out of his home shortly before the assassination meant that Ruth had a spare room to accommodate Marina Oswald. Ruth spoke fluent Russian and took the girl under her wing. She was also, of course, a part of the White Russian group in Fort Worth and Dallas and knew the de Mohrenschildts. The incriminating photographs, supposedly taken by Marina, of Oswald in the backyard with rifle, pistol and Communist literature, were found in Ruth's house and she owned a station wagon similar to the one seen by several witnesses near the Book Depository on the day of the assassination. Oswald's famous warning to the Dallas police – 'leave her out of this. She didn't have anything to do with it' – seems a little lame, all things considered.

'Only one person,' Ruby's smuggled letter goes on, 'could have that information [Oswald's job overlooking the motorcade route] and that man was Johnson ... because he is the one who was going to arrange the trip ...'

Again, technically, the choice of Dallas for the Kennedy visit was not Johnson's alone, but the idea of Governor Connally and Senator Yarborough. The actual motorcade route was decided by the Secret Service, acting in conjunction with the Dallas Police Department and the FBI. 'You may learn quite a bit about Johnson,' Ruby wrote, 'and how he has fooled everyone ...'

Sixty years on, we do indeed know a lot more about Johnson. He was a foul-mouthed bully, using his height, bulk and infamous stare to cow opponents. He was a prize liar in a world where lying was the norm and when asked why he wanted to go to war in Vietnam, unzipped his fly and exposed himself, growling, 'This is why!' Any man who can do that and believe that international diplomacy is all about a 'mine's bigger than yours' competition, is certainly not what the office of president is all about. Does that mean that he is the kind of man who would engineer the removal of his boss in so brutal a fashion? We will discover this in Chapter 13.

But in the meantime, Jack Ruby had another bombshell to burst. Dying of cancer as he was, he claimed that he had been deliberately injected with a deadly cocktail of drugs to keep him quiet about Johnson's involvement in the Kennedy killing. And he may have told this story to investigative journalist Dorothy Kilgallen who interviewed Ruby in jail. She told friends that she would soon 'break open the Kennedy case'. Kilgallen was found dead in her New York apartment on 8 November 1965 (see Chapter 11), just the day before the equally sudden death of her friend Florence Smith. Smith's cause of death was unresolved; Kilgallen's was due to 'ingestion of alcohol and barbiturates'.

The deaths of these two women are among those mysterious ends met by a surprising number of people connected with the Kennedy case and will be investigated later, but the coincidences are astonishing – 'I wouldn't try to speak for Dallas,' the journalist wrote, 'but around here [New York], the people I talk to really believe that a man has the right to be tried in court' – and Ruby's death and Kilgallen's stem from that. Conspiracy theorists Richard Belzer and David Wayne believe that the journalist was silenced in view of her threatened exposé of the Kennedy assassination. Whether this was related to Johnson or Kilgallen's alleged research on the Ruby interview is unknown.

In the dark and unknowable world of the deep state there were rumours that super-cancer drugs were being developed as part of a biological warfare programme in the 1960s and that Kilgallen, Smith and Ruby were all guinea pigs for that experimentation. This is as lunatic as the fringe gets, but if we focus on Ruby, his death does seem fortuitous.

We know from his meeting with Earl Warren that Ruby was in fear for his life in the Dallas jail. Deputy Sheriff Al Maddox reported that he had told him that he had been injected for a cold, but that he had deliberately been given cancer cells. Maddox said, 'You don't believe that bullshit?' Ruby replied, 'I damn sure do.'

Chapter 10

The Warren Omission*

The words sounded grand – 'This is a sad time for all people. We have suffered a loss that cannot be weighed. For me it is a deep personal tragedy ... I will do my best. That is all I can do. I ask for your help – and God's.' This was Lyndon Johnson soon after Air Force One touched down in Washington on 22 November 1963. Unfortunately, the best that he could do was to set up the Warren Commission, a body of men straight out of the 'system's' playbook, without time, adequate resources or any breadth of vision to find out what *really* happened in Dealey Plaza.

Johnson was effectively in a fix. The moods of nations and the sweep of international politics are constantly changing and there are relatively few alive today who remember the chill of the Cold War. It was less than ten years since Senator McCarthy of Wisconsin had struck terror into the hearts of millions of Americans by claiming that there were 'reds under the beds' at all levels of American society. The sociopath Joseph Stalin was dead, but few in the West thought much better of Nikita Khrushchev and his successors in the Kremlin. What we now know – and very few did in 1963/4 – was that assassination of world leaders was an active policy of both the Russian and the American governments. The Kennedy brothers had given their blessing to attempts on the life of Fidel Castro; what if he, independently or backed by Russia, should use Dallas as payback time? Such realpolitik could lead to World War Three. In that context, Johnson was anxious

---

* Historian Walt Brown's book title from 1996.

to prove that the killing of Kennedy was a domestic affair – there was no worldwide conspiracy. It was intriguing that Castro himself, in a speech the day after the assassination, agreed; the Americans had killed their own president.

That was why Johnson had rung Captain Will Fritz of the Dallas police at lunchtime on the day after the assassination – 'You've got your man. The investigation is over.' Either Johnson knew a lot more about Oswald than he was letting on or this comment was wishful thinking. But he clearly passed the same message on to Assistant Attorney General Nicholas Katzenbach. Briefly paralyzed by grief as Robert Kennedy was (or, if you believe author Seymour Hersh, desperately busy covering up his brother's indiscretions), Katzenbach effectively took over Bobby's duties. This played into Johnson's hands; he detested Bobby as much as he detested JFK. In the words of one Mafia Mobster, the Mob's *bête noire* was now 'just another lawyer'.

On 25 November, with Oswald dead and the world ready for the grandmother of all cover-ups, Katzenbach wrote a memo to Johnson's press secretary, Bill Moyers:

It is important that all of the facts surrounding President Kennedy's assassination be made public in a way which will satisfy people in the United States and abroad that all the facts have been told and that a statement to this effect be made now. 1) The public must be satisfied that Oswald was the assassin; that he did not have any confederates who are still at large; and that the evidence was such that he would have been convicted at trial. 2) Speculation about Oswald's motivation ought to be cut off and we should have some basis for rebutting thought that this was a Communist conspiracy or (as the Iron Curtain press is saying) a right-wing conspiracy to blame it on the Communists. Unfortunately, the facts on Oswald seem too pat – too obvious (Marxist, Cuba, Russian wife etc). The Dallas police have put out statements on the Communist conspiracy theory and it was they who were in charge when he was shot and thus silenced. 3) The matter has been handled thus far with neither dignity nor conviction. Facts have been mixed with rumour and speculation.

It would be difficult to find a more damning document than this. Katzenbach's role, as Acting Attorney General, was to administer justice. Yet, without trial and with conflicting evidence, 'Oswald was the assassin'. All in all, you do not get more 'deep state' than Nicholas Katzenbach.

So, Lyndon Johnson set up the Warren Commission not to find answers to difficult questions, but to prove Oswald's guilt. No wonder researchers like Harold Weisberg have condemned the whole fiasco as a whitewash. Weisberg's first book of the same name was published in 1965, just over a year after the Commission's twenty-six volumes appeared. The volumes had no index, making it difficult for critics and researchers to analyse it. One of the researchers was Sylvia Meagher who not only wrote an excellent book of her own, *Accessories After the Fact* (1967), but provided an index for the first time.

Weisberg apologizes for the physical appearance of *Whitewash*. The typesetting is directly from a typewriter, there are no conventional page margins and the reproduction of photographs and diagrams is poor. Weisberg had no choice in this. Self-publishing in the mid-1960s was not the behemoth it has become today, where even the most egregious rubbish looks glossy and polished. He approached a total of 103 publishers, magazines and newspapers in the United States, Britain, France and Germany, but although editors were frequently and genuinely excited by what they universally acclaimed to be an important book, no one would actually publish it. This woeful inactivity on the part of mainstream media (especially in the States) is examined in Chapter 14.

Committees of the Warren type do not have the power of a court of law. If a witness was proved to have perjured himself/herself, all the Commission could do was to recommend investigation by an actual law enforcement body. There is no doubt, with evidence we now have, that several witnesses did indeed lie, for a whole host of reasons, but the real culpability lies with the Commission itself. We have already seen, from Katzenbach and Johnson, what its real brief was – pin the murder on Oswald, the lone gun-nut. Anything else was ruled out.

Various people have pointed to the integrity of the Commission, as though famous names are beyond reproach. But it was a *presidential* body, not one created by Congress and that curtailed its extent and powers. Of the seven members of the panel, only three – Senator Richard Russell, Senator John Cooper and Representative Thomas Hale Boggs – showed by their conduct and questions an admirable degree of impartiality. The other four sang from the government hymn sheet.

Chief Justice Earl Warren did not want the job as chairman, to the extent that there were embarrassing tearful exchanges in Lyndon Johnson's office. For the Chief Justice of the Supreme Court of the United States, Earl Warren seems to have had an astonishingly warped idea of the concept of justice. Using his usual bullying tactics, Johnson leaned on him and spoke of millions of American dead if it was discovered that Oswald was working for a foreign (Communist) power. With Nicholas Katzenbach's very similar words ringing in his ears, Warren left the Oval Office sobbing and appointed staff on his Commission who would evaluate the evidence against Oswald as presented by the FBI, whose Director, J. Edgar Hoover, had said that law and order has very little to do with justice. The fact that Warren could not *quite* pack his panel with yes men (Russell, Cooper and Boggs rejected him) did not deter the Chief Justice from partial appointments on the panel and among staffers who made the Commission little more than a trial of Lee Oswald in which Oswald had no rights to a defence. This is the man who created the Commission and who was defended for years by blinkered apologists like Vincent Bugliosi and Gerald Posner.

As Warren told a reporter who asked him when all the documents in the Kennedy case would become available, '... not in your lifetime'. And, as researcher James DiEugenio adds, 'One wonders just how many lifetimes Warren was talking about.' When given an opportunity to get the truth from Jack Ruby by moving him for his own safety from Dallas to Washington, Warren flatly refused.

Representative Gerald Ford, who went on to become president himself in 1974, was arguably the most stupid man ever to enter the White House, which Lyndon Johnson attributed to his having played too much football without a helmet! Ford has the distinction of being the only president who was once a male model and who pardoned the most corrupt president of them all, Richard Nixon. In the context of the Warren Commission, he personally moved the recorded position of Kennedy's back wound to one in the neck, so that all the 'shots from behind' scenarios would be believed.

James DiEugenio refers to Ford, Allen Dulles, John McCloy and J. Edgar Hoover as 'four of the most repellent characters in post-war American history' and it is difficult to disagree with that. All four had a murky history of covert activity that is completely at odds with the concept of an honest, free and democratic America that Kennedy was trying to foster. When Ford published his own book on the killing – *Portrait of the Assassin* – it was not only one of the dullest books ever written, it was simply a rehash of the Commission's findings before the records of the Commission were declassified. Nobody had the ammunition to challenge it.

Dulles had cosied up to Nazi big business in the 1930s, hob-nobbing with millionaires like Hjalmar Schacht, I.G. Farben and Fritz Thyssen. When the war ended, as head of the OSS in Germany, he turned his attention to Soviet Russia, ordering his subordinates to 'find out what the Commies are up to'. One of those subordinates was Richard Helms, who featured heavily as head of the CIA in 1963. It was Dulles who engineered the escape of Nazi Intelligence chief Reinhard Gehlen from Bavaria in 1945 because Gehlen had the goods on Soviet espionage. As DiEugenio writes, 'a man who should have been in the dock at Nuremberg was now allowed to start and exacerbate the Cold War.'

Without doubt, Dulles made money – a lot of it – out of his directorship of the CIA. Wags said that the acronym stood for Corporate Interests of America. It was under Dulles that the 'Executive Action' programme was developed, the term a euphemism for political assassination of enemies. Two underlings involved in this were David Atlee Phillips (see Chapter 13) and E. Howard Hunt, both of whom were up to their necks in the events in Dealey Plaza.

Clearly the man had learned nothing from his firing by Kennedy after the Bay of Pigs. When researcher David S. Lifton challenged him concerning gun smoke having been at the top of the grassy knoll, Dulles scoffed, 'Now, what are you saying, someone was smoking up there?'

Allen Dulles should never have been on the Commission at all. The CIA's involvement in the murder of Kennedy is undeniable, however much the mainstream media still denies it. Whenever Commission witnesses strayed remotely near covert operations or Intelligence activity, Dulles was there to deflect them, to the extent that some have claimed the body should have been called the Dulles Commission. When he was subpoenaed by Jim Garrison, the District Attorney of New Orleans in the trial of Clay Shaw, Dulles had such contempt for the law that he simply ignored it.

John McCloy screamed establishment. He was a former president of the World Bank, an assistant secretary of defence and a former high commissioner for Germany. All you need to know about his attitude to justice is summed up in the phrase that America was not 'a banana republic, where a government can be changed by conspiracy'.

Therefore, there could be no conspiracy at all and the guilty Oswald acted alone. McCloy was a Harvard commercial lawyer who joined a Wall Street firm handling the business of the Rockefeller estate. He married into money because he obviously liked the stuff and in this obnoxiously rich enclave became bosom buddies with Allen Dulles. He pushed hard for one of the most shameful injustices in American history – the internment of several thousand Japanese Americans after Pearl Harbor. When reminded that his actions had been unconstitutional, he replied, 'If it is a question of the safety of the country or the Constitution of the United States, why, the Constitution is just a scrap of paper to me.' Which rather echoes Harold Ickes' view of the man in the 1930s, that he was 'more or less inclined to be a fascist'. Such men have a warped view of justice. But McCloy went further. In the de-Nazification programme instituted by Konrad Adenauer, West Germany's chancellor, McCloy reviewed a number of cases where the death penalty had been proscribed. He lessened the sentence by commutation in half the cases, even though the guilty were members of the Einsatzgruppen, the extermination squads responsible for the murder of thousands of Jewish civilians.

'The monumental record of the President's Commission,' Ford wrote later, 'will stand like a Gibraltar of factual literature through the ages to come.' In fact, it was already being described as a government whitewash by the end of 1964. Astonishingly, as recently as 2018, the same cover-up nonsense was peddled by Nicholas Nalli, senior research scientist at IMSG Inc. (a company set up to help governments plan for climate change impact through feasibility studies). Not only does he cling to the universally discredited verdict of Professor Luis Alvarez in 1988 that the backward jolt of Kennedy's head shown clearly in the Zapruder film was a 'recoil effect', but he claims that all official investigations into the shooting, including the Warren Commission, 'were comprised of [sic] upstanding civil servants of high ethical standards, who, in spite of difficult circumstances, by and large got the basics of the case correct'. What right a physicist has to comment on the probity of politicians I do not know, but in the context of Warren, Dulles, Ford and McCloy, 'how's that,' as sceptical Americans ask, 'working for ya?'

Virtually everybody else, including the fourteen assistant counsel and twelve staffers, had a legal background. And lawyers, whatever they try to tell you, are not much interested in justice; they work for a client. And in the case of the Warren Commission, the client was Lyndon Johnson's government. J. Lee Rankin led the legal team and was omnipresent; that was because the panel members were busy men with commitments elsewhere. None of them was present for the duration of the Commission's sitting and so the spade work was done by lawyers. *They* decided who to call as witnesses and who to ignore. *They* badgered witnesses whose answers they did not like. Three of these stand out. Joseph Ball, from California, did his best to pin the guilt on Oswald, ably abetted by David Belin of Iowa. The most aggressive was Arlen Specter of Philadelphia. Known for his bullying tactics, he created the nonsensical 'single bullet theory' to match the number of shots fired in Dealey Plaza. It is deeply ironic that this ultra-conservative figure should be the instigator of the most ludicrous example of conspiracy in the whole tragic story of the Kennedy assassination. At the time, the system and most of the media believed it. And Specter went on to become a senator, just as Gerald Ford went on to become president!

Others, like Wesley Liebeler, were tasked with trying to disentangle Oswald's torturous back story. When he uncovered the man's links to Silvia Odio, the Cuban exile, J. Lee Rankin shut him down with, 'At this stage, we are supposed to be closing doors, not opening them.' So much for due process and the rule of law. And Liebeler himself was hardly squeaky clean. 'The best evidence,' he said, 'that Oswald could fire as fast as he did and hit the target is the fact that he did so.' I would not find this piece of 'logic' impressive in my 6-year-old grandson!

With painstaking patience, Harold Weisberg takes us through the day of the assassination, as reported by the Warren Commission's report alongside the reality. For anyone interested in justice and the truth, it makes depressing and terrifying reading. Not even Belin and Specter could shake the Connallys in their recollection of events, but the governor's memories of the shot sequence (he was an ex-military man and a hunter) were concluded to be mistaken, probably as a result of shock. On the morning of 22 November, Oswald's co-worker Buell Wesley Frazier and his sister Linnie Mae Randall were both mistaken as to the length of the curtain rod package that Oswald carried.

As for Troy Eugene West, who had worked as a wrapper at the Book Depository for sixteen years and swore that Oswald had come nowhere near his desk in pursuit of tape later found on the package, his testimony did not appear in the report at all. It was not until Sylvia Meagher carried out the huge job of indexing the Commission's report that such anomalies emerge. Gerald Posner, as could be predicted, refers to Meagher as a 'committed Leftist' and has apparently found that bias even in her index.

For those who see no elements of 'Big Brother' in the Land of the Free, two FBI agents were sent to interview the wife of Joachim Joesten in New York. He was living in Bonn, Germany, and had published one of the earliest books on the case in 1964, while the Commission was still sitting. *Oswald: Assassin or Fall Guy* clearly ruffled feathers in Washington. To Posner, needless to say, Joesten is 'a German Leftist'. It was Joesten who discovered that Oswald's dingy little apartment had no curtains, which explains the rods in the man's package. As to the existence of these, it was not until 31 August 1964, just before the Commission report went to press, that the Dallas office of the FBI were *looking into* interviewing the Depository supervisor, Roy Truly, as to whether any rods had been found there. Unsurprisingly, nine months after the assassination, Truly did not know anything about them.

So far, the Commission's case had collapsed. It could not shake the Connallys on the number of shots fired or the sequence. It could not prove that Oswald had brought a gun into the Book Depository. In a court of law, a jury would have already decided Oswald's innocence – that is, if the judge had not already thrown it out. But in the Commission, the 'judge' was Earl Warren and he danced to Lyndon Johnson's tune.

In the context of Oswald's ability as a gunman, the Commission turned itself inside out to invent a cold, callous killer of impeccable credentials. It was unfortunate for the man's reputation that he scored 'sharpshooter' level in the Marine Corps, because to most civilians that means an expert, a crack shot. In fact, it is the middle grade of three and Oswald only managed it once, using a new state-of-the-art weapon, shooting at a stationary target that was not the president of the United States! The Warren Commission would have us believe that Oswald fired three shots with his 20-year-old, mail-order, Mannlicher-Carcano bolt action in the space of seconds that no other marksman could achieve in practice tests weeks, months and even years later. In fact, according to his scores with the Marines, Oswald's skill with the rifle *deteriorated* as he went on, which may explain why he became a communications technician before he left the service. The rifle itself cost $10, a trivial sum in 1962/3. Ignoring for the moment why Oswald brought this by mail order rather than from any of Dallas's many gunsmiths, tests carried out by Robert Frazier, the FBI's own arms specialist, proved that the gun was inaccurate and that the sight had been removed, presumably by the Dallas police, in that only they, with the FBI, had access to it. The list of exhibits used by the Commission refers to shims which had been used to attempt to correct the sight defect. These were not present on the gun when it was found in the Depository.

The Carcano was believed to have fired three bullets, which coincides with the number of shots *some* of the Depository witnesses (but by no means all) heard in Dealey Plaza and the three spent cartridge cases on the sixth floor of the Depository. The fourth, (a Western Cartridge Co. make) was still in the breach. Where were all the others? Bullets are bought by the box, yet there is no record of Oswald buying any. Neither were any found at his home, the Paines' home or the Depository itself. As Weisberg sums up the ballistic evidence, 'There is no single thing that is beyond reasonable doubt about the marksman, the rifle, the ammunition, the shooting or number of shots. Except that President Kennedy was killed, Officer Tippit was killed and Governor Connally was wounded.' And that is simply not good enough.

One of the imponderables of the Kennedy shooting is how quickly a description of his killer was made available to all police personnel, which (allegedly) led to the murder of Officer Tippit. The description does not actually fit Oswald – he was younger and lighter than the all-points bulletin – but it allegedly came exclusively from the eyewitness account of construction worker Howard Brennan, who was standing across Elm Street directly opposite the Book Depository. That said, no policeman nor any Secret Service agent could be found who remembered Brennan talking to them immediately after the shooting. He told the Warren Commission that one of them was agent Forrest Sorrels, but Sorrels was not there.

Gerald Ford described Brennan as *the* most important witness in an article in *Life* magazine in October 1964, which is bizarre for a number of reasons. First, Brennan calculated the height of the killer, even though he was looking up to a window six floors above him. On his own admission, he never saw the man below the waist. Second, Brennan could not positively identify Oswald at the police line-up, even though he had seen his face several times on television. Third, and most damningly, he did not see the actual shooting. When John McCloy, anxious to pin the whole thing on Oswald, asked Brennan, 'Did you see the rifle discharge? Did you see the recoil or the flash?'

Brennan answered, 'No.' Yet to Gerald Ford, that most perspicacious of politicians, Brennan was the Commission's best witness.

Having got Oswald into the Depository building itself with a welter of spurious information about the curtain rods, the Commission had to get Oswald out. They claimed he walked casually out of the front door, having shot the president minutes before, and caught a bus. But there were at least four other doors to the building, which led to marshalling yards at the back. There were no crowds there and virtually no risk of the killer being apprehended. Much was made at the time of the shooting and during the Commission's activity of the police sealing off the Depository. But the fact is that this never happened – policemen, Secret Service agents, even members of the press sauntered in and out of the place at will. Umpteen photographs were available to the Commission of the front of the Depository, yet they used none of them. Still and moving images taken by Abraham Zapruder, Ike Altgens and Phillip Willis form a fascinating and accurate montage of events in Dealey Plaza. Yet the Commission was selective in its use of these. Only those that hinted at Oswald as the lone gunman were used. But there were *no* photographs of Oswald at the crime scene. As far as the camera was concerned, he might as well have been on the far side of the moon.

Most contentious of all the evidence the Warren Commission looked at was the Zapruder film, taken from a concrete bollard at the end of the pergola between the Depository and the grassy knoll. The 8mm footage is the clearest evidence we have of what happened. Despite that, a number of problems arose. The Stemmons Freeway sign formed a visual obstacle immediately after the first shot that hit Kennedy. We can see his reactions and those of others in the car. We can see the moments when Governor Connally was hit twice and, above all, the horrendous backward jolt of Kennedy's body and explosion of blood and brain when the fatal head shot hits home. At each shot, Zapruder's camera jerks visibly with the shock of the noise.

The first shot (which was fired from behind Kennedy) was fired at Zapruder frame 155. The second shows Kennedy's hands come up and a reaction only from Jackie. This was fired from the front and hit the president just above the tie knot (the notorious wound obliterated by the tracheotomy insertion), which the Warren Commission insisted was an exit wound of the bullet fired from behind. The third shot hit Kennedy nearly 6 inches below the shoulder line to the right of the spine and was fired from behind. The fourth shot was also from behind and hit the president in the head. It blew out the piece of skull which is clearly shown over the right ear, still attached to the head, at the autopsy. The fifth shot (Zapruder frames 312 and 313) was fired from the front and blew out the back of Kennedy's head. This shot was fired within 1/10 of a second of the previous one and could not possibly have been fired from the same gun.

There is considerable evidence that Zapruder's film was tampered with. Frames 155 (the first shot) and 156 no longer exist. That is because it was spliced either by a government agency or Time Inc., who bought the rights to the film from Zapruder. The Warren Commission decided that the first shot could not have been fired until frame 210 because there was an oak tree obstructing the shooter's view from the sixth floor of the Depository. This supposes, of course that that was the firing position and despite the best efforts of the FBI and the Dallas police that was never established. The oak tree story comes from the FBI files on which the entire Warren Commission investigation was based, specifically from Director J. Edgar Hoover himself. In fact, it was nonsense; there was no tree in the way. The Commission also ignored the evidence of police motorcycle McLain's Dictabelt tape recording, which pinpointed the first shot at frame 155. The Commission and subsequent attempts to exonerate its incompetence and criminality often contend that Dealey Plaza was a giant echo chamber, and that what we hear on the recordings are merely echoes of only three shots fired. There were at least seven shots, one striking the Lincoln's windshield frame (from behind Kennedy) and another hitting the kerb next to witness James Tague, who was hit by flying debris (again from behind the president). Likewise, Zapruder frames numbers 208–11 have been removed. Time Inc.'s explanation for all this is that having paid Zapruder a small fortune for the film, a junior technician worked on it and damaged the film. Why? All he had to do was run it – anything else amounted to deliberate tampering with evidence. Unsurprisingly, the technician was never named. The third shot, at Zapruder frame 226, is the one that caused the most impossible wound of all time, the one involving the 'magic bullet'.

This is clearly shown in the weighty tome by researchers Harrison Livingstone and Robert Groden. Arlen Specter expected the world to buy into the fantasy that a killer (whom he and everyone else in 1964 assumed was Lee Oswald) fired downwards at a moving target 60 degrees below his position in the sniper's nest. It hit Kennedy 5¾ inches below the collar, then travelled upwards, having hit no bone tissue, to exit through his throat, just above the tie knot. Not content with that, the bullet then sharply turns to the right to hit Governor Connally near the right armpit, shattering his fifth rib. Undeterred, the missile exits below Connally's right nipple and shatters his right wrist, raised because he is still waving his Stetson at the crowd. Having now hit two lots of bone, it has the right to change direction again to enter Connally's left thigh. So one bullet caused seven wounds and emerged as Warren Commission No. 399, a missile almost completely undamaged, which corresponded to the calibre of Oswald's Mannlicher-Carcano. The magic bullet had to be created because the authorities were hopelessly wedded to only three bullets having been fired in Dealey Plaza. How Specter expected to persuade his fellow counsel and commissioners to go along with this travesty remains a mystery. Had the Commission been a court of law rather than a mere (toothless) inquiry, opposing counsel would have torn it apart. As it was, the single bullet fired by a single gunman was duly entered into the Commission's report, and not until the House Select Committee on Assassinations twelve years later was that theory demolished. Even then (1976), the HSCA was only prepared to lend speculative support to the notion of a second gunman and made no attempt to exonerate Oswald.

The Zapruder film was a problem, but tinker with the frame sequence and its impact can be reduced. The magic bullet makes no sense, but for at least twelve years, America and the world bought it. Even today, thanks to bad physics and the dog-in-the-manger attitudes of writers like Vincent Bugliosi and Gerald Posner, there are those who believe the Commission was right.

But what about the witnesses? Hundreds of people had been in and around Dealey Plaza on 22 November 1963. Cynics would say the place was chosen because it was at the end of the motorcade's run and there would be fewer people there than, say, Main Street. Dozens were in Oak Cliff where when J.D. Tippit was killed. Many more had information which was relevant to both murders. The problem for the Commission, if they were to follow the direction insisted upon by Johnson and Katzenbach, was to ignore or intimidate anybody who appeared not to be singing from the 'Oswald Did It' playbook. The archetypal example of this intimidation and/or neglect of witnesses is provided by Richard Carr, who was watching the motorcade from girders on the Courts Building then being refurbished. He saw a thick-set man with glasses on the sixth floor of the Depository who walked down Houston Street and got into a grey Rambler station wagon. When he told this to the FBI, an agent said, 'If you didn't see Lee Harvey Oswald in the School Book Depository with a rifle, then you didn't see it.' Carr was arrested by Dallas police on trumped-up charges and his sons were temporarily removed from his care. He was attacked several times over the weeks and months that followed, which may of course be a coincidence ...

Eyewitnesses are notoriously poor at observation. The almost constant rejoinder in fictional television series and films is the witness response to police – 'It all happened so fast.' Seven shots were fired in Dealey Plaza in the space of as many seconds. No one, not even the Secret Service, trained to look out for trouble, was ready for what happened. Some eyewitnesses were confused, shocked and frightened. Others misremembered weeks, months or sometimes years later when asked to describe their experiences. Supposedly, we all remember where we were when Kennedy was killed, but we do not remember the colour of the shirt worn by the man – or was it a woman? – who stood next to us. Some of the witnesses had reasons of their own to avoid publicity or not to work with the police. Some never came forward. Badge Man, Black Dog Man, a smattering of Secret Service and FBI agents, have never been identified. Then there are those who lie to the authorities about their mythical presence in Dealey Plaza because they want their fifteen minutes of fame.

In the case of the Warren Commission, however, the counsel and staffers decided who should be called, both for the Kennedy and Tippit shooting. Large numbers of witnesses who heard shots coming from the grassy knoll and even ran up the slope in pursuit of a would-be killer were conveniently forgotten. Such people, in the words of J. Lee Rankin, would be opening doors, not closing them. Even Wesley Liebeler, one of the less partisan Commission members, reminded witness 'Virgie' Baker that contrary to her hearing shots from the grassy knoll that 'the shots actually came' from the Book Depository. Refreshingly, even when faced with a heavyweight lawyer like Liebeler, Mrs Baker refused to back down entirely – 'Well, I guess it could have been the wind, but to me it didn't [sound that way].'

In some cases, contrary evidence was submitted and ignored by the Commission. When cab driver William Whaley, who sat next to Oswald for 3 miles driving to Oak Cliff on the day in question, could not positively state that Exhibit 383-A, was Oswald's ID bracelet, Counsel Joseph Ball admitted it into evidence anyway and Congressman Ford endorsed it. On such minor irregularities, men have been hanged or in this case their reputations trashed. Whaley was so hazy on the clothes that Oswald was wearing that the pants moved from a khaki colour to blue to grey so that he could have passed for a Confederate soldier, notoriously casual dressers. Mary E. Bledsoe, Oswald's former landlady (for five days) who saw him get on the bus before leaving it for Whaley's cab, usually answered 'I don't know,' 'I didn't care,' 'I didn't pay any attention.' She had had a stroke (which may have diminished her ability to remember accurately) and clearly (for unclear reasons) did not like Oswald. She has him grinning like a maniac on the bus. At one point, she produced written notes while being examined by Ball. This rattled even him, and her attorney explained that this was because she easily got confused. Having a lawyer present in such a situation is probably common sense and is certainly the American way. But it also smacks of testimony given to a prearranged agenda. Bizarrely, Mrs Bledsoe was subjected to the longest and most detailed examination of the entire proceedings. Most of the Commission's counsel had a go at her, as did her own lawyer, and most of it was about Oswald's clothing, carried in two bags, none of which had any bearing on the events of 22 November at all. When asked if she had seen Oswald carrying a package, her answer was no. She assumed that Marina was Spanish and that her pregnancy was a matter of shame because she was unmarried. She said that she had not seen the shirt shown to her by the Commission before, even though Oswald had it on! There was clearly reason to doubt the landlady's cognitive ability, but little things like that did not unduly bother the Commission.

Counsel David Belin got himself in knots when he tried to pin down the exact time frame in which Book Depository worker Elizabeth Reid saw Oswald in the building. The fact that she was in the lobby, which she claimed was deserted, seconds before Dallas policeman, Marrion Baker, gun drawn, had to fight his way through the crowd, was glossed over by Belin. She was adamant, however, that Oswald was wearing only a T-shirt and not a brown shirt with long sleeves over it (which witnesses like Whaley had testified to). In the two minutes that Mrs Reid *ran* excitedly back into the building, Oswald had time to get his shirt, drink a bottle of Coke or discard it and leave the premises by 12.33. This was only three minutes after Kennedy was shot, but the exact time was necessary for the Commission to establish a precise time frame. Her answers to her lunchtime, what she ate and with whom were vague in the extreme. Considering that she had worked there for seven years, she seemed to have only a rudimentary grasp of the building's structure.

While the Commission was able to fudge the Connallys' testimony and was suitably respectful to Jackie, the one person they could not ignore was Mark Lane, a New York lawyer who represented Marguerite Oswald in defending her dead son's name. His book, *Rush to Judgement* (1966) is one of the landmark accounts of the case and exposes a number of cover-ups by the authorities which have become more obvious – and widespread – as time goes on. Lane demanded to be present at the Commission hearings and they could not stop him. He also uncovered the inconvenient fact that the medical findings at Parkland did not square with those at Bethesda. Much of the medical evidence that you have read already in this book is available thanks to Lane's research and tenacity. He reminded everybody that the FBI still had Mary Moorman's photograph which had not been returned to her; that the Dallas police identification of the murder weapon was still a 7.65 Mauser; and that the testimony of Helen Markham over the Tippit shooting was contrary to what she had told him in various interviews. In a clash with J. Lee Rankin on 2 July 1964, Lane said, 'I am amazed, quite frankly, Mr Rankin, that the kind of harassment which I have been subjected to since I became involved in this case continues here in this room ...' He accused the FBI of the same overbearing approach. Rankin was treading on dangerous ground in the context of lawyer-client privilege – 'And, I think you know,' Lane said, 'that the questions you are asking are quite improper.'

Lane pointed out that he uncovered more in a two-day trip to Dallas than the FBI, the Secret Service and the DPD had uncovered in six months. His research had been at great financial cost to him and when Warren accused him of handicapping the Commission by not giving the names of his informants (something which no lawyer is obliged to do), Lane replied, 'I understand very fully your position, Mr Chief Justice.' Sixty years on, we all do.

When Liebeler quizzed Helen Markham on her telephone interview with Lane, she became hysterical, denying several times that they had ever taken place. Even when Liebeler played her a tape recording, she denied that the voice was hers. Her performance was so garbled and hysterical that it makes Mary E. Bledsoe seem quite rational. In a court of law, Helen Markham would have been found unfit to testify, but the Commission's report found her testimony reliable. And anyway, they said it hardly mattered because there was so much other evidence against Oswald in the Tippit murder that she was irrelevant.

As Harold Weisberg points out in *Whitewash*, the Warren Commission actually tended to find Oswald innocent rather than guilty by the way it steamrolled its way through American jurisprudence – 'How [the Commission] could accept without question or comment so much nonsense, fantasy and outright perjury is beyond comprehension.' Weisberg poses questions which the Commission should have posed and tried to answer. They managed none.

Most damning of all is the 'rigged' artwork the Commission produced. I have included the most obvious of these along with my alternatives based on *actual evidence*, not tentative speculation. The altering of angles of Kennedy's head, of the position of his body, vis-à-vis Connally in the car, the 'lining up' of the back and throat wounds to mark the supposed path of the magic bullet, all that pointed to a single gunman firing from the rear. The Warren Commission was so horrified by the mortuary photographs that they failed to investigate the autopsy work in detail.

'Never in history,' Harold Weisberg wrote, 'have such crimes been "solved" by such consistent disregard for truth, honesty and credibility, with so much avoidance of the obvious and such dependence on the incredible and palpably undependable, with such a prostitution of science, and with so much help from misrepresentation and perjury.'

It would be refreshing to think that later enquiries, such as the House Select Committee on Assassinations (1977–8) would have more regard for actual evidence and the truth, but sadly, that is not the case. Congressman Richard Russell and Thomas Hale Boggs, never part of the Dallas 'troika' on the Commission, expressed their displeasure with the Warren Commission's findings. As Boggs famously said, 'Hoover lied his eyes out to the Commission – on Oswald, on Ruby, on their friends, the bullets, the gun, you name it.'

By 1977, a number of conspiracy theorist books had emerged and the extraordinary movie *Executive Action*, starring Burt Lancaster and Robert Ryan had been screened. Told in a stark documentary format, the film contained all the elements missing from the Warren Commission – a shady clique of conspirators, composed of oil men and government agents, an Oswald lookalike causing scenes at shooting ranges, car dealerships and on the streets with Cuban leaflets. There were three gunmen, in the Depository, the Courts Building and the grassy knoll – none of them was Oswald. Surprisingly, considering the outspoken criticism of the Warren Commission, there was far less public outrage over this than Oliver Stone's *JFK* in 1991 which was slammed by conservative critics even before it was released.

The HSCA was formed against a backdrop of opposition from Warren Commission supporters. The original idea, proposed by Congressman Tom Downing, was to investigate all three assassinations that had rocked the 1960s, those of JFK, RFK and Martin Luther King. It also supposed to look at the conduct of the Warren Commission, but that never happened. There was no enquiry into the murder of

Bobby Kennedy either. The new panel consisted of twelve members but there was so much in-fighting that three directors were in and out of post in rapid succession. Philadelphia prosecutor Richard A. Sprague was the best of these, but he resigned after opposition from Texas Congressman Henry Gonzalez. Robert Tanenbaum then resigned rather than preside over another Warren-style cover-up. The third director was G. Robert Blakey, a Cornell University law professor, but under him, the Committee's priorities slewed to one side. It was limited by time and money and the Warren Report, rather than being ignored as whitewash, was taken as a professional yardstick. The CIA in particular were as difficult as they could be. Knowing that the Committee had only two years to function, it stonewalled as much as possible. Blakey was either naïve or complicit when he said, 'I've worked with these people [the CIA] for twenty years. You don't think they'd lie to me, do you?'

Photographic expert Robert Groden, who had uncovered clear evidence of tampering with the official morgue photographs from Bethesda, was not allowed to testify to the panel. Blakey himself kept the press out of the picture and the whole Committee worked in an atmosphere of secrecy. Even Henry Gonzalez said that the HSCA was 'a put-up job and a hideous farce that was never intended to work'. Nevertheless, hard evidence such as the enhanced Zapruder film and the police Dictabelt recordings could not be swept under the carpet in the late 1970s and Blakey had no choice but to keep the media in the loop in a series of brief press conferences.

The star of the HSCA was undoubtedly Gaeton Fonzi who became an investigator for the Committee and wrote an excellent book on its workings (or lack thereof!) *The Last Investigation* in 1998. He was led down a blind alley by Clare Boothe Luce, Joe Kennedy's ex-mistress, who claimed to have all sorts of information on the Cuban connection; this got nowhere. The other star was Dr Cyril Wecht, a member of the nine-man forensic pathology panel. He radically opposed the single bullet theory, often being the only dissenting voice, which either proves the stupidity of the others or the fact that the spirit of Arlen Specter cast a long shadow.

The upshot of the HSCA disappointment was that there was indeed the likelihood of more than one shooter in Dealey Plaza and that Kennedy had been killed as part of a conspiracy. As to who was involved, it was anybody's guess, the Committee decided and it recommended that a new enquiry should be launched by the Justice Department. Forty-five years later, that department has done precisely nothing.

Chapter 11

The Silence of the Dead

O ne of the most bizarre aspects of the Kennedy case is the number of witnesses who died mysteriously, often when they were due to testify for the Warren Commission or the HSCA. There is no universally agreed number of these victims, but over the years conspiracy theorists have happily added to the total, not only making the premise of Kennedy-related murder less likely but playing into the hands of debunkers who ridicule the whole concept.

The PR for the 1973 movie *Executive Action* cited eighteen such cases, material witnesses who died suddenly between 1963 and 1966. Six were shot; three were killed in car crashes; two committed suicide, one died from a karate chop; three from heart attacks and two from natural causes. An actuary working for *The Times* newspaper calculated that the probability of these deaths within three years of the killing of Kennedy was 1 in 100,000 trillion!

Debunkers questioned this figure and were proved to be right; the odds/ratio is *far* lower, In *Hit List* (2013), authors Belzer and Wayne spend several pages in their Introduction on the arcane mathematics that actuaries deal with. Their figure stands at a mere 1 in 167 trillion – which is still absolutely extraordinary.

Belzer and Wayne discuss in detail the deaths of fifty witnesses whose deaths are suspicious. In these cases, 'natural causes' like heart attacks and accidents like car crashes may not be as straightforward as they seem. Even in obvious cases of murder, there is no hard evidence that these are Kennedy-related; the United States is a violent country with an exceptionally high murder rate. We would need to look at a much wider mathematical field to see this in context. For example, two men died on the same day in Dallas, Friday, 22 November, both by gunshot. But how many other deaths were there in the city that day? And can we *prove* that they had no connection with those of Kennedy and Tippit?

I have rejected all members of the Mafia or Mob underworld from Belzer and Wayne's list because such men (and women) lived on the edge. The Mob specialized in violence – eliminating opposition with a gun was standard practice. For instance, Jack Zangretti was a motel manager in Altus, Oklahoma. According to conspiracy theorist Penn Jones, he had claimed, the day after the assassination, that three men had killed Kennedy and that Oswald was not one of them. He predicted that Ruby would kill Oswald the next day and that Frank Sinatra's son would be kidnapped to act as a smokescreen, at least for the media, on the Kennedy/Oswald killings. Zangretti's body was found in Lake Lugert two weeks later with two bullets in the chest. What is vital in all this is to whom Zangretti gave this information and how (in Oklahoma) he got to know it. Without this knowledge, *anybody* could have 'whacked' Jack Zangretti for any number of reasons.

Likewise, Sam Giancana, Johnny Roselli and Charles Nicoletti. We know that Giancana shared a mistress with Kennedy and may have (at least according to journalist Seymour Hersh) helped rig the 1960 election ballot which saw Kennedy win the White House. His murder (clearly an inside Mob job) in June 1975 could have been ordered and carried out by any one of a dozen Mafia opponents. Roselli had probably known Jack Ruby for years and had agreed to testify to the Senate in the HSCA hearings. He never had the chance because his dismembered body was found in an oil drum off the Florida coast in 1976. Nicoletti was shot three times in the back of the head and his car was fire-bombed. He was due to testify to the HSCA on CIA and Mafia plots against Fidel Castro. George de Mohrenschildt shot himself in the mouth (or did he?) on the same day – 29 March 1977.

Although I have rejected Mob deaths they may well have had stories to tell and they *may* have been related to the killing of Kennedy; but all these men had clever lawyers each able to advise and defend their clients in court. 'Pleading the fifth' is one of the most disgraceful elements of the American legal system, but it is enshrined in the Constitution and does not, in the eyes of the law, imply guilt. The Mob were hard men who had faced court before; they knew how easy it was to buy off corrupt policemen and even the judiciary.

Others cannot be dismissed so easily. Some were intimidated into changing their testimony. Warren Reynolds could not identify a man he saw running away from the Tippit shooting. When he himself was shot in the head in the basement of his used-car salesroom, he changed his mind – surprise! surprise! The man *was* Oswald. Harold Russell had been there too, working for Reynolds. He could not identify Oswald either, but in 1967 he went berserk at a party, screaming that he was going to be killed. As we have seen, he was, by a police officer who beat him to death with his pistol on 23 July 1965 in Oklahoma.

I have analysed what is left of Belzer and Wayne's fifty and concede that the jury is still out on most of them; their deaths *may* have been suspicious or not – evidence is lacking. But in just nine cases, I believe that it was in somebody's interests to make sure that their testimony in relation to the Kennedy killing was not heard.

The first of these is Dorothy Kilgallen, in conjunction with her friend Florence Smith, who died the next day – the 8 and 9 November 1965. The official verdict in Kilgallen's death was suicide or accidental overdose, evidenced by the high levels of barbiturates and alcohol in her bloodstream. Predictably, Gerald Posner dismisses the woman and her death in seven lines. He claims that her 'private' interview with Jack Ruby happened quickly in a crowded courtroom and that she had no impending scoop which she threatened to reveal, 'by the time,' Posner writes her off '[she] drank herself to death.' As for Florence

Smith, her cause was heart failure and the links with Kilgallen just a coincidence. The truth is rather different.

Dorothy Kilgallen was a nationally syndicated columnist with an immaculate reputation. Having interviewed Ruby (at his request alone, in his cell, as well as in the courtroom) she told friends that she was 'about to blow the JFK case sky high'. She was working on a book, provisionally called *Murder One*, and she gave a copy of her JFK chapter to Florence Smith. Kilgallen was an awkward 'witness' to silence. There was no murky Mob connection. She was not a 'Commie' or a Cuban exile. She was, however, high profile, a powerful and popular Hollywood journalist, appearing regularly on the television show *What's My Line?* And she was preparing to tell the world what she knew within five days. We know from unimpeachable evidence that Ruby wanted to tell the truth, but that Earl Warren refused to move him to the safety of Washington to do so. Ruby was not a stupid man; did he tell Kilgallen all as a fall-back position should anything happen to him?

Kilgallen was found dead in her third-floor apartment off Park Avenue, New York, shortly before she was due to visit New Orleans. Red flags in the crime scene were everywhere. She was found dead in a bed she never slept in. She was wearing a peignoir over her nightgown – something she never did. She was wearing full make-up, although apparently ready for bed. She had a book in her hand, but no reading glasses (which she needed for close work). The air conditioning was on, which it never was at night. From the lividity noted in her autopsy, it was clear that her body had been moved after death. Three barbiturates were found in her bloodstream – triunal, nembutal and seconal. This combination would cause death in less than half an hour, but the amount equated with the *exact* dosage that would kill. If she had swallowed the necessary 15–20 pills, either in a suicide attempt or by accident (?) she would have vomited and yet the crime scene was particularly sterile.

Suicide seems highly unlikely. Kilgallen was excited about the forthcoming JFK revelations and had appeared on television earlier in the evening. She made a completely coherent and normal phone call to her editor at 2.20 a.m., but was dead by 4. Dorothy Kilgallen's book was published after her death, but there was no chapter on JFK. Neither was any such paperwork found in her apartment.

Florence Pritchett Smith had a copy of that missing chapter too. She was found dead on 9 November, the official cause given as cerebral haemorrhage, perhaps due to leukaemia. There were rumours that Smith was one of the many liaisons of John Kennedy and there is at least one photograph of them together at a nightclub. Pretty and dark, she was certainly his type. Posner claims her death was due to a heart attack, which it was not – and there was no chapter of Kilgallen's book in her home either.

Gary Underhill had worked for the OSS before its transition and was still called upon by the CIA afterwards. He had also been military affairs editor for *Life* magazine which had bought the Zapruder film rights and which exerted an extraordinary influence on the handling of the case (see Chapter 14). Gerald Posner claims that Underhill's CIA connection is non-existent, but researchers like Belzer and James DiEugenio have proved him wrong. Within twenty-four hours of Kennedy's death, Underhill left Washington and went to New York. There, he told a friend, Charlene Fitsimmons, 'This country is too dangerous for me ... Oswald is a patsy. They set him up ... The bastards have done something outrageous. They've killed the president! ... I know who they are. That's the problem. They know I know. That's why I'm here.'

The group that Underhill was afraid of was a rogue element within the CIA who had a lucrative sideline in gun and drug running in Southeast Asia. He was found dead in his Washington apartment with a bullet in his brain. It was ruled a suicide, which was odd because the bullet wound was behind the left ear. And Gary Underhill was right-handed.

Lee E. Bowers may well have been in the wrong place at the wrong time. He had been in a uniquely important position on 22 November, in a railway tower 14ft up overlooking the marshalling yards and car park behind Dealey Plaza. He was one of sixty-five witnesses who believed he heard shots and saw smoke coming from the fence area on top of the grassy knoll. He saw three cars cruising the car park half an hour before the assassination. They all had out-of-state plates and one of them was covered in mud. One of the men in one car appeared to be talking into a hand-radio set. The irony of all this is that the car park actually belonged to the Dallas Police Department and had been supposedly sealed off by them on the day of the president's visit.

At the top of the grassy knoll, Bowers saw two men, both looking up Elm in the direction of the motorcade. One of them was late middle age, heavy set with a white shirt and dark trousers. The other was younger, perhaps mid-twenties in a plaid shirt or jacket. Bowers testified to this effect to the Warren Commission, but on 9 August 1966, his car left the road. Mortally hurt at the crash scene, he still had the strength to tell paramedics that he thought someone had drugged his coffee at a stop some time earlier. One ambulanceman said, 'He was in a strange state of shock … I can't explain it. I've never seen anything like it.'

Debunkers, of course, write this off as the sort of accident that happens on highways every day. Except that Charles Good, of the Texas Highway Patrol, testified that Bowers' car had been deliberately forced off the road. Why would a conspirator kill Bowers when he had already testified and before there was any suggestion of another official enquiry into Kennedy's death? The implication is that Bowers knew more than he was letting on. What if he recognized at least one of the men on the grassy knoll? What if he could positively identify him? What if he had memorized at least one of the number plates on those cars in the car park? His own brother, Monty, came out with the rather lame and prosaic solution – Lee suffered from allergies and a sneezing fit may have resulted in a loss of control at the wheel!

If Florence Smith once had a romantic fling with JFK, what about Mary Pinchot Meyer? When she was killed on 12 October 1964, she was described as a 'stunning 43-year-old bohemian aristocrat'. She was certainly an interesting character. The former wife of Cord Meyer, a CIA operative, she had a serious affair with John Kennedy and there was talk of his leaving Jackie and setting up home with her (which would, of course, have stopped his career in its tracks). Author Leo Damone wrote of her in the *New York Post* in 1991 – 'She had access to the highest levels. She was involved in illegal drug activity. What do you think it would do to the beatification of Kennedy if this woman said "It wasn't Camelot, it was Caligula's court."' A reason perhaps for her to be silenced *before* JFK's death, but why afterwards? Posner dismisses her in three lines, but he has missed a rather crucial point. Meyer believed that the Warren Report was a whitewash. This is widely accepted today, but in the year of its publication it was not and certainly not from a woman whose husband walked the corridors of power. And Mrs Meyer kept a diary ...

She moved in the circles of Ben Bradlee, the editor of *Newsweek*. Both he and the paper were highly influential in the east coast media long before he went on to the *Washington Post* and outed Richard Nixon's Watergate conspiracy. And of course, she and Cord were personal friends of the CIA's counterintelligence chief, James Jesus Angleton. By 1958, the Meyers were in trouble and she filed for divorce, citing mental cruelty. She believed that Cord had bugged her apartment and that Angleton was aiding and abetting him.

On 12 October, Meyer left her home as usual for her morning jog. While running along a canal, she was shot twice, at close range with a .38 calibre gun, once in the back of the head, then in the heart from the front, probably when she was on the ground. A suspicious-looking black man, Raymond Crump, was seen near the body and taken in for questioning. He had been fishing, he claimed, despite no fishing equipment having been found, and had fallen in the Potomac River that ran near the canal. No forensic evidence was found on him and no weapon either, but Crump was tried for murder anyway.

With such a high-profile killing, the media went into overdrive. Meyer had been killed during a robbery that had gone wrong, despite no evidence for this. She was the victim of a sex maniac, with even less evidence for that. Cord Meyer nevertheless went along with the latter view – 'Mary had been the victim of a sexually motivated assault by a single individual and that she had been killed in her struggle to escape.'

The judge in the case, a personal friend of Lyndon Johnson, ruled that Mrs Meyer's private life could not be introduced in court. No mention of Kennedy; no mention of the CIA. The method of execution was highly proficient and accurate – hardly the random shooting of a 'gun-nut'. The lack of a weapon indicated that the shooter brought his own weapon and knew how to hide it and himself. Although Meyer was not identified until 6 p.m. on the day of the murder, both Ben Bradlee and James Jesus Angleton knew about the situation four hours earlier. Bradlee's *Newsweek* produced several articles in the weeks ahead proclaiming Crump's guilt and both he and Angleton lied about the existence of Meyer's diary, even though both men were frantically searching for it on the day of her murder.

Crump was found not guilty (a rare example of America's justice system actually working) and the case is still officially classified as both open and unsolved. According to the supposed deathbed statement of CIA man E. Howard Hunt, Lyndon Johnson orchestrated the Kennedy killing and his number two was Cord Meyer. Author Peter Janney, the son of Wistar Janney, a CIA operative at the time, has claimed that the Meyer murder was a professional hit to keep the woman quiet and that it was carried out by an assassin whose codename was William L. Mitchell, a specialist working for the CIA and the National Security Agency.

Two years later, there was another suspicious death, this time officially a suicide, which made no sense at all. Lieutenant Commander William B. Pitzer is summarily dismissed by Gerald Posner because his name is not included in those present at the Bethesda autopsy. And such is Posner's naivete; if it is not in the official record, it does not exist. According to the records that Posner loves, Pitzer shot himself in the head on 29 October 1966 soon before his retirement from the navy and prior to his taking on a lucrative new post in the media.

In the chaos of the Bethesda fiasco, Pitzer's job was to take a video of the process. Dr Humes asserted that there had been surgery to the president's head and said this in the presence of FBI agents Sibert and O'Neill. The fact that Humes later retracted this statement is proof enough of a cover-up; somebody got to him. As we have seen, the still photographs and X-rays available today are not consistent with evidence at the time from medical professionals at Parkland Hospital.

Pitzer confided to friends that he was threatened by anonymous members of the Intelligence services not to reveal what he had seen – and filmed – from the autopsy. Looking forward to his $45,000 a year new job with a network television station, the inveterate note-taker left no suicide note, gave no hint of depression to family or friends, and shot himself in his office at Bethesda, a .45 calibre pistol lying on his desk. There was no gunshot residue on his right hand, but his left hand was so badly mangled that doctors could not remove his wedding ring. The FBI found that the fatal shot, to the temple, was fired from 3 feet away! The gun was not Pitzer's; he had borrowed it, with a note about it which was his trademark modus operandi, but no note for ammunition. There was a heel print in his blood on the floor which did not match the lieutenant commander's.

Pitzer's widow was also threatened soon after her husband's death. The lieutenant commander's routine on the day he died was mundane.

He made breakfast and raked leaves on his lawn, had a haircut, did a little shopping and left notes for various colleagues at his office, including one to himself – 'Remind me to return gun to the sec[urity] office.' He never did.

Between 1995 and 2005, Lieutenant Colonel Daniel Marvin of the US Army Special Forces produced a number of articles and two autobiographical books relating to his work in covert operations. In one of them, he claims to have been ordered by the CIA to kill Pitzer to stop him exposing the conspiracy once he left the navy. We have to be wary of exposés like Marvin's; if he openly acknowledged his part in a murder, why was no action taken against him?

William C. Sullivan's death had a strange – and ancient – parallel in English Medieval history. On 2 August 1100, William II, king of England and known as Rufus (the red-head) was killed in the New Forest while hunting deer. No one believed that such a rapacious and vicious ruler could die by accident; all the evidence points to political assassination. So does it in the case of Sullivan, number three in the FBI hierarchy under J. Edgar Hoover. There was no love lost between Sullivan and his boss; on at least one occasion, they nearly came to blows. Sullivan's speciality was counterespionage, where the Bureau's work overlapped with National Security and he was directly involved with the Executive Action programme concerning attempts on Castro's life.

Sullivan died, having been 'mistaken for a deer' in woods near his home in Sugar Hill, New Hampshire, on 9 November 1977. He had already testified to the HSCA but was scheduled for a second grilling. His killer, Robert Daniels, was charged with 'shooting a human being by accident' and was released into the custody of his father, a state trooper. There was no further action, except that Daniels, described as an experienced hunter, lost his licence for ten years and paid a fine of $500. What makes the whole thing suspicious is that Sullivan had told a friend, Robert Novak, 'someday you will read that I have been killed in an accident, but don't believe it; I've been murdered.'

We have already noted what a mass of contradiction George de Mohrenschildt was and this is as true of his death as it was of his life. With his multilingual skills, contacts and White Russian pedigree, the baron was a very unlikely friend for Lee Oswald and his wife. That was because, almost certainly, de Mohrenschildt was, as researcher Mark Lane puts it, 'the baby-sitter for Oswald for the CIA'. Jackie Kennedy called him 'Uncle George'; he had George H.W. Bush's number in his phone book and they belonged to the same club. Yet, on 29 March 1977, de Mohrenschildt blasted his face with a shotgun.

There is considerable evidence to show that the baron was a go-between for the CIA and the oil business, creating a framework for those conspiracy theorists who believe that the Agency was in cahoots with big business in the Military-Industrial Complex angle. In a way, de Mohrenschildt's 'suicide' is not surprising, considering his rapid physical and mental decline. The suave socialite degenerated during the 1970s into a 'human vegetable', afraid of his own shadow. His wife, Jeanne, was convinced that this was the work of mind-bending drugs administered to her husband by Dr Charles Mendoza in the spring or summer of 1976. De Mohrenschildt's personality changed – he became petulant and angry and Mendoza refused to let Jeanne attend their sessions together. Neither would he tell her what exactly the treatment was.

Mendoza himself is an enigma. He registered in Dallas in April 1976 and was gone by December by which time Jeanne had stopped her husband having any more treatment. The baron had been subpoenaed to testify to the HSCA and his behaviour became increasingly neurotic as a result. On 5 September, de Mohrenschildt wrote to George Bush, asking for help. He believed he was being followed by the FBI, had written an unwise (and ramblingly chaotic) book on Lee Oswald and believed that Bush, who had been director of the CIA, could sort the situation out. Bush's reply professed total ignorance.

On the day he died, Gaeton Fonzi, investigator for the HSCA, visited the de Mohrenschildts' villa near Palm Beach, Florida, but found him not at home. He was apparently talking to researcher Edward Jay Epstein who had written *Inquest* in 1966 in which he accused lawyers Joseph Ball and Wesley Liebeler of falsifying who did what in the Warren Commission's work. Because of this, Fonzi missed him. But somebody else did not.

Just as we have a Dictabelt recording of the shots in Dealey Plaza on 22 November 1963, so we can hear the shotgun blast on 22 March 1977. The de Mohrenschildts' maid had left a tape recorder running to record a television soap and the sounds of the entry to the room by person or persons unknown are unmistakeable. The security system delivers several beeps as someone enters the room from outside. Seconds later, the shotgun blast. If Dr Mendoza had been allowed to continue his use of drugs, de Mohrenschildt would probably have been considered too ill to testify to the HSCA. But, as it was ...

If George de Mohrenschildt was the archetypal dodgy character, Roger Craig was not. Researchers Belzer and Wayne believe that there should be an entire book on this Dallas policeman because his story is fascinating. Craig was one of Bill Decker's deputy sheriffs and soon after the shots died down in Dealey Plaza, he heard a piercing whistle. He saw a man run down the slope alongside the Book Depository from the rear entrance and jump into a white Nash station wagon with a luggage rack on top. The driver was black or Hispanic. He was later able to identify the man as Oswald, which is, of course, at odds with the bus and cab testimony of Mary E. Bledsoe and William Whaley.

Craig spoke to Captain Fritz while he was interrogating Oswald and Oswald snapped at him, 'That station wagon belongs to Mrs Paine. Don't try to tie her in with this. She had nothing to do with it.' Ruth Paine's station wagon was actually a Chevrolet, but Oswald's abrupt closing down of the conversation effectively brought that line of enquiry to an end. The officer was with colleagues Boone and Weitzman in the Book Depository when the rifle was found and, like them, maintained that it was a 7.65 Mauser. Captain Fritz called Craig a liar, contending that he was never in the interrogation room, but then Fritz was very good at covering his back and knew that his failure to follow up on Craig's testimony could cause him problems.

In the Warren Commission enquiry, Craig was badgered by David Belin, but his evidence on the gun (the station wagon information was ignored) held firm. He had not seen a bag anywhere in the Depository and the rifle was not a Mannlicher-Carcano. When Craig eventually read his testimony, he found that there were fourteen alterations to what he had said.

Three years later, he was a prosecution witness at Jim Garrison's trial of Clay Shaw/Bertrand on charges of conspiracy to kill the president. During this testimony, Craig's story became more detailed. He said that the man driving the station wagon was Hispanic and that he had seen the same man being summarily interviewed by Dallas police officers on Elm Street moments before.

In view of his exemplary record with the sheriff's office (he was cited for good conduct in 1960) more people should have listened to Craig. After Dallas law enforcement hounded him out of his job, he went back to New Orleans to talk to Garrison. A bullet had grazed his head in Dallas while he was walking in a parking lot and he had reason to believe that one of his own colleagues had shot at him, but could not prove it. Craig reiterated his testimony to Garrison about the confrontation with Oswald and Fritz. 'This man saw you leave,' the captain had said, which instigated Oswald's outburst in defence of Ruth Paine.

Craig was a pain in the backside of the DPD and the Warren Commission. He was still in the Book Depository on 22 November when he heard reports of Tippit's death on his radio. He noted the time – 1.06 – which effectively destroyed the prosecution's time frame for Oswald's being Tippit's killer.

After the hoo-ha had died down, Craig moved back to Dallas, which was, after all, his home town. His car blew up, with him inside it, but miraculously, he survived. In 1973, his car was forced off the road, badly injuring his back. The following year, he was fired on again, with a shotgun in Waxahachie, Texas. Shortly after appearing on a radio talk show about the Kennedy assassination, he was found shot dead at his home, on 15 May 1975. The verdict, as you will not be surprised to hear having read this chapter, was suicide. The *Dallas Morning News* reported that Craig's father had found him, a rifle beside his body and a note which said he could not stand the pain any more (from the car 'accident' two years earlier).

I agree in general with historian Walt Brown's verdict – '... I'm not a strong subscriber to the "300 dead witnesses" story. There was never any guarantee of immortality because someone was in proximity to a JFK event.'

But in the case of the nine individuals discussed in this chapter, I am prepared to make exceptions.

Chapter 12

'I Was the Second Gunman on the Grassy Knoll' (Ace Ventura, Pet Detective)

In his 1977 movie *Annie Hall*, comedian Woody Allen conjures up a scene in which he is talking to his ex-wife:

Allison: Okay. All right, so whatta yuh saying, now? That everybody on the Warren Committee is in on this conspiracy, right?

Alvy: Well, why not?

Allison: Yeah, Earl Warren.

Alvy: Hey, honey, I don't know Earl Warren.

Allison: Lyndon Johnson?

Alvy: Lyndon Johnson is a politician. You know the ethics these guys have? It's like a notch underneath child molester.

Allison: Then everybody's in on the conspiracy? The FBI and the CIA and J. Edgar Hoover and oil companies and the Pentagon and the men's room attendant at the White House?

Alvy: I would leave the men's room attendant out.

This dialogue is quoted in David Aaronovitch's *Voodoo Histories* (2009) in which the journalist rubbishes all such ideas as though they come from a parallel universe rather than hard, rational evidence. He buys into Vincent Bugliosi's flawed mathematics – 42 different groups, 82 separate assassins and 214 individuals – who would have had to be part of the conspiracy against Kennedy if such a thing existed. But

Bugliosi does not understand conspiracies. They do not work like that. We are looking at disparate, compartmentalized groups of people, who are only concerned for their tiny orbit of experience. There is no point at which any two of Bugliosi's vast numbers get together to plot.

The decision reached by the Warren Commission in 1964 was that John Kennedy was killed, as was J.D. Tippit, by Lee Oswald and that no one else was involved. This decision was based on defective investigation carried out by the FBI and the outcome was pre-ordained. It had nothing to do with justice or the truth.

Given that situation, speculation began almost at once. In fact, it began within hours of the president's death and has spiralled out of control ever since, especially via the Internet, because of the system's refusal to accept the obvious. The debunkers, spearheaded in the US by Vincent Bugliosi and Gerald Posner have been amply backed by American mainstream media who are perfectly happy for secrets to remain buried in an agenda of their own which will be discussed in Chapter 14.

Doubts about the Warren Commission were expressed first in Britain, free from the constraints of the American mindset, its thralldom to a two-party system and a lingering fear of Communism. It came from unlikely and heavyweight sources. Mr Justice Devlin, a high court judge, and the philosopher Bertrand Russell both went into print to express their concerns. America rejected their criticism; what did a bunch of limeys know?

This chapter looks at the range of existing theories, virtually all of them involving conspiracies and evaluates their plausibility.

1 – The Russians

Who would want to see Kennedy dead? On the surface, a Russian assassination contract looked highly likely in 1963 at the height of the Cold War. It was this fear that Lyndon Johnson was anxious to quash.

Ever since photographs were taken of American GIs shaking hands with Russian soldiers over the ruins of Nazi Germany in the spring of 1945, relations between the new superpowers had deteriorated quickly. With Hitler dead and the Nazi threat eliminated, the world locked horns in the East vs West confrontation with which my generation grew up. In March 1946, former British Prime Minister Winston Churchill gave a speech in Fulton, Missouri, in which he said, 'From Stettin in the Baltic to Trieste in the Adriatic, an iron curtain has descended across the Continent.' And no one in the West knew what lay behind that curtain. All that seemed apparent was that Joseph Stalin was a sociopathic dictator who seemed to be trying to spread the grip of Marxism across the world, exactly as Karl Marx himself had hoped.

The United States was the land of the free (although such a term was relative) and the forces of capitalism and greed, still referred to positively as the American dream, stood four square against Stalinism. Senator Joe McCarthy spearheaded a witch-hunt of Communists which outed talented, thoughtful people and destroyed them. Showing solidarity with him were right-wing groups like the John Birch Society, one of whose members, Joseph Milteer, was in the throng lining Houston Street, Dallas, that day in November when the president came to town.

Kennedy was accused by such people as being too liberal and too soft on Communism. This criticism, vouched by Allen Dulles of the CIA (whom Kennedy had fired) and General Edwin A. Walker (who, according to Marina Oswald, had been an earlier target of her husband) was not only unfair; it was unjustified. Kennedy had, albeit reluctantly, backed the Bay of Pigs and gone head to head with the Soviet leader Nikita Khrushchev in the Cuban Missile Crisis in the year before the assassination.

The reaction of the Russian government to Kennedy's killing is informative and by no means follows what most Americans expected. Initially, the two most powerful rulers in the world, each capable of pressing a nuclear button, did not see eye to eye. The American government's apparent espousal of an invasion of Communist Cuba in 1961 (actually launched by the CIA under Eisenhower) was hardly calculated to lead to détente and a peaceful world. Neither did the setting up of Soviet nuclear missile bases in Cuba, only 90 miles from the American mainland. A Russian fleet was on its way and the world held its breath. Then, as Secretary of State David Dean Rusk said on 24 October 1962, 'We're eyeball to eyeball and I think the other fellow just blinked.' The 'other fellow' was Khrushchev who responded, 'How can it be that we suffered defeat when revolutionary Cuba exists and is growing stronger? Who really retreated and who won this conflict?'

But behind the rhetoric, common sense prevailed. The Russians pulled out their missile bases and Kennedy agreed to leave Castro's Cuba alone, even punishing his own people who tried to subvert that. He and Khrushchev had developed a mutual respect for each other by the middle of 1963. Both men had to contend with hawks pushing for a nuclear war via the Kremlin and the Pentagon and both men were far too canny to allow that to happen. We know from private, internal correspondence released years later that the Politburo was genuinely shocked by Kennedy's death. He was a man they could and did work with; who knew what might follow? We are a long way from the current age of Russian political murder, where hit squads poison dissidents in foreign towns and rafts of failed generals quietly disappear. With hindsight, even the nuclear, happy-hippy 1960s seem so much more civilized.

2 – Castro's Cubans

Pinning Kennedy's murder on Soviet Russia makes little sense, but when it came to Cuba and its Marxist ruler Fidel Castro, the American government (and specifically the Kennedy administration) had form. Since the 1890s, Cuba had been an unofficial state of the Union, used as a casino-studded playground by American big business and money. The Mafia in particular had benefited from the holiday atmosphere and nobody had many concerns for the native population. All that changed in 1958 when the corrupt government of Fulgencio Batista was overthrown by a young Communist 'freedom fighter', Fidel Castro. With his trademark beard and combat fatigues, aided and abetted by every 1960s student's poster boy, Che Guevara, Castro kicked the Mafia out and set up a Marxist state, courting the Soviet Union.

We know something now that was barely dreamed of in 1963, that the American government had, from the late 1950s, an official policy, as part of their international relations programme, of carrying out political assassinations, euphemistically termed 'executive action'. The CIA had an assassination manual, drawn up in 1954, in which various murder methods were evaluated. We shall look at the CIA's role in the Kennedy killing later, but the essence of this conspiracy theory is that it was payback time on the president for trying to kill Castro first.

After the failure of the Bay of Pigs in 1961, when Kennedy had refused to provide vital air support for the CIA's botched invasion of the island, General Maxwell Taylor wrote in his report, 'There can be no long-term living with Castro.' Before the end of the year, Robert Kennedy had set up Operation Mongoose to have Castro removed by any means. Edward Lansdale of the CIA was in charge of this, but the shock of the Cuban Missile Crisis brought everything to a standstill in the autumn of 1962. Throughout these weeks and months, neither Kennedy brother actually used the words 'kill Castro'. 'Get rid of' was as direct as it became, leaving far too much leeway to dogged, Communist-hating spooks like James Jesus Angleton and Richard Helms of the CIA. The whole thing was called 'plausible deniability'. Should everything have been exposed and the Kennedys ever put in the dock of a court, they could say, hand on heart, that they knew nothing about it.

Under Operation Mongoose, a variety of assassination methods were used. A fountain pen was rigged up to become a poisoned dart. A machine gun was hidden in a press camera. A bomb was to be placed in an airport ashtray. These plots, some extraordinarily amateur, went on for years, long after the Kennedy administration. Was Dealey Plaza simply a Castro plot thrown into reverse?

Certainly, the Cubans were in the frame. They were Communists; their leader was touted by the American press as dangerous and homicidal. And the Cubans were all over Lee Harvey Oswald. There was the 'dark complected' man sitting in Dealey Plaza watching the motorcade. He was allegedly using a walkie-talkie and after the shooting merely sat down on the kerbside, apparently unmoved by what he had just seen. Just as likely is that he was in shock. A number of men in and around the Plaza were described as 'Hispanic', but whether that makes them Cubans is another question altogether. David Ferrie, the bewigged man who was probably a CIA asset, certainly worked for Mob boss Carlos Marcello and was often in Jack Ruby's Carousel Club, was involved in training for the Bay of Pigs invasion, knew Oswald and ran guns to Cuba in his private plane even after the president had outlawed that kind of activity.

When Oswald was alleged to have visited Mexico, his intention was supposedly to travel either to Cuba or Russia. In the last week of September 1963, Silvia Odio was visited by two Cubans and an American. She lived in Dallas and was the daughter of a high-profile anti-Castro agitator. The American was allegedly Lee Oswald, who said nothing during the meeting, but the next day, one of the Lantinos, Leopoldo, rang Odio and asked her what she thought of Oswald. She had no comment about him, but Leopoldo told her that he was an ex-Marine sharpshooter and was about to be introduced to the Cuban underground and, pledged to remove Castro. Oswald's view, according to Leopoldo, was that Kennedy should have been killed after the fiasco of the Bay of Pigs. Gaeton Fonzi was still investigating Odio as late as 1977.

Nowhere is the Cuban connection more obvious than in the one-man organization Oswald set up in New Orleans. This was the Fair Play for Cuba Committee and Oswald was photographed several times handing out leaflets with the FPCC logo and contact details. There is no evidence that anyone joined the group or that any meetings ever took place, but the odd thing is that the leaflet address was the same (544 Camp Street) as the offices of William Guy Banister, a police superintendent in New Orleans who had worked for the FBI and closely with the CIA and the Office of Naval Intelligence. So we have the bizarre situation that Oswald, supporting Castro by leafletting (as perhaps a good Communist should) operating from the same building as someone on the edge of the 'spook' community pledged to wiping out such people and their operations.

On 9 August 1963, Oswald got into a fight while leafletting, with Carlos Bringuier, an anti-Castro activist. Egged on by the crowd, Bringuier hit Oswald, who seemed to welcome the attention and Oswald was arrested. Both men appeared on a radio chat show on Cuba in New Orleans on 21 August.

The smart money today is on the fact that Oswald's Cuban connections were fabricated, that he was set up to appear to be pro-Castro, whereas he was actually anti. Given the febrile attitude to Hispanics in the United States in 1963 (and since), it did not take much to persuade the average American that Cuba was involved. But nothing came of this, even though there were undoubtedly various redneck generals at the Pentagon who would have liked nothing better than to launch an all-out invasion of the island which would have achieved what the Bay of Pigs did not. Officially, Cuba's involvement in the Kennedy assassination, like that of Russia, was repudiated by the House Select Committee on Assassinations in 1978.

As for Castro himself, the day after the assassination, the president made an extraordinary speech. Naturally, he denied any involvement, as might be expected, but pointed the finger at an internal coup. He said that Oswald might be innocent and was merely being used 'as a cat's paw, in a plan very well prepared by people who knew how to prepare these plans.' 'Who?' Castro asked, along with the ghost of Marcus Tullius Cicero, 'can benefit from this ... if not the worst elements of US society? Who could be the only ones interested in this murder?'

As James DiEugenio points out, Castro was, ironically, 'being a better American citizen than anyone of the Warren Commission'.

3 – The Far Right

'The worst elements of US society'. Today, thanks to the Civil Rights movement and a radical shift in America's cold, hard look at its racial problems, there is no doubt that those elements would be regarded by many people as anti-Communist, racist, 'good ol' boys' of the South. This is putting it too crudely, but there is no doubt that Texas, in particular, had a redneck reputation based on white supremacy and segregation. Both Kennedys were seen as bastions of the liberal elite, if anything to the left of the Democrat party, soft on Communism both in the United States and around the world. The fact that Martin Luther King was a frequent visitor to the White House proved the point and filled some elements of 'white' America with dread.

It was Earl Warren himself who had said in 1954 that 'in the field of public education, the doctrine of "separate but equal" has no place. Separate educational facilities are inherently unequal.' Much of white America was not listening. A Southern Manifesto two years later condemned mixed-race education, although Lyndon Johnson, then a senator, refused to sign. James Morris said on national radio, 'We [whites] have to preserve ourselves ... Anyway, the nigrahs can never run the place – they're congenitally incapable of it. They've never produced a single genius.'

Six months before Kennedy was killed, George Wallace, the governor of Alabama, posted troops outside the doors of the state university to prevent black students' admission – 'Segregation now! Segregation tomorrow! Segregation for ever!' The government official sent to argue with him was the Assistant Attorney General, Nicholas Katzenbach.

Martin Luther King may have had a dream, as he told a crowd of 200,000 in the summer of 1963, but it was not a dream shared by Edwin A. Walker, Joseph Milteer, the John Birch Society, the Ku Klux Klan and the vast majority of the inhabitants of Dallas that year. When John Kennedy arrived in Dallas, he faced adverse criticism in the local newspapers. Three months earlier, Democratic presidential candidate and US ambassador to the United Nations Adlai Stevenson had been heckled and jostled when he visited the city. One woman hit him over the head with a placard. 'Nut country' indeed, and Dallas was made all the nuttier by the presence of ex-General Edwin A. Walker, whom Kennedy had forced to resign from the army because of his distribution of John Birch Society right-wing propaganda among his troops. Similar literature, 5,000 leaflets, were stuffed under windscreen wipers and into news-stands all over Dallas on 22 November, accusing Kennedy of treason.

The specific charges overlapped or repeated themselves and most of them ranted about the president's supposed softness on Communists. There was a particularly deranged slant, however, accusing Kennedy of being Antichrist (an attack on his Catholicism that had not been seen in Europe since the Reformation of the sixteenth century). In a country that had consciously (and wisely) separated church and state, this was an archaic and idiotic stand to take. Kennedy, said the leaflets, had lied to the American people (I would suggest in common with every president before him – such is the nature of politics) but it got personal. In 1947, at least according to his critics, Kennedy had married a Palm Beach socialite, Durie Malcolm. The marriage lasted only days before divorce proceedings ended it. Seymour Hersh, a warts-and-all biographer of JFK, could find no evidence for such a divorce in any surviving papers. Walker's Birchers brought this up.

The newspaper advertisements and the leaflets were printed by Robert Surrey, Walker's aide, and sponsored with oil money. Other than Walker, the only high-profile right winger that Friday was Joseph Milteer, photographed in the crowd along Houston. He was the man who had told the authorities of a potential assassination plot against the president and he was ignored. Since several of the Dallas Police Department were themselves Birchers, this is hardly surprising.

The Right could easily have orchestrated the Kennedy shooting, but the scale of the cover-up, extending to Bethesda and beyond, would have been beyond them.

4 – The Mafia

There can be fewer more obvious titles in the world of Kennedy conspiracy than David E. Scheim's *The Mafia Killed President Kennedy* (1988). In a huge, erudite tome filled with impeccable sources and a thick bibliography, Scheim lays out the evidence of the Mob's involvement.

The Sicilians brought their warped code of 'justice' with them to Ellis Island and from the 1890s expanded 'business' into every conceivable facet of crime, preying on human weakness. Gambling, prostitution, drugs, protection, gun-running and much more came under the ambit of 'friends and family' to the extent that some Mob leaders claimed to be more powerful than the government. The 1920 Volstead Act played directly into their hands by making alcohol illegal. Speakeasies sprang up overnight providing illicit booze and the Mafia headquarters of the USA was Chicago under Al Capone.

By the 1960s, the days of machine-gun battles between gangs had all but disappeared and 'organized crime' (one of the slimiest euphemisms ever created) had become almost respectable, with expensive lawyers and corporate images. The Mafia's tentacles were everywhere, buying the silence of witnesses to crimes, giving handouts to police departments and high court judges. But the violence never went away. If a man could not be bought off, he was simply murdered and the method was usually a bullet to the heart and a bullet to the head.

The FBI had turned a blind eye to the Mob's activities for years. J. Edgar Hoover as the Bureau's Director for life was perfectly happy to bask in the reflected glory of his 'G-Men' in the context of lone criminals like John Dillinger and 'Pretty Boy' Floyd. When it came to organized crime, however, Hoover denied that such a thing existed. Robert Kennedy, the new Attorney General in 1961, knew better and declared war on the Mob. For the first time since Eliot Ness in the 1930s, law enforcement across the States cracked down on the Mafia, rounding up everybody from hitmen to corrupt lawyers (of which there were many).

Not unnaturally, the Mob spoke of retaliation and the focus in 1963 was on four Mobsters: Momo Salvatore (Sam) Giancana, Santo Trafficante, Johnny Roselli and Carlos Marcello. Some researchers have thrown in Jimmy Hoffa, the Teamsters' Union boss, as a rather limp fifth.

Sam Giancana peers out of contemporary photographs as a weasel in big glasses and an obsolete fedora. There is every possibility that he offered the services of his heavies to the CIA for their disastrous Bay of Pigs debacle. And it is even more likely that Giancana did business with Joe Kennedy, the president's corrupt businessman father, who may or may not have swung votes for JFK in the election of 1960. And it is undoubtedly a fact that the Mobster shared a mistress with Jack Kennedy in Judith Exner, who told researcher Anthony Summers, that for eighteen months in 1960 and 1961, she literally carried letters between the president and both Giancana and Roselli. There were also meetings between Kennedy and Giancana, one in the White House. Exner speculated that these meetings were about the Mafia's proposed assassination attempts on Fidel Castro. If any of this is true, it not only paints an unflattering portrait of Kennedy (which the Birchers had entirely missed), but must have made life doubly difficult for Bobby, who was doing his best to rid America of Giancana's ilk.

The book *Double Cross* (1992) spells out Giancana's supposed connection with the assassination. It was written by the Mobster's half-brother and nephew and tells us that Giancana sent a team of killers to Dallas in November 1963. The fatal head shot was fired by Richard Cain from the sixth floor of the Book Depository. Cain himself was killed 'gangland style' in 1973. Not content with making Kennedy a Giancana victim, Marilyn Monroe, like Exner, the sometime 'property' of the Mobster, was also murdered on his orders with the (distinctly un-Mafia) method of a poisoned suppository. We know from a thorough medical analysis in the Kennedy killing that the fatal shot was from the front, not behind, and it has never been established that any shots came from the sixth floor of the Depository. Like Cain, Giancana came to a sticky end. In June 1975, while under police protection, he was shot dead with a .22 calibre pistol at his home while cooking in the kitchen. Somebody had switched off the alarm system and it is likely that Giancana knew (and trusted) his killer. There were six bullet holes around his mouth – the message that he talked too much was loud and clear.

Santo Trafficante was the Boss in Florida although his remit extended more widely to include Louisiana and parts of Texas. He also had direct links with Cuba and was one of those Mobsters who lost heavily when Castro closed the island's casinos. In 1978, the HSCA, more amenable than the Warren Commission to the idea of a conspiracy, investigated the Mafia connection closely. It reported that Trafficante was in the top ten Mobster leader list targeted by

Robert Kennedy and acknowledged that, like Giancana, the man had offered his services to the CIA against Castro. The HSCA conceded that Trafficante's background and connections made it possible that he could have been implicated in Kennedy's death. In terms of the old police analogy of means, motive and opportunity, Trafficante had them all. Hitmen skilled in firearms usage were everywhere; Dallas was payback time for closed casinos and Kennedy's failure to reopen them; and Dealey Plaza was one wide-open space. While admitting to the Castro plots, the Mobster denied any involvement with Kennedy.

CIA information uncovered the fact that Jack Ruby had visited Trafficante in a Cuban jail in 1959 and there were rumours (as ever, unconfirmed) that Trafficante worked for Castro, in the narcotics racket. The Mobster died in his bed following heart by-pass surgery in 1987 and is said to have made a deathbed confession to his lawyer, Frank Ragano. 'Carlos [Marcello] f*cked up. We should not have killed Giovanni [JFK]. We should have killed Bobby.' I have no faith in deathbed confessions. They are sometimes taken seriously even by courts of law but we only have Ragano's word for what Trafficante told him and that, it could be argued, was still covered by lawyer-client confidentiality. In the case of Ragano himself, he was a Mafia lawyer for years, both for Trafficante and Jimmy Hoffa. Can we trust *anything* he says?

Carlos Marcello was born Calogero Minacero. He ran America's oldest Mafiosi family and was based in New Orleans where Lee Oswald lived for a time. He had a personal grudge against Bobby Kennedy for having him deported in April 1961. He was, in effect, kidnapped and had a grim time in Guatemala, flown back, according to some sources, by David Ferrie. His famous line, delivered in Italian, was 'Take the stone out of my shoe,' which purports to mean remove the Kennedys but of course could refer to anything that was causing the Mob annoyance. On the day of the assassination, Marcello was in court being acquitted on immigration fraud charges.

In 1979 and 1980, the Mobster was hit by an FBI sting operation involving 1,350 tapes. In three of these, Marcello is heard discussing the assassination with an unknown confederate and the pair leave the room to continue the conversation in the car – 'We don't talk about that in here' – which may imply he knew he was being bugged. The tapes themselves remained sealed by the dead hand of American bureaucracy, first by Judge Morey Sear and second when the FBI itself appealed against a Freedom of Information Act request to have the tapes released. To date, therefore, we have no idea what they have to say.

According to Frank Ragano, on the day of the assassination, Jimmy Hoffa (whose lawyer he then was) phoned him to say, 'Have you heard the good news? They killed the SOB. This means Bobby is out as Attorney General.'

Oswald's uncle, Dutz Murret, had worked for Marcello which may be another tortuous link in the assassination story. Oddly, considering Marcello's power base in New Orleans, DA Jim Garrison did not investigate him as part of his case against businessman Clay Shaw. Admittedly, that case collapsed, largely through the huge criminal opposition to Garrison, but Garrison's avoidance of Marcello may be that he too was in the Mobster's pocket. Marcello died peacefully in March 1993 at the age of 83.

Johnny Roselli was not so lucky. He had probably known Jack Ruby since childhood and met him twice in Miami in the autumn of 1963. He told journalist Jack Anderson that Ruby had killed Oswald in order to silence him, but did not go into details. Roselli's dismembered body was found floating in an otherwise empty oil drum off the Florida coast in July 1976. He had been garrotted and stabbed.

I have made a point, since beginning research on this book, to ask any Americans I meet who they think killed Kennedy. The answer is usually 'the Mafia'. This is because the various quotations from Bosses are now widely available, about stones in shoes and so on and because the Mafia is a safe and comfortable answer. Traditionally, the Mafia are the bad guys, on the wrong side of law and order. *Of course*, they are guilty of such a deplorable act as the murder of a president.

But two things preclude this. First is the fact that the actual hit is nothing like the usual 'gangland slaying'. The triangulated fire in Dealey Plaza smacks of the military, not organized crime. Second is the complexity of the cover-up. The Mafia was powerful, but it could not possibly have extended itself into the corridors of power to ensure that secrets were kept for, to date, sixty years and very possibly for ever. Many researchers have rejected Mafia involvement for these reasons; Matthew Smith, for instance, dismisses the idea in five paragraphs.

5 – The Dallas Police Department

To British eyes, there is appalling confusion over American law enforcement. The FBI holds court over the whole of the United States, but is all too often at loggerheads with local forces. In Texas, there were the Rangers, first set up to protect citizens against native Americans when Texas was still an independent republic. In Dallas, there was the County Sheriff's Department, spearheaded by 'Bill' Decker and recognized immediately in contemporary photographs by their white Stetson hats and the Dallas police themselves, wearing the traditional dark blue uniform of all American policemen, led by their chief, Jesse Curry. All law enforcement in Texas in 1963 carried guns, usually the standard .38 calibre Smith and Wesson revolver, although some preferred a 9mm automatic, usually of Colt manufacture. How well these various agencies got on is anybody's guess, but, while the FBI were seen as outsiders, the common Texan heritage probably held them together. And the FBI had offices in Dallas.

In 1963, the DPD was typical of its time and place. Texas had never been at the heart of 'Dixie' but it was geographically and spiritually in the south and that meant that the 'Black problem' was a continuing one and there were no black officers in the force. It is likely that the safety and comfort of black Texans was not high on the list of priorities for the DPD. In the 1920s, the majority of officers were members of the revitalized Ku Klux Klan, including senior officers, and many of them forty years later were members of the John Birch Society.

When the president came to town in November, he was on the DPD's patch and it was their job, as well as that of the Secret Service, to protect the man. But, from Love Field onwards, things went wrong. There were insufficient motorcycle outriders to cover the whole motorcade and the crowds were so great along Main Street that many of them had to fall back and change position to avoid colliding with people. As the motorcade swept down Main, one of the three motorcycle cops carried straight on, ignoring the planned turn along Houston. Who he was and why he did that was never ascertained.

The actions of Bill Decker that morning are highly suspicious. He was in the lead car of the motorcade with Chief Curry and had given explicit instructions to his deputies to 'take no part whatsoever in the security of the presidential motorcade'. Was that because he thought the Secret Service and Curry's men had it covered? Or did he want to see John Kennedy dead for reasons of his own? He was more 'on it' after the shooting, ordering every available man out of his office up to the railroad yard at the top of the grassy knoll. It may or may not have been his fault that police activity was then re-focused on the Book Depository (from which, by that time, any assassins had gone). Then, there was the strange, unexplained meeting with Captain Will Fritz of Curry's men. Fritz was interrogating Oswald in the afternoon when Decker rang him and ordered him to a meeting in his office fifteen blocks away. Whatever the point of the meeting was, it apparently could not be discussed over the phone, and the pair had met face to face half an hour earlier.

What Decker also did was to order police marksman, Deputy Harry Weatherford, to the roof of the County Jail building where he had a clear view of the motorcade and the Plaza. Weatherford had had a silencer fitted to his gun a few weeks earlier. Three things stand out about this. Why, if Decker had told his deputies that they should not take part in the motorcade's security, should he put his best shot in a position that overlooked it? Why would a police marksman, allowed to use a firearm in pursuance of his duty, need a silencer? And why is there no record of Weatherford's report of what he saw as the motorcade passed beneath him? From his vantage point, he should have seen the rifle in the Depository sixth-floor window, gun smoke coming from the grassy knoll and even possibly the departure of a gunman from that area via the railroad yards. He may have seen all that, but he said nothing. When a researcher rather flippantly asked Weatherford whether he had shot the president, he snapped, 'You little son of a bitch. I shoot lots of people.' Perhaps one of them, for reasons unknown, was John Kennedy. That Weatherford was a crony of Decker's cannot be doubted; he was at the man's bedside as he lay dying in 1970.

Following the day's events for Weatherford is a superb example of the obfuscation in the Kennedy killing. James Bowles was a sergeant in the DPD at the time, in charge of the radio division. Much later, he told researchers that Weatherford was on the roof with another deputy and pointed out that, unless *both* men were in on the conspiracy, Weatherford could not possibly have fired any shots. He rubbished conspiracy theorist Penn Jones, editor of the Texas *Midlothian Mirror*, by saying that Weatherford as a possible hitman was merely in Jones's imagination. But then, the same James Bowles (later promoted, as many cover-uppers were) told another researcher, Harrison Livingstone, that Officer McLain's Dictabelt which recorded the shots in the Plaza, was at the Trade Mart and not in the Plaza at all.

On the JFK Assassination Debate website, he is quoted as saying, 'President Kennedy was killed by a head shot from the right rear, fired by Oswald from the Texas School Book Depository. Unfortunately for conspiracy buffs, that's all there is to it.' In other words, Bowles is an out and out debunker with a spectacularly closed mind. We cannot therefore accept the veracity of his two deputies on the roof contention. Elsewhere, Weatherford is quoted as saying that he was outside the courthouse (presumably on the ground) and responded to shots he believed came from the grassy knoll. There is no mention of a rifle. Yet a third sighting of him allegedly shows him climbing into a second floor of the Depository via a window! Why he should do this (or even how he got there) is unclear – the front door was wide open and the place crawling with policemen after the shooting. Incidentally, since the photograph only shows a man's legs, it could be of the Man in the Moon.

Researcher Matthew Smith, along with many others, finds it suspicious that the three tramps found in the railway car were taken into custody by Dallas police wearing incorrect insignia – 'Also,' says Smith, 'when did Dallas police officers carry rifles?' I cannot comment on the insignia (although many officers that hot, sunny afternoon wore white-topped hats) but photographs taken randomly of the police and crowds show several rifles. Bearing in mind that the APB had said that the president's killer was carrying a rifle, it made sense to issue them, although I have not come across evidence of when this happened or under whose orders.

Then there is the strange behaviour of Captain Will Fritz. The man was a detective with years of experience, nearing retirement. Lee Oswald was probably the most high-profile suspect he had ever interviewed, given that the assumption was made that he had killed the president. Yet, having grilled him for nearly twelve hours in all, no tape recording was made (Fritz claimed, rather lamely, that he had been asking for one for months) and the captain's report was based on rough notes he had made which have never been made public. Did Oswald, indeed, as researchers Ray and Mary La Fontaine mention, talk? Did he tell Fritz of his role in the assassination under orders from someone in the corridors of power? And was Fritz, very much part of the conspiracy, determined not to let any of this reach the outside world?

All the suspicious behaviour of the Dallas Police Department, however, pales into insignificance in the context of the murder of J.D. Tippit. On the face of it, he was an honest cop going about his business in Oak Cliff, Dallas and perhaps responding to the APB description of the president's killer he had picked up on his radio. That went badly wrong and Tippit was simply in the right place but at the wrong time. If only it were that simple!

We know that Tippit's behaviour that lunchtime was odd. He was not where he claimed to be and failed to answer his dispatcher's calls for no apparent reason. Eyewitness accounts of his murder are highly confused, relying, as the Warren Commission did, on the hysterical Helen Markham, who said she comforted the dying officer for twenty minutes when there were in fact others at the scene and the post-mortem showed that Tippit died instantly. If Tippit did indeed roll down his car window and chat to Oswald, did he know him? At least two witnesses believed that he frequented the same coffee house as Jack Ruby, who lived near Tippit. He was also, according to one of Ruby's girls, a regular at the Carousel.

It would have been impossible for Tippit to have been involved directly in the shooting of Kennedy, but what about the follow-up? One conspiracy theory runs like this. Tippit was told (by whom is unknown) to meet up with a young man in Oak Cliff and take him to Red Bird airfield where a private plane would get him out of the country. This in itself, if true, does not mean that Oswald shot anybody, but merely that he was involved in some way. Such a private plane was indeed waiting at the edge of the runway at Red Bird, its engine annoying locals so much that someone called the police! The plane was never used because something had gone wrong.

Enter Officer Roscoe 'Rock' White, a surly-looking man with thinning hair who was a colleague of Tippit. In fact, Tippit's wife was a bridesmaid at White's wedding. In August 1990, White's son, Ricky, claimed that his father had been a CIA plant (he had joined the DPD two months before the shooting) and had shot the president twice from the grassy knoll. He was not alone; his two confederates had the codenames 'Saul' and 'Lebanon'. He himself was 'Mandarin'. The triangular field of fire was the most likely scenario in terms of trajectories and success rate. The shooter in the Depository (let in presumably from the rear by Oswald) had the most difficult shot because of the angle involved (and may have been the shot that missed). The other was firing from the County Records Building which was a more direct trajectory altogether. Those were the shots that hit Kennedy in the back of the head and back, and hit Governor Connally. White's shots from the knoll hit Kennedy in the throat and in the right temple, blowing out the back of his head.

Ricky White claimed that he had his father's rifle (Roscoe died in an industrial fire in 1971, having left the DPD) which fired ammunition of the same calibre as the Mannlicher-Carcano. He also claimed to have messages sent to Roscoe by US Intelligence ordering the hit. The link between Roscoe and Oswald was that they had served in the Marines together, travelling to Japan on the same ship.

Roscoe's wife, Geneva, was a stripper at the Carousel and overheard her husband discussing the plan to kill JFK with Jack Ruby. According to the Reverend Jack Shaw, White confessed to a number of murders on his deathbed (see my comments above on the validity of this). The CIA of course denied any involvement, saying that White had no links with them whatever. Another deathbed interview, this time with Geneva, led researcher Harrison Livingstone to the scenario that Tippit got cold feet at the last moment, having realized that the president was dead and tried to pull out. The police car sounding its horn earlier in the day outside Oswald's house in North Beckley, was Tippit's (the vehicle's number was not 107 but 10) and the two men seen in it by Oswald's landlady Earline Roberts, were Tippit and

White. When witness Domingo Benavides saw a man sitting in a red Ford Falcon six cars down from Tippit's, was that Roscoe White? And other witnesses saw a man with bushy dark hair running away from the scene of the shooting in the opposite direction from 'Oswald'. White was known to wear a wig to hide his baldness, according to Matthew Smith.

The problem with all this, like so many theories, is that it is thin on evidence. Where is the rifle that White owned? Where are the messages from US Intelligence? Where is the diary which Geneva White claimed that her husband kept? And would any self-respecting CIA agent working as a hitman who had just killed a president and then a police colleague to shut him up, actually commit any of this to paper?

6 – The Secret Service

In the interval of *Our American Cousin*, the play being performed at Ford's Theater, Washington on 19 April 1865, John Frederick Parker of the Washington Police Force went off to the nearest tavern with the president's footman and coachman. It is unlikely that he ever returned to his post outside the presidential box and in his absence, the actor John Wilkes Booth crept into the box and shot Abraham Lincoln in the head. The president died hours later.

Ironically, one of the last orders that Lincoln had signed was to set up a Secret Service with partial responsibility for the protection of the president himself. But the main job of the new service that came into operation in July of that year was to do something about the huge flow of counterfeit currency being used in the United States at the end of the Civil War. As such, the Secret Service came under the remit of the Treasury Department.

Lincoln had his own bodyguard, the enormous and enigmatic Ward Hill Lamon, but he was off duty that Friday night, as was Lincoln's aide William Crook. No one took the protection of the president very seriously – even though there had been at least two attempts on Lincoln's life already – and it was not until William McKinley's assassination in 1901 that security was stepped up. The Secret Service as we know it began life the following year. In the macabre history of assassinations, including attempts, the bodyguard of a powerful leader is crucial. If the guard is loyal and efficient, all well and good. If it is not ... In ancient Rome, the Praetorians acted as the emperor's bodyguard, but when Caligula ridiculed one of them, they killed him. As the poet Juvenal wrote in his *Satires*, '*Quis custodiet ipsos custodes?*' – who guards the guards? Bodyguards have regular personal access to their charges, know protocols and routines inside out and are armed and used to taking risks. Who better to kill Kennedy than the men assigned to protect him?

Agents Forrest Sorrels and Winston G. Lawson were assigned to organize the motorcade and its route through Dallas. Working in conjunction with the Dallas police they determined the route from Love Field via Main Street and across Dealey Plaza. But the motorcade took a dog-leg turn, right on to Houston, then a sharp left on to Elm, a more than 90 degree turn which was *verboten* in the Secret Service manual. Sorrels and Lawson both knew that but allowed it (or perhaps instigated it) anyway. There was the vague suggestion later that the dog-leg was to give the president maximum connection with the crowd, but the crowd would go wherever the motorcade went and that argument held no water.

Then there was the matter of the bubble top of the president's Lincoln. The warm, sunny afternoon meant that the top could be left off (again, to let the crowds see their president) and that decision was made by Special Agent Emory Roberts who was in charge of the follow-up car behind Kennedy's. When Secret Serviceman Don Lawton remonstrated with him at Love Field, Roberts shouted him down. We have this on film, the agent spreading his arms in disbelief. At various times along Main Street, Secret Servicemen like Clint Hill had hopped on to the Lincoln's bodywork (standard procedure) but Roberts ordered them off. He did so again at the first sound of gunfire on Elm, when Agent John Ready instinctively jumped off the follow-up car and ran towards the Lincoln. He explained this later by saying that he did not think Ready could reach the car in time, even though it was only doing 11 miles an hour and clearly, from its brake lights, slowing down. The photograph taken by Ike Altgens, which forms the cover of this book, is very telling. Kennedy's hands are up at his throat (the equivalent of Zapruder film frame 155) because he has been hit there from the front. Two of the Secret Service agents on the follow-up car's running boards, are turning to look behind them, directly towards the entrance to the Book Depository. One of them is Paul Landis. John Ready has yet to move.

Roy Kellerman was the agent riding alongside the driver in the Lincoln. He was one of the few people to be present in the motorcade, at Parkland Hospital and at the Bethesda autopsy. His memories were confused. He heard Kennedy say, 'My God, I am hit,' when no one else in the car did and the wound in the throat would make this very unlikely. Kellerman was an experienced officer, having served three other presidents, but his responses that day in Dallas were lamentably slow.

Not as slow, however, as those of driver Will Greer. Secret Service protocol demanded that, in the event of shots at a motorcade, the president's car should be driven at speed out of harm's way. Greer did the opposite, braking after the first shot and looking behind him. His focus should have been on the road ahead. And why, after giving his testimony to the Warren Commission the following year, did he come out of the building laughing?

The only Secret Service agent to emerge with any credit is Clint Hill. Ignoring Agent Roberts' earlier order, he dashed forward, missing his footing at first, then leapt on to the Lincoln's bumper, forcing Jackie Kennedy back into her seat as she was reaching for part of her husband's skull on the bumper area. Altgens photographed this too and it forms the back cover of this book. Hill stayed clinging on over both Kennedys until Parkland when he did what he could to comfort Jackie – 'Oh, Mr Hill, you know he's dead.' The character played by Clint Eastwood in the movie *In the Line of Fire* is based indirectly on Hill.

Another agent who acted with commendable speed was Rufus Wayne Youngblood. Riding in Lyndon Johnson's car, he recognized the apparent 'firecrackers' for the shots they actually were and leapt on Johnson and his wife, pinning them both to the car floor. But did he react so quickly because he knew the shots were coming as some conspiracy theorists have contended?

To one extent, the lid was blown off the Secret Service by one of their own. Abraham Bolden was the first black member of the Secret Service (which does not say much for Kennedy's much-vaunted espousal of civil rights) and the general tenor is that he was much resented as an outsider because of his ethnicity. Bolden heard of a plot by four Cuban gunmen to kill Kennedy during his visit to Chicago. High-powered rifles were to be used. His warnings were ignored, as nothing happened in Chicago during the president's visit there in February, but Bolden accused the Secret Service of laxity. In August 1964, he was found guilty on federal charges of trying to sell government files and served a six-year sentence. Were the Secret Service trying to shut him up?

7 – The Federal Bureau of Investigation

The FBI is the Marmite of America; people love it or hate it. Because of the federal system, where each state of the Union had its own laws and regulations, law enforcement agencies such as sheriff's offices had limited legal jurisdiction. Depending on the nature of the felony, a criminal only had to cross state lines and he was safe. In 1908, the Bureau of Investigation was set up to override this. Various crimes had the 'federal' label, which meant that the Bureau could chase bad guys from coast to coast. This was sharpened in 1935 when the FBI proper emerged. That, in itself, has been seen as a cause for alarm. The baby of aviator and national treasure Charles Lindbergh was kidnapped and murdered in 1932 and after a woeful investigation by local police, the Bureau took over. Its arrest of German immigrant Bruno Hauptmann which led to the man's execution, was every bit as flawed as the original investigation, but Lindbergh was America's darling at the time and, as a result, kidnapping was elevated to a federal offence which was far above its status in the world of crime.

By that time, J. Edgar Hoover had been the Bureau's Director for eleven years. More than any other American institution, the persona of the director dominated policy and attitude. And J. Edgar remained in post until 1972 by which time he was *way* past his sell-by date. In the 1920s, the era of gangsterism and Prohibition, the G-Men who worked for Hoover were seen as heroes, but over time, the Bureau became involved in a number of scandals, all brazened out by Hoover who seemed to have an extraordinary hold over presidents.

That hold was due to a 'black book' of indiscretions carried out by those presidents and data carefully collected by Hoover, largely by the process of wire-tapping (recording private telephone conversations) which Congress continually voted illegal, then legal, depending on any given situation. In the case of the Kennedys, it did not help that both the president and his brother the Attorney General had a string of mistresses whose very existence made life awkward for the men in their lives. We have already seen Judith Exner's ambivalent position of being in bed with both JFK and Sam Giancana. Bobby's clandestine affair with Marilyn Monroe also fell within Hoover's ambit, which was doubly unfortunate because technically Hoover was responsible to Bobby as Attorney General. The pair detested each other, which explains Hoover's incredibly off-hand phone call to Bobby to tell him that his brother was dead.

Today, Hoover's most glaring abuse of power was his growing list of 'sex deviants' compiled in 1950. At first, it was limited to rooting out homosexuals in any federal office but the remit grew wider. What was particularly galling in all this was that it was pots calling kettles black; Hoover was himself homosexual, his lover Clyde Tolson actually working with him in the Bureau. Though stories of J. Edgar in a dress are probably malicious hearsay, the probity of the director was always doubtful. Yet no one seems to have had the gumption to turn the tables on him.

Nowhere was Hoover's paranoia so obvious than in the growing clamour of the Civil Rights issue. He seems to have taken a personal dislike to Dr Martin Luther King, pre-eminently *the* Civil Rights leader in the 1960s and the FBI wasted no time planting bugs in hotel rooms to provide a platform for blackmail.

One of the problems of the FBI in the Kennedy case was its overlap into espionage. While the CIA was concerned with overseas Intelligence, the FBI was internal and domestic, but was pledged to keep America safe from any external espionage threats, rather like MI5 in Britain. At the height of the Cold War, Hoover's detestation of Communists was as visceral as his hatred of Martin Luther King.

And the FBI was ordered by Lyndon Johnson to handle the case of his predecessor's murder. And once again, we face the question – who guards the guards? The FBI already knew a great deal about the Kennedy murder. According to conspiracy theorists, although hard evidence is, as always, hard to come by, Lee Oswald was an FBI informant. What is beyond doubt is that the Bureau had its hooks into Marina Oswald, looking after her safety in a way that could be construed, ironically, as kidnapping. In this respect, the principal agent concerned was James Hosty.

The Warren Commission reported that on 6 November 1963, Oswald wrote Hosty a note which read, 'If you want to talk to me, talk to me. Do not talk to my wife when I am not around. If you do not cease and desist, I will have to take the matter up with the proper authorities.' Who guards the guards? Exactly who 'the proper authorities' were in this instance is difficult to pinpoint. Hosty's superiors, from his immediate boss James Gordon Shanklin to the director himself, had scant regard for people's liberties, for all they were pledged to uphold the Constitution.

We are clearly not looking at a rogue agent here but somebody singing from the Bureau's authorized hymn sheet. Oswald's mysterious defection (if that was what it was) to the USSR and his subsequent return made him an obvious target for FBI interest, but if all this was above board and routine procedure, why did Shanklin, in charge of the Bureau's Dallas office, insist that Hosty destroy Oswald's note?

Hosty was certainly everywhere in November 1963. He was seen on Main Street, Dallas, forty-five minutes before the motorcade arrived, talking to an army intelligence officer. His name and car registration number appear in Oswald's notebook. He was an associate of Robert Surrey, General Edwin Walker's aide, who had printed and distributed the 'Wanted for Treason' literature which appeared just prior to Kennedy's arrival. And of course, he was there in police headquarters while Captain Fritz was interrogating Oswald.

Hosty's own book on the Kennedy killing, unsurprisingly, sheds no light on the killing or much on the background to it, but he did hint that all FBI agents were ordered to stop cooperating with the Dallas police and that this order came from the Bureau's Assistant Director William C. Sullivan. Sullivan was in Dallas on 22 November and was killed in a hunting accident in 1977 just before he was due to appear before the HSCA (see Chapter 11).

The problem with FBI agents, like anyone involved in espionage and official secrets, is that evasion and obfuscation became a way of life. Two FBI men who appear straight as a die are James W. Sibert and Francis X. O'Neill who were present during most of the autopsy at Bethesda. Sibert spoke of a bullet removed from Kennedy's body, which is not mentioned in the official report, and wrote of the apparent surgery to the top of the president's head. O'Neill saw the same thing, but in his book *A Fox Among Wolves* he still contends that 'there has been no hard evidence to date, nothing to support any conspiracy theories in a court of law, nor a scintilla of fact that would prove otherwise'. Either agent O'Neill is seriously deranged or the attitude of J. Edgar Hoover ran deep and pervaded for years.

Did the FBI provide the shooter(s) to kill Kennedy? To answer *that*, I have to agree with O'Neill – there is no evidence. The cover-up, however, of somebody else's involvement, is another matter altogether.

Chapter 13

The Guilty Men?

In the tortuous world of research into the Kennedy murder, where few people are quite what they seem and some may have a problem with the truth, three interlinking groups of men stand out as having the most to gain from the president's death. Those who subscribe to the 'lone nut' theory have no need to establish a motive; Oswald was 'bonkers', 'a basket case', 'a whack job' and all those other layman's terms for the psychologically disturbed. But Kennedy's killing does not conform to that pattern. Whatever the Warren Commission would have you believe, the murder of JFK was carried out with forward planning, proficiency and professionalism; it was, in effect, a military operation.

The great Roman orator Marcus Tullius Cicero, whenever he acted as counsel in a law court, posed the question '*Qui bono?*' (Who benefits?) A large number of people could be said to fill this category in the case of Kennedy, but few could orchestrate it and cover it up with such efficiency that we are still reading, writing and arguing about it today.

1 – Lyndon Baines Johnson

The office of vice president of the United States is a peculiar one. Nominally and certainly on paper, the vice president is the president's number two, his second in command, who undertakes various duties on behalf of the president himself. Should the president be ill or otherwise indisposed, it is the vice president who steps up to the plate.

In practice, however, the two are often at loggerheads and rarely was this more evident than in the case of John Kennedy and Lyndon Johnson. Both men were Democrats, but that was virtually all they had in common. Kennedy chose Johnson as his running mate in 1960 because the Texan could win the South for him. Kennedy, with his Irish background, his Ivy League education, his Catholicism and Martha's Vineyard accent, was not remotely popular in Texas and his liberal stance, on Communism and Civil Rights, for example, found few supporters in the Lone Star State. The 'Wanted for Treason' posters which appeared in Dallas prior to Kennedy's visit resonated with thousands across the South and, bizarrely as it seems, Johnson had it in his remit to do something about it.

'Listen, Godammit,' he snarled in his usual belligerent way, 'my ancestors were teachers and lawyers and college presidents and governors when the Kennedys in this country were still tending bar.' The jibe was in reference to the fact that the earliest Kennedy family to cross from Ireland to America did indeed keep a saloon, in Boston, where they gravitated to 'lace curtain' Irish before Joseph Kennedy made a fortune (much of it illegal) and set his boys up in office. There was no Ivy League for Johnson. He left school at 16 and eventually ended up at a teacher-training institute in San Marcos, Texas.

Johnson made a shrewd move in marrying Claudia Taylor – 'Lady Bird' as her family called her – because she was smarter than he was and far better educated. For all his bulk and swagger – Johnson was 6ft 3in – he smarmed his way around Franklin D. Roosevelt, the New Dealer president in the 1930s and drank 'good ol' boy' bourbon with Sam Rayburn, the House Majority Leader. A shrewd businessman, he made a fortune in construction in the 1930s and war-technology in the 1940s. He was a civilian passenger in a B-26 on a bombing raid over New Guinea in 1942 and his plane was hit. He became perhaps the only civilian in the Second World War to receive the Silver Star, even though none of the actual crew did.

In 1948, he ran for the Senate in Texas and scraped home by the tiniest of margins after a vicious and dishonest election. Scoffingly, his opponents called him 'Landslide Lyndon'. In politics, as in business, Johnson's tactic was 'The Treatment' – shouting, growling, looming physically over the opposition. Ben Bradlee of the *Washington Post* described it 'as if a St Bernard had licked your face for an hour'. He referred to Kennedy when he met him as a 'little scrawny fellow with rickets', which was wrong on every count.

While he stood four square on the Civil Rights issue (something in which he opposed most of his fellow Texans) his business dealings were decidedly murky and at the time of Kennedy's assassination he was about to be investigated by Congress and the president was rumoured to be about to drop him from the ticket. Dealey Plaza changed all that.

We have ample film footage of Kennedy's visit to Texas. Next time you see it, look at Johnson's face during a press conference in Fort Worth. He stands back from the president with a look of utter contempt on his face. Johnson, who had been governor of Texas himself, was a friend of John Connally, but he could not stand Senator Ralph Yarborough and tried to change the riding protocol of the motorcade so that Yarborough would be in Kennedy's car, not Connally. Was this just childish schoolboy politics or was there something more sinister involved? Kennedy himself intervened; Yarborough was to ride in LBJ's car or walk!

As it was, Johnson's car was far back in the motorcade. Did this annoy him, as writer Jonathan Mayo surmises in *The Assassination of JFK: Minute by Minute* or did he arrange this distance deliberately? Johnson was sitting in the rear seat with Lady Bird; Yarborough and Secret Service agent Rufus Wayne Youngblood in front of them. Youngblood noticed the clock on the top of the Hertz advertising sign on the Depository roof read 12.30. That time sequence is crucial, because once the shooting started, Secret Service agent Roy Kellerman radioed Youngblood, 'Dagger [Youngblood's codename] cover

Volunteer [Johnson]'. But Youngblood had already reacted, forcing LBJ down in the seat and lying over him. This meant that Youngblood had dashed into action after the first shot and which most people thought sounded like a firecracker. Why would the bodyguard react so quickly when nobody else did? There is a theory that it was because Johnson was already on the car's floor *before* the first shot, knowing in advance who was firing, when and where from. Yarborough, on the other hand, stayed upright and smelt gunpowder as LBJ's car sped up down Elm Street. That could only mean a shot from ground level, not six floors up in the Depository.

Only a minute later, Youngblood received a message over his radio. 'He's hit! Hurry, he's hit! Let's get out of here!' This was probably Roy Kellerman, urging Greer to get the Lincoln out of the line and get to Parkland. As was proper in desperate security situations, Youngblood was now in charge in the vice president's car – 'I want you and Mrs Johnson to stick with me and the other agents as close as you can. We are going into the hospital and we aren't gonna stop for anything or anybody. Do you understand?'

'Okay, partner, I understand.'

Once it was established that Kennedy was dead, Johnson was driven at speed to Love Field where he had himself sworn in as the 36th president of the United States, in a position to pardon himself for all but the worst of crimes and begin to dismantle most of what John Kennedy stood for. By the time he had finished, 50,000 Americans were dead.

Two weeks after JFK's death, Lyndon Johnson performed a spectacular U-turn in American foreign policy. He scrapped Kennedy's National Security Memorandum 263 and replaced it with his own, 273, which not only halted JFK's removal of 'observers' (in practice, troops) from Vietnam, but increased them and built up to a full war situation. The point about NSAM 273 was that it was printed on 26 November, four days after the shooting but the rough draft *pre-dated* it (21 November). The vice president did not have the authority to do this and, had he seen it, Kennedy would have torn it up and removed Johnson with immediate effect. Johnson wrote the draft because he knew that Kennedy would never see it.

Johnson was, in effect, shafted by his mistress, the enigmatic Madeleine Brown, a Dallas businesswoman in the world of advertising. In 1992, she appeared on an American chat show, *A Current Affair*, to claim that LBJ had clear advance knowledge of an attempt on Kennedy's life. True to form, the debunkers have lined up to denounce Brown, with the usual dismissals – she is disturbed, she is a liar, she is in it for the money and so on. According to Brown, a party was held at the home of oil billionaire Clint Murchison on the night before the assassination. The guest list at Murchison's bash looks like the cast of the usual suspects. Brown attended with LBJ who took time out from his Fort Worth hotel, where the president's party was staying, to meet up with Texas cronies. Two others who were there raised eyebrows. One was Richard Nixon, who had been beaten by Kennedy in the 1960 election and who was in Dallas on business. Nixon's presence in Dallas, at a business convention, has been verified by a number of sources. The other was J. Edgar Hoover and I can find no honest reason for him to be in Texas at all. Researcher Mark North claims that the FBI were investigating the Mafia's Carlos Marcello of New Orleans, but New Orleans is not Dallas (or even in the same state) and, according to Hoover, the Mafia did not exist. Two days after the assassination, Hoover wrote to Johnson – 'The thing I am concerned about ... is having something issued so we can convince the public that Oswald is the real assassin.'

According to Madeleine Brown, the others were surprised to see Johnson there and a handful of them went into a separate room. When LBJ came out with 'smoke coming out of his ears' (Brown) he whispered to her that, 'after tomorrow those damn Kennedys will not be poking fun at me any more.' Does this explain Johnson's attempt the next day to swap Connally for Yarborough? Does this explain his pre-emptive diving to the floor of his car in Dealey Plaza?

Johnson's swearing in on board Air Force One was carried out with what may be called embarrassing speed. In the charged atmosphere of the day, perhaps this was understandable; if this was a wider coup, perhaps involving a foreign power, then Johnson himself could be a target and he needed the full powers of the president's office to act. But, given the situation, he was *de facto* president anyway; why the rush? Was it, as some have surmized, so that he could bury the charges of financial fraud against him and pardon others around him?

On the day of the assassination, the *Dallas Times Herald* ran stories about Bobby Baker, one of Johnson's aides who had been forced to resign in October because of insider trading involving the Mob. Baker had made $2million before he was outed and the general feeling was that Johnson knew all about his racketeering. Then there was Billie Sol Estes, a corrupt businessman who had defrauded the government over contracts for grain and cotton. Once Johnson was dead, Sol Estes, who served fifteen years for fraud in 1967, was facing charges of complicity in the murder of agricultural government agent Henry Marshall. He wriggled out of it, claiming that the whole thing had been set up by Johnson.

There is no doubt that LBJ had some dubious friends, but one who has stayed resolutely under the radar is Malcolm Everett Wallace, known as 'Mac'. He does not feature in Michael Benson's *Who's Who of the Kennedy Assassination* (1993) and rarely in any other works. Gerald Posner ignores him altogether. But his links to LBJ are undeniable, as is his homicidal track record.

Look again at eyewitness accounts in Dealey Plaza. Richard Carr was a construction worker sitting on the scaffolding around the Courts Building in Houston Street. He saw, on the sixth floor of the Book Depository, a heavy-set man wearing a hat, a tan-coloured sports coat and horn-rimmed glasses. By the time he had climbed down to the ground, Carr saw the man again, this time with two others, 'walking very fast' towards Record Street. Here, the three got into a 1961 or 1962 grey Rambler station wagon with Texas plates and with a black driver. Carolyn Walther saw him too – 'a man in a brown suit coat'. So did James 'Dickie' Worrell. The man in the brown suit was hurrying out of the back of the Depository and heading south on Houston soon after the shooting.

Clothes can easily be changed, but photographs of Mac Wallace show the thick-set neck and shoulders and the distinctive horn-rimmed glasses. Was he the man on the sixth floor of the Depository and what was he doing there? Researchers Glen Sample and Mark Collom unearthed the fact that Wallace had attended Woodrow Wilson High School in Dallas. He played quarterback for the school's football team and was 'tough as nails' according to a contemporary. He had dark hair and an olive complexion, easily passing for Mexican or Cuban. From school, he attended the University of Texas in Austin and joined the Marines. He was a member of the Dallas Gun Club. He attended Columbia University in New York and became an economist for the Department of Agriculture. And he worked for Lyndon Johnson.

Wallace's first clash with the law was a serious one. In 1952, he was charged with the murder of a love rival, professional golfer John Kinser, in Austin. Kinser was having an affair with Wallace's wife; Wallace found out and shot him. For reasons that are unclear, Johnson arranged for John Cofer, a high-profile lawyer, to defend Wallace, which he did so successfully that the sentence was only five years, which was suspended! According to Madeleine Brown, Wallace did not even appear in court, but 'the judge gave him a ... suspended sentence for a capital murder ... in Texas!' The Lone Star State was not famous for its clemency.

When Henry Marshall investigated the frauds being carried out by Sol Estes, he was found dead on 3 June 1961 at his home in Robertson County. His death was officially ruled a suicide, despite five bullets being found in his abdomen. According to various sources years later, Wallace was hired to kill Marshall, to fake a suicide by carbon-monoxide in his car, but something went wrong, Wallace panicked, shot the man with the official's own rifle and ran.

Lawyer Douglas Caddy, working for Billie Sol Estes, wrote in August 1984 that Wallace was the triggerman in no less than eight murders, including Kinser, Marshall and Kennedy. Confusion arises in two areas. First, Clifton Carter, the aide who had ridden in the motorcade with Johnson and Youngblood, told Sol Estes that Wallace had a Communist background which is most unlikely in a Texan university culture and that he (Wallace) had recruited Jack Ruby who in turn recruited Lee Oswald. Second, Carter allegedly told Sol Estes that Wallace fired from the grassy knoll. Clearly, he could not be in two places at once and no one reports a figure resembling him behind the fence.

Wallace's university career is in the public record. He *may* have met George de Mohrenschildt there, since the baron was at the college in 1944 studying oil geology. Wallace was president of the students' union and campaigned for greater academic freedom for Blacks. No doubt in the eyes of many white Texans, that made him a Communist.

By 1964, the tide had turned against Mac Wallace. He lost his security clearance in a missile programme because of 'criminal, infamous, immoral and notoriously disgraceful conduct'. This included the murder conviction (Kinser), the two drunk-driving charges, Communism and homosexuality. About all they did not accuse him of was shooting the president!

Researchers Sample and Collom tracked down Joe Bloombury who had worked under Wallace for years. He remembered the reactions of various colleagues hearing the news of Kennedy's death – the office was closed down and everybody went home – but Mac Wallace was not in that day. Wallace's wife, Virginia, did not know where he was either, but they were estranged by then so that is hardly surprising.

Whatever the involvement of Mac Wallace as a hitman, one man was in no doubt that the power behind the killing belonged to Johnson. In the History Channel's television documentary, *The Guilty Men* (November 2003), Barr McClellan said to camera, 'I know, as attorney for Lyndon Johnson, that he murdered John Kennedy. He murdered John Kennedy to become president and to avoid prison and there is no doubt in my mind.' The programme caused outrage (and probably not a little panic) in the States. People threatened to burn down libraries that stocked the DVD. Sales were halted. Various notables, including ex-president Jimmy Carter and ex-president Gerald Ford (who had, of course, already carried out the fraud of the Warren Commission) slammed the 'very bad journalism, the worst they had ever seen'. Presumably, they had not read the mainstream media's eulogies over the whitewashing books of debunkers like Bugliosi and Posner. To date, the only copies of *The Guilty Men* can be found on YouTube. Three historians were chosen to rebut the ideas in the programme and their scrutiny was lamentable, ignoring key points of evidence. One of them twice got the date of the Warren Commission report wrong. One viewer wrote, 'The American public has been denied the truth once again. The evidence is out there and *The Guilty Men* only scratched the surface. Mac Wallace was a murderer, [Sol] Estes and Baker were extortionists and LBJ was their leader.'

One tantalizing piece of evidence has come to light. The Dallas police could only find vague palm prints of Lee Oswald on the boxes in the 'sniper's nest'. This is hardly surprising, in that the man worked there. On one of the boxes (Box A in evidentiary chain terms) there was an unidentified single print, subsequently labelled #29. Despite various attempts to prevent comparison, researchers were able to compare this print with those of Mac Wallace from his 1952 murder trial. Fingerprint expert Nathan Darby found thirty-four points of comparison between the two prints. British law demands sixteen points for a criminal case; American law only eight. Did Mac Wallace have a legitimate reason for being in the Texas School Book Depository in November 1963?

No, he did not.

2 – The Military-Industrial Complex

In a number of dystopian/sci-fi movies over the last few years, there have been predictable plots involving attacks on the United States by foreign powers/aliens/you name it. In almost all of them, there is at least one five-star Pentagon general, his chest encrusted with military decorations, whose only answer to everything is to 'nuke' the opposition. Such caricatures are based on real people, so blinkered by the awesome technological capability of the United States that they believe themselves – and their nation – to be invincible. This kind of thing led America to wield the 'big stick' and become the world's policeman (not until President Biden was this officially denied) – it also led to the humiliation of Vietnam.

In movie terms, nowhere is this better expressed than in the brilliant political thriller *Seven Days in May*, a story that so impressed Jack Kennedy that he allowed a camera crew access to the White House one weekend to film it. James Matoon Scott (Burt Lancaster) is the five-star general who could have been a stand-in for Edwin A. Walker, the general and right-wing activist effectively fired by Kennedy in 1961 for disseminating right-wing propaganda to the men under his command. The 'weak sister' president (played by Frederic March) is despised by Scott for his liberalism and the general hatches a plot to depose him. Thankfully, there is an honest, straight-as-a-die colonel (Kirk Douglas) who spoils Scott's party and all ends happily. It did not end happily for Kennedy.

Such stuff of course is bread and butter for conspiracy theorists. Of course, America is led by right-wing bigots. Of course, there are trigger-happy generals in the Pentagon. Of course, they wanted to remove the 'weak sister' Kennedy in 1963. And there to aid them were the fascists of the John Birch Society and opponents of black Civil Rights.

President Dwight Eisenhower had warned people in his farewell speech in 1960 – 'The conjunction of an immense military establishment and a large arms industry is new in the American experience. We must guard against the acquisition of unwarranted influence, whether sought or unsought, by the military-industrial complex.'

'Ike' was up to his neck in all this. As a war hero and former general himself, he knew all about the power of the military. He had also sanctioned an invasion of Cuba which became, under Kennedy, the Bay of Pigs debacle. Perhaps, in his twilight days in office, he realized that the Frankenstein's monster he had helped create was out of control. America liked wielding the 'big stick' and had been doing it in Central America since Theodore Roosevelt's administration. It also saw itself as the 'land of the free', the champion of liberty against (especially) Communism around the world and that ancient right, which the Romans and Nazis had also espoused, to invade any country on the flimsiest of excuses. Remember LBJ's coarse explanation for American involvement in Vietnam, when he pulled out his penis for reporters and growled, 'This is why!'

Because of the huge demand for materiel during the Second World War, the armed forces had grown exponentially. There had been no air force in the 1920s when General Billy Mitchell was court-martialled for demanding one. American involvement in the First World War amounted to little more than a single division on the Western Front. But the armaments industry, providing bullets, planes, tanks, surface warships, submarines and bombs rose spectacularly to the occasion and the 'draft' increased the number of Americans in uniform as never before.

Obviously, with the war's end, this was scaled down, but war and the threat of war had not gone away. The Cold War began almost immediately with flash-points in Korea and elsewhere. American troops found themselves on duty all over the world, to combat the Communist threat and to protect American interests. It would be over-stretching it to call the post-war world an American empire, but the situation was certainly a form of imperialism. Immediately in the eyeline of the military in 1961 was Cuba. General Lyman Lemnitzer, chairman of the Joint Chiefs of Staff (aka the Scott/Lancaster character in *Seven Days in May*) had submitted a detailed plan to Robert McNamara, the Defense Secretary, for a full-scale invasion of the island to topple Fidel Castro. This was the start of over half a century of 'regime change' which America believed it had the right to undertake. The plan involved fake outrages, supposedly committed by Cubans, on American soil against American citizens and had the code name Operation Northwoods. When JFK discovered this, Northwoods and Lemnitzer were shown the door.

As Kennedy's administration continued, the rednecks determined to wage war – and to make money out of it – became more and more embittered. The president had avoided war with the Soviet Union over the Cuban Missile Crisis by tough and judicious 'jaw-jaw', not 'war-war' and it had paid off. The words of his inaugural address were tough – 'Let every nation know, whether it wishes us well or ill, that we shall pay any price, bear any burden, meet any hardship, support any friend, oppose any foe to ensure the survival and success of liberty. This much we pledge ...'

There was unrest in Africa (when is there not?), and in Berlin they built a wall to separate the Eastern and Western zones, a physical concrete barrier between freedom and oppression. By the summer of 1963, Kennedy had come to realize that working *with* the opposition was infinitely preferable to conflict. To that end, he scaled down the number of 'observers' in Vietnam and pledged to remove them. The first 1,000 men came home before Christmas, just before Lyndon Johnson sent them all back again – and then some!

On 22 November, Dallas newspapers 'welcomed' Kennedy with a black-bordered series of questions about his policies. There were also a number of posters around the town (quickly taken down when they could be found) calling the president a traitor. The American Fact-Finding Committee which had placed the advertisement in the *Dallas Morning News* was composed of a group of fascist lunatics headed by Bernard Weissman who, according to some sources, had been at a two-hour meeting at the Carousel on 14 November with Jack Ruby and Officer J.D. Tippit. Weissman annoyed Ruby, first because of the disrespect it showed to Kennedy and second because he could not understand how a fascist could have a Jewish name. Weissman's ad was paid for by a right-wing cabal led by Bunker Hunt – and this leads us to the industrial element of the men behind the Pentagon.

In an attempt to curb inflation, Kennedy had persuaded the steelworkers who were making wage-increase demands, to reduce those demands and told their bosses to hold the price of steel steady. In the true spirit of American greed, the bosses ignored that and put up prices, for no legitimate reason, by $6 a ton. Quite rightly, the president told the bosses in a televised speech that they were showing their utter contempt for 185 million Americans. Steel, of course, was one of the basic elements of hardware necessary for military use. So was oil. Texas ran on oil and serious money was being made hand over fist by a corporate cabal confident that they were supported by the government with the oil depletion allowance. This was a system whereby generous tax allowances were given to the oil industry to compensate them for the risks they ran. Kennedy intended to curb this. After all, *all* businesses and their owners take financial risks – it makes capitalism what it is. With Dallas as the epicentre of oil, the president was riding into serious opposition on 22 November.

At the heart of the epicentre was Haroldson Lafayette Hunt, an oil billionaire who was a friend of Baron George de Mohrenschildt and accompanied around the city by George Butler, ex-head of the

Dallas Policemen's Union and member of the Ku Klux Klan. Hunt's money was used to back both Gerald Ford and Richard Nixon in their respective bids for the presidency in the years ahead. He was also, needless to say, in bed with Lyndon Johnson (a man always attracted to money) and had been a fervent supporter of Senator Joe McCarthy's hysterical anti-Communist witch-hunt, spending over $2 million a year to thwart the Red threat. Hunt's sons, Lamar and Nelson Bunker, were very much chips off the old block, Bunker paying $1,465 for the full-page anti-Kennedy ad in the *Dallas Morning News*.

Then there was Clint Murchison, who may or may not have hosted the notorious party with LBJ, Hoover and Nixon on the day before the assassination. After Ruby shot Oswald, a distraught Marina was whisked away by Murchison's partner Bobby Winn and the FBI and kept in a secluded motel until her appearance before the Warren Commission months later. According to researcher Pete Brewton in *The Mafia, CIA and George Bush* (1992) Murchison had links with both the CIA and Carlos Marcello.

Any oil billionaire had reason to want Jack Kennedy dead. They also had the money to hire hitmen and enough contacts to ensure that a cover-up would work.

Tantalizingly, a note found by the FBI among Oswald's property was addressed to 'Dear Mr Hunt' and asked only for information. This *may* be any of the Hunt boys referred to above. Equally, it could be E. Howard Hunt, he of the many aliases. *This* Hunt worked for the CIA. And there the tale becomes appreciably more entangled.

3 – The Central Intelligence Agency

Every country has its Intelligence units. The United States, like Britain, has one for each of the three armed forces – army, navy and air force. There is also the National Security Agency and, more politically skewed than any of them, the Central Intelligence Agency (CIA).

I once met a CIA man, on a cruise in the Mediterranean. To make conversation, I asked him what he did for a living. 'Oh, I'm CIA,' he smiled. As I expected, no more information was forthcoming, which is as it should be for an operative whose whole raison d'être is about secrecy. The problem with that is that it is music to the ears of conspiracy theorists because the CIA very quickly morphs into the Illuminati, a sinister, unaccountable and largely faceless force that operates above the law and the power of elected governments and whom we came across in Chapter 1.

The CIA developed from the Office of Strategic Services (OSS), a combined Intelligence unit for the United States combatting the Nazi Intelligence of the Abwehr and the Sicherheitsdienst. At the end of the war, Allen Dulles was promoted from within its ranks to run OSS in Germany. He personally 'turned' a number of Abwehr agents into OSS operatives, just as his bosses in Washington were all too happy to employ Nazi intelligentsia in other walks of life, such as space technology.

By the time Dulles became Director of the CIA (as it was now called), his older brother John was a Cold Warrior of unrivalled bigotry, the most hawkish of advisers in Truman's and Eisenhower's administrations. As we have already seen, the obsession with the Communist threat which manifested itself in the McCarthy witch-hunts and the creation of Congress's Un-American Activities Committee, also led to a near declaration of war against Communist Cuba.

There is something hysterical about the American government and there always has been. No one can imagine, say, MI6 in Britain launching the Bay of Pigs invasion. But that was exactly what the CIA did. They put undue pressure on Eisenhower's administration to back the training and preparation for an assault on Fidel Castro's territory. On the one hand, it was a naked act of aggression. On the other, it was what the American government had been doing in Central America since the 1890s, an extension of the Monroe Doctrine which smacked of Hitler's invasion of umpteen European states in the name of *lebensraum* (living space). The CIA's own Intelligence gathering was woefully inept. With the arrogance that only men like Allen Dulles possessed, they assumed that the Cuban defences would crumble quickly. They were, nevertheless, careful – and both Eisenhower and Kennedy insisted on this – that only Cuban exiles should be involved. What was necessary for success, however, was air cover against Castro's admittedly ramshackle air force – and that meant the deployment of highly trained Americans. Kennedy baulked at this and would not provide it, so the Cuban guerrillas were stopped in their tracks on their own beach-heads.

The shock waves were felt around the world. America's allies – and even some Americans – found the situation untenable. As for Kennedy himself, he famously promised to 'smash the CIA into a thousand pieces' and began by firing Dulles and a number of his cronies from key positions. Could there be a better example of Cicero's '*Qui bono?*' The very existence of the CIA was under threat from the only man who could take them down, John F. Kennedy. How could they *not* have been involved in Dallas?

The most detailed research on CIA involvement was carried out by John Newman in *JFK and Vietnam* and *Oswald and the CIA*. Since the 1960s, we have become aware of the extent of the 'deep state', the arcane workings of Intelligence agencies generally. For instance, it became policy during the Eisenhower era to use political assassination as a means to an end – 'executive action'. The almost farcical attempts on the life of Fidel Castro, all of them organized by the CIA, is proof of this. These are not rogue agents, of the kind beloved by the James Bond franchise, but the central policy of an organization created and backed by the White House. Although neither Jack nor Bobby Kennedy used the word 'assassinate' or 'kill' ('removal' or 'elimination' were the *mots de jour*) both brothers in fact sanctioned such skulduggery.

The whistle on all this was blown by Colonel Leroy Fletcher Prouty, Chief of Special Operations for the Joint Chiefs of Staff who wrote his own book on CIA involvement in 1992. Dismissed as a crank by debunkers, Prouty was at the heart of the paranoid group of warmongers like the Dulles brothers and knew where espionage bodies were buried. He was the liaison officer between the CIA and the Pentagon and minced no words when he asserted that Oswald was an undercover agent on special assignment since his training days with the Marines in Atsugi, Japan. In the late 1950s, the CIA were selecting and training men for undercover operations. Oswald was among them and his supposed 'defection' to the USSR (and, one assumes, his return) were all part of that. The ease with which he came and went, at the height of the Cold War, makes no sense otherwise.

As Matthew Smith says, 'trying to get the truth from [the CIA] is difficult beyond belief. They are skilled at "dirty tricks", deceit, lies and covering their tracks.' By the time it came to the Warren Commission, James Jesus Angleton, the paranoid alcoholic counterintelligence chief of the CIA, had all the angles covered and coached various witnesses on what to say. According to Richard Haldeman, President Nixon's aide later involved in the Watergate debacle, Angleton leaned on William C. Sullivan, senior FBI agent, to that end.

It was the CIA, say conspiracy theorists, who sent a fake Oswald to Mexico City where he tried to obtain a visa to take him to either Cuba or Russia. Routine security photographs of 'Oswald' seen leaving and entering the Cuban embassy in the city are clearly of an older, heavier-set man who bears no resemblance to Lee Harvey at all. Grilled as he was by embassy staff, the visitor's command of the Russian language was poor, whereas George de Mohrenschildt testified to the Warren Commission that the real Oswald's Russian was excellent. This line of reasoning – including the fake Oswald's loud and memorable appearances at car dealerships (the real Oswald could not drive), rifle ranges and even restaurants – is all part of the CIA's setting Oswald up as a 'patsy'. Here was the unstable, paranoid, anti-US ex-Marine who was precisely the 'lone nut' who would try to kill the president.

To add to the murkiness, Valery Kostikov, a KGB assassin and saboteur, was based in Mexico City at the time and 'Oswald' may have met him. Kostikov belongs in the 'the Russians did it' theory, but the overlap with 'Oswald'/Mexico is fascinating. And Mexico was the stomping ground of David Atlee Phillips, the CIA's man in the city. He may have operated under the code name 'Maurice Bishop' and he testified to the HSCA that Oswald had meetings with a number of Cuban agents. Phillips was a propaganda specialist and had himself operated in Havana, where he worked with E. Howard Hunt (another future Watergate burglar). Mark Lane's book *Plausible Denial* (1991) contends that Hunt was directly involved in the Kennedy killing although G. Robert Blakey, who eventually chaired the HSCA, defended him to the hilt. As 'Maurice Bishop', conspiracy theorists contend, Phillips was involved with Alpha 66, a terrorist group of Cuban exiles continuing to work with the CIA long after Kennedy's death, to kill Castro. Men like Phillips are masters of deception, plotters so devious and careful, that the truth about them is likely never to come out.

Murkier still, the CIA is believed to have been experimenting with mind-altering drugs in the 1960s in the process then known as 'brainwashing'. This was the MK-ULTRA programme which every CIA operative, from planner Richard Helms on downward denied existed. Unfortunately, as with the movie *Seven Days in May*, *The Manchurian Candidate* destroyed for ever our ability to investigate what was really going on in the corridors of power. Debunkers could easily deflect genuine research (and have done so) by claiming that a political coup in America and the programming of someone's mind by organizations is the stuff of deranged fiction, the most bizarre of conspiracy theories. Similarly, when Oliver Stone's movie *JFK* (1991) caused such a furore, it was an unfortunate piece of casting that the character 'X' was played by Donald Sutherland. 'X' is clearly Leroy

Fletcher Prouty but Sutherland, excellent actor though he is, has played so many duplicitous 'baddies' that we cannot believe a word he says. Someone like Rob Lowe would have been more convincing!

There is no doubt that the CIA had the means to orchestrate the assassination of John Kennedy (and, if necessary, J.D. Tippit too). They actually had an assassination manual which offered advice on the weapons and logistics involved in a variety of scenarios. A triangular hit in Dealey Plaza, gunmen placed in the Book Depository, the Dal-Tex or Court Building and the grassy knoll, was archetypally military. True, one is left wondering why the various attempts on Castro were so inept, when the Kennedy hit was not, but the mechanics of assassination were known to the CIA and used by them. Hitmen were not in short supply and there was no need to involve the Mob in this context. The real strength of the CIA, however, was in the cover-up, which no organization other than the FBI could do. Why, for instance, was Allen Dulles, the director fired by Kennedy, appointed to the Warren Commission? The simple answer is that he was there to deflect probes into CIA activity by whatever means, and, as we have seen, he had a lot of help in that context from shady lawyers like David Belin and Arlen Specter and 'useful idiots' like Congressman Ford.

Chapter 14

The CYA* Conspiracy

As I wrote in my Author's Introduction, I do not know who killed John Kennedy or precisely why. When I was teaching and I taught the Dealey Plaza story to a group of 13-year-olds and asked them who they thought was responsible, one girl said she thought it was Jackie Kennedy because of her husband's affair with Marilyn Monroe. Still another believed the shooter was a mysterious man called 'Grassy' Knoll! Perhaps I hadn't taught the thing too well …

In the vast literature on the assassination of President Kennedy, several researchers (at least those who do not accept the 'lone nut' theory) are more concerned with the organizers, the instigators, the men behind the scenes who orchestrate and pull strings than with the hitmen who actually carried out the job. This is understandable and conforms to the idea that the man at the top is ultimately responsible. As another president, Harry S. Truman said, 'The buck stops here.'

But I believe the real tragedy behind the killings of Jack Kennedy, J.D. Tippit and Lee Oswald is the way in which the little people – you and me – covered up their own complicity in order to feel good about themselves. In the end, it was all about covering their asses, as the Americans say and that, too, is a large part of a conspiracy of a different kind, but one which has masked the truth for sixty years.

How did it work?

---

* CYA – Cover Your Ass, in other words, protect yourself at all costs.

1 – The Secret Service

The job of the Secret Service was to keep the president safe. In Dallas, they did a singularly bad job, not because there was a plot by agents to kill their boss, but because human nature being what it is, too many of them were sloppy and mistakes were made. It was more cock-up than conspiracy.

The night of Thursday, 21 November was cold and wet. Nobody in the Kennedy entourage in Fort Worth expected crowds to be out, in the wet and the dark, but there they were. The Secret Service were caught slightly off guard by this, the night on which Jack said to Jackie that someone with a high-powered rifle could easily shoot from a high building and disappear into the darkness. At 11.35 outside the Hotel Texas, a crowd of 2,000 wanted to shake the president's hand. Knowing how important glad-handing in this alien state was, the Secret Service let it go ahead. Helen Ganss was an old lady who lived on the eighth floor of the hotel and the Secret Service let her stay there when all the other guests had been moved out. But it was an old lady who had bashed Adlai Stevenson recently with a placard in Dallas ...

At ten past midnight on Friday morning, with the Kennedys safe in their suite, a group of Secret Servicemen went off with reporter Roy Stamps to the Fort Worth Press Club. Conspiracy theorists have seen something sinister in this, that the men were lured there by conspirators. Actually, it was good old-fashioned carelessness, of the type Abraham Bolden, back in the White House, would lodge a complaint about in the coming days. The Press Club normally closed at midnight, but nine of the agents were still there at 1.45 a.m., along with Mac Kilduff, Kennedy's acting Press Secretary, who was, perhaps, not acting responsibly that night.

Undeterred, seven of the nine went on, at 3 a.m., to the Cellar Coffee House. According to their testimony, they only drank Salty Dicks, non-alcoholic beer. Nobody left until 5.05.

Clint Hill reported for duty as Jackie's personal bodyguard at 7.40. She was having a bit of a lie-in as Jack gave a breakfast speech downstairs. He grabbed a roll and some coffee. Roy Kellerman, in overall charge of the trip to Dallas, had to make a call about the bubbletop of the president's Lincoln. The rain was easing by mid-morning.

At Love Field, the 'We Love Jack' placards mingled with 'Your [*sic*] a Traiter [*sic*]' and 'I hold you in complete contempt'. The agents did nothing; the president would have been the first to remind them that America was a free country. The motorcade was always a problem, but the formation for Dallas was not the usual one. Behind the president's limo was the Secret Service car 'Queen Mary', 5 feet away, packed with eight agents and two of Kennedy's aides, O'Donnell and Powers. One of the Secret Service men was George Hickey, with an AR-15 automatic rifle at his feet. Conspiracy theorists have cited the work of ballistic expert Howard Donahue who spent twenty-five years to 'prove' that Hickey killed the president by accident, his rifle going off as the limo slowed and accelerated. This ignores two things – Hickey was an experienced shot and the fatal wound came from the front, not the rear.

Agent Lawton had already been reprimanded by his boss Emory Roberts, a jobsworth who made some bad decisions that day. Removing agents from the president's car was a mistake, giving an assassin a clear shot. The motorcycle outriders too should have been further forward, as they had always been in other motorcades. It is not clear whose decision this was, but either the Secret Service or the Dallas police must take responsibility.

Concerned about this, Clint Hill dashed forward on Main Street and clung on to the Lincoln's bodywork just alongside Jackie; Roberts ordered him back to the Queen Mary. The turning on to Houston was tight enough, but the one on Elm was worse and Will Greer slowed to an estimated 5 miles an hour. At 55, were his reactions too slow for what was about to happen?

Ike Altgens captured the moment of the first shot. Some Secret Servicemen are half turning to the sound of gunfire; others are not moving. Glen Bennett was the first to react, seeing the bullet wound explode in Kennedy's back – 'He's hit!' Hickey had the rifle, so he drew his revolver. By that time, Kennedy had been shot twice and Connally once. Then Hill dashed forward to grab the Lincoln and cover the First Lady with his own body.

At Parkland, one account among the hysteria has Will Greer sobbing his apologies to Mrs Kennedy. If this is true, he is the only Secret Serviceman to acknowledge guilt in what had just happened. Forty-five minutes later, with the president declared dead, the guilt showed itself in a different way and it showed the Secret Service in a bad light. Kellerman threw his weight around, haranguing Dr Earl Rose and telling him that there would be no autopsy in Dallas. In that, he was actually breaking the law and certainly exceeding his authority. The Secret Service wheeled the casket out of Parkland.

In the president's cabin aboard Air Force One, at 2.36 on that dreadful afternoon, Jackie Kennedy took both of Clint Hill's hands in hers. 'What's going to happen to you now, Mr Hill?'

'I'll be okay, Mrs Kennedy. I'll be okay …'

Outside, Paul Landis was crying. 'Pull yourself together, Paul.' Kellerman snapped. 'You're witnessing history.'

For me, the *only* Secret Service agents to behave properly that day in Dallas were Clint Hill and Rufus Wayne Youngblood in LBJ's car. The others badly let their president down, but there was no enquiry and nobody took a rap of any kind. And why, we have to ask, were there no Secret Servicemen on the ground in Dealey Plaza?

2 – The Dallas Police Department

How hard, in the end, did they try? We have already noted Jim Leavelle's disparaging comment on Kennedy's death – to a policeman, Tippit was far more important, which is odd bearing in mind the mistakes they made in that murder too. For experienced police officers, both Jesse Curry and Bill Decker were woefully lacking. They both gave orders over their radios for their men to get to the top of the grassy knoll, then they abandoned that in favour of the Book Depository. They did not have the car park beyond the knoll searched or check the cars. They did not seal off the Depository and allowed Assistant District Attorney Bill Alexander to poke his nose in where it had no business. Whoever transmitted the APB describing the president's assassin, the information was inaccurate and appears to be based on a brief sighting by one witness, Howard Brennan, although the officer who relayed it, Inspector Herbert Sawyer, could not remember who told him and did not make a note of the man's name. 'He was a white man and he was there' was as good as it got. They did not authorize a search of the Dal-Tex building or the County Court Building next door, both of which offered excellent platforms for a marksman. Sheriff Bill Decker had told his men to offer no assistance with the motorcade.

Down the hierarchical chain, one anonymous motorcycle cop veered off from the motorcade, going the wrong way across Dealey Plaza. At the Tippit murder scene, Officer J.M. Poe almost certainly forgot to scratch his initials on the two shells he was handed by witness Domingo Benavides. When the Warren Commission produced them as evidence on 12 June 1964, there were no initials at all. Poe had been clearly told to do this by his boss, Sergeant Gerald Hill.

Collectively, the Police Department were unimpressive. Many of them were members of the John Birch Society, some of them possibly Ku Klux Klan. An estimated 50 per cent of them knew Jack Ruby personally and regularly attended the Carousel Club. The ease with which Ruby could get into Headquarters, at all hours of the day and night defies belief. 'You all know me; I'm Jack Ruby,' he said having shot Oswald and he was right; they did. In encouraging his force to be helpful to the media, Chief Curry went too far. Despite assurances to the contrary, security in the station was lamentable. Ruby entered at least three times with a gun in his pocket. He mingled with pressmen, even though virtually every cop there knew that he was not one of them. Roy Vaughn specifically denied letting Ruby pass him on the Main Street ramp, even though other officers said they *had* seen a man walking there.

We have already looked at the odd movements of J.D. Tippit on the day he died. And we have the bizarre story of Roscoe White's family, convinced that he was actually the shooter on the grassy knoll. And what about Badge Man caught on camera by Mary Moorman? Was that White or another of Dallas's finest who should not have been where he was?

No doubt there were some dependable, hardworking and honest cops in the DPD, but as the names emerge in the ghastly events of that Friday, I cannot think of one who stands out; except Roger Craig - and somebody killed him.

3 – The Federal Bureau of Investigation

The rot starts at the top. J. Edgar Hoover had been in post as the Bureau's Director for too long. He was a dinosaur, ignoring the existence of organized crime, further to the right than any of the usual suspects we have encountered so far in this book. His attitudes, hypocrisy and methods were all highly suspect and all of this seeped downwards throughout the entire organization. He snooped personally on his men, checking their private lives and berating them if they ever appeared in public without suit, tie and hat. Long before *Men in Black* became a highly lucrative (and very funny) film franchise, the men in black suits *were* the FBI. The unofficial motto was 'Don't embarrass the Bureau', which explains why James Gordon Shanklin, head of the Dallas office was so hysterically intent on destroying the complaining note that Oswald had sent his operative, James Hosty.

Virtually all the evidence presented to the Warren Commission came from the FBI, so the enquiry began life as a lop-sided, preconceived stitch-up. There is actually no evidence to suggest that the Bureau was instrumental in the death of Kennedy, but what mattered most was the reputation of the Bureau. It is redolent in agent Francis X. O'Neill's contention that, despite having seen the extent of Kennedy's head wounds at Bethesda, he could still cling to the nonsense that there was no evidence of a conspiracy in the man's death.

Likewise, James Hosty, muscling in everywhere in the case, was perfectly happy to go along with orders from above (in this case not Hoover but his number three, William C. Sullivan) not to cooperate with the Dallas police. The problem with the multiplicity of American law enforcement is that, at the very least, it encourages a rivalry underpinned by jealousy, bitterness and pettiness. 'Justice is only incidental to law and order,' Hoover once said and his agents agreed – if they did not, they would not be agents for long. Even Vincent Bugliosi, an Establishment apologist if ever there was one, admits that Hoover was 'beset by obsessions, paranoia and insecurities', yet, unaccountably, he ran 'perhaps the finest, most incorruptible law enforcement agency in the world'. This must be one of the greatest non sequiturs of all time.

It amounted to a personal vendetta. The Bureau's obsessions focused on Communists, 'uppity n*ggas' like Martin Luther King and a denial of the Mob. Robert Kennedy, who, as Attorney General, was effectively Hoover's boss, was described by the director as an 'arrogant whipper-snapper' and a 'sneaky little sonofabitch'. There is little doubt that, had JFK lived to be re-elected, which seemed likely, Hoover would be forced out. Under Johnson, his post was secure, despite his being past retirement age.

On the day after the assassination, so concerned was Hoover that he went to the races with Clyde Tolson. The report on the killing that the FBI produced was only 100 pages long, with double spacing and wide margins. The murder of Tippit is covered in two pages, with only two of the dozen witnesses listed and one of these (probably Helen

Markham) not named. There is no mention of any of the anomalies here, or the finding of Oswald's two wallets or the confusion over shells/bullets and the kind of gun involved. The report places absolute confidence in the (conflicting) statements of Marina, especially her unverified claim that her husband had shot at General Walker. When it came to Oswald's own death, 'Ruby refused to advise the FBI how he got into the basement or what time he entered', as if the 'finest, most incorruptible law enforcement agency in the world' just took a killer's non-compliance with a shrug; what can you do?

Duplicitous characters like George de Mohrenschildt, Ruth Paine and David Ferrie get no mention at all. Most of the report centres on Oswald and his Communist leanings, as if that is all you need to know about an assassin's motive.

Some writers assert that the Warren Commission could not accept this one-dimensional piece of investigation, but in essence they did. The FBI found no evidence of a conspiracy; neither did the Commission. One or two agents felt guilt and embarrassment in the years ahead, but it was all too little and too late. William C. Sullivan, before being killed mistakenly for a deer, wrote, 'There were huge gaps in the case – gaps we never did close.' 'Looking back,' said agent Laurence Keenan, 'I feel a certain amount of shame. This one investigation disgraced a great organization.' And another former agent, Congressman Don Edwards, said, 'There's not much question that both the FBI and the CIA are somewhere behind the cover-up. I hate to think what it is they are covering up – or who they are covering for.'

J. Edgar Hoover knew. And he was not talking.

4 – The Central Intelligence Agency

While the FBI intimidated witnesses (like Nelson Delgado who had served with Oswald in the Marines and knew him to be a poor shot) the CIA had even more destructive power because of the secrecy of their organization and the existence (little understood in the mid-1960s) of the deep state or the depths to which it could sink. In the corridors of power, the CIA's position in November 1963 was a difficult one. After the Bay of Pigs, it knew it was on borrowed time and that Kennedy had promised to 'smash it into a thousand pieces'. He had started that process by firing Allen Dulles and other key men. But, rather like the FBI, the paranoia of its leader filtered down to all levels. And just as Hoover had the goods on the Kennedy boys because of their sexual misdemeanours, so the CIA was indispensable to the president because of the executive action programme that he never actually abandoned.

Debunking authors like Bugliosi trot out the agency's line that Oswald was never on their payroll. That ignores the ease with which he was able to 'defect' to the USSR and to return as easily. Not only could the man not afford the travel arrangements, *no one* crossed the Iron Curtain so effortlessly as Lee Oswald. And why, on the last night of his life, did Oswald try to ring John Hart, an Intelligence officer, from the Dallas police station?

American Marines do not routinely learn Russian, which is what Oswald did. As Jim Garrison put it, the man would normally have as much use for the language 'as a cat would have for pajamas'. Unless Lee Oswald worked for the CIA. Unless he was under orders, quite possibly up to and including the assassination day itself. Oswald did not go to the Texas Theater that afternoon because he liked Van Heflin films – cinemas were standard meeting places for Intelligence operatives and their handlers. The Lopez Report, produced for the HSCA in 1977, makes it clear that the CIA covered up a great deal in the Oswald story. They have always denied that he worked for them, because if they acknowledged that, fingers might be pointed at them as being instrumental in Kennedy's death. The way the evidence stacks up, however, means that Oswald was not the assassin and if the CIA were behind it, used other people entirely as the hitmen.

Below Dulles was a raft of shady operatives, many of whom had been in the spying game for years, under Eisenhower and even Truman. Richard Helms, who told the HSCA that his organization knew nothing about Oswald, was the brains behind the MK–ULTRA mind control programmes. James Jesus Angleton, counterintelligence chief, sat down with William C. Sullivan of the FBI and rehearsed the questions they were likely to get from the Warren Commission and the answers they should give. E. Howard Hunt claimed that he was at home with his children watching television, whereas in fact he was in Dallas on 22 November (not, despite conspiracy theorists' hysteria, posing as a tramp in a box car). Was he the 'Mr Hunt' to whom Oswald wrote shortly before his death? Then there was Frank Sturgis who went by a number of aliases and was later up to his neck (along with Hunt) in the Nixon-ordered Watergate burglaries. He too, he claimed, was watching television at the time of the assassination (curious how many CIA 'spooks' have a penchant for day-time TV!) but in one account, he was in Miami; in another, Washington. Dodgiest of them all was David Atlee Phillips, aka Maurice Bishop who had been working for Dulles since the Guatemala coup of 1954.

Just as the Warren Commission relied on Hoover's distorted FBI report, so James Jesus Angleton was CIA liaison to the same group. He may have been superfluous, in that Dulles himself was on the panel, but Angleton could be relied upon to have all the details of cover-up at his fingertips.

Remember researcher Matthew Smith's view – 'trying to get the truth from [the CIA] is difficult beyond belief. They are skilled at "dirty tricks", deceit, lies and covering their tracks.' And that is exactly what they have done to this day. 'Oh, I'm CIA,' their smiling operatives will tell you openly. Beyond that, everything is smoke and mirrors.

5 – The Mainstream Media

Presidents and their visits are big news. So it is hardly surprising that television, radio and newspapers/journals were all over John Kennedy's visit to Dallas is November 1963. We are so used to the media today that we barely think about it. It is all-encompassing, from the belligerent and mindless 'social' arm to the 'one-eyed monster' that is television. Across the bottom of our screens is the phrase 'breaking news'; as a society, man has never been so informed as we are today.

But we have to pause. Literally all the information we have, on current affairs, the weather, politics, war, climate and regime change, fashion, entertainment, sport and just about everything else, we only see through the prism of the media. This is, of course, highly selective. Media moguls, executives, programme editors only show us what they want us to see. And they have their own agendas and angles on just about everything. There is no such thing as impartial media coverage and there never has been. On 11 May 1941, the British Broadcasting Corporation, accepted by everybody as the trustworthy voice of the nation, told radio listeners (there was no television, even though a Scotsman, John Logie Baird, had invented the thing!) that in last night's bombing raid on London (the heaviest in the Second World War, as it turned out) twenty-eight enemy aircraft had been shot down. In fact, the number was seven. This was a lie, but because it was done to raise morale at a time when Britain stood alone against Nazi Germany, nobody queried it or even doubted it for a moment.

Since then, and almost certainly before, thousands of lies have been peddled by the BBC and the world's media, for whatever reason and following whatever agenda. Realistically, we have no effective means of checking the veracity of what we are told. There are, no doubt, some people who ignore the media altogether, in which case, they inhabit a world of perpetual darkness which most of us cannot understand.

It was not quite like that in 1963, but the roots of the problem were there. Dallas only had two local newspapers, but there were plenty of radio and television studios across Texas who were already in the city when the shots rang out. And once they had, the media scrum we have all seen at great events on a daily basis, began in earnest. The American media is most relevant here, although news teams from all over the world descended on Dallas and Washington, hungry for news. That hunger fed greed and various branches of the media vied with each other, fighting tooth and nail for centre stage. That was why Merriman Smith, in the president's motorcade, pulled his wire, so that other journalists could not reach their stations. That was why so many people thrust their microphones into Lee Oswald's face and asked him, 'Did you kill the president?' Did they seriously expect him to say, 'Yes. And I'll tell you all about it but only exclusively to you at [add the name of any media station you like]'?

On that fateful Friday, the television networks abandoned all advertising and entertainment programmes. The smaller ones could not keep this up for long because their revenue derived solely from this source, but the larger ones could afford the luxury. Wire services were red-hot. Newspapers covered the story for pages. Essentially, nothing else was happening in the United States that weekend. People were interviewed on the ground in Dallas who had seen nothing, heard nothing and knew nothing but such was the media frenzy that large numbers had their fifteen minutes of fame.

The chaos that developed in Dallas police headquarters was attributable partly to the pressure of so many newsmen. The media and the police collaborated in an hysterical atmosphere which had probably never been seen before in America. And because of the press presence, Jack Ruby was able to sneak past the authorities and kill the only man who might have had some answers to the whole thing. The Dallas police had mistakenly given the press the green light, streaming the public's much vaunted 'right to know'. At the same time, of course, by the actions we have seen already, they were denying them that right.

Television dominated. Between 22 and 25 November, the average American home had their sets turned on for 31.6 hours. An estimated 166 million people, in 51 million homes, watched, horrified and enthralled as various details emerged. Anger, sorrow and anxiety were the feelings recorded at the time, which, obviously, receded as time went on, but there was, oddly perhaps, very little in the way of dread of a political coup or a foreign invasion, which were the fears that the new president and the White House reportedly had.

In one of many groups of ordinary people interviewed by researchers in the months ahead, a participant said, 'After the TV went off last night [22 November] I thought about … why I had spent the whole day and it struck me that I was waiting for somebody to explain why this happened.'

In a sense, we are still waiting. But the media did not wait. It had a duty to report events as they happened, but then it had a duty to evaluate. Whatever discussions were going on, in Lyndon Johnson's Oval Office, in J. Edgar Hoover's FBI, in Richard Helms's CIA, in Chief Curry's DPD offices and all the other corridors of power, these were, by definition, happening behind closed doors, which, after all, is the symbol of the deep state. What emerged from behind these doors, piecemeal and over time, was the story that a deranged Marxist ex-Marine, for reasons that made little or no sense, had shot the president. He had also killed a policeman who was probably trying to arrest him. And a patriot who owned a Dallas nightclub had, in turn, killed the assassin.

This was the myth that the DPD and the FBI gave to the world and to the Warren Commission and it was only slowly that another interpretation began to emerge. A series of books appeared, as early as 1965, which criticized the Warren Commission report and exposed holes in the prosecution's case. Mark Lane, Harold Weisberg, Jim Marrs, Sylvia Meagher, Jim Garrison, David E. Scheim, David

Lifton, Harrison Livingstone, Robert Groden and James DiEugenio only form the tip of the iceberg of a long list of men and women who have sifted through the evidence, spent a fortune, travelled miles and interviewed scores of people in an attempt to get to the truth. As you will have read of Harold Weisberg's experiences, very few publishers and newspapers want to know about this careful and erudite work. It does not fit a newspaper's agenda, it is 'not one for us', that smug dismissal of publishing editors throughout time.

The Church Committee of 1975 exposed for all time the shady and illegal measures carried out by the CIA and other Intelligence agencies in the deep state. The HSCA of the following year uncovered so much evidence that it *had* to acknowledge that there *was* a conspiracy in the murder of John Kennedy.

Then, just as the light of truth and common sense was beginning to burn more brightly, two books threatened to extinguish that light. The first was Gerald Posner's arrogantly titled *Case Closed* in 1993, massively long, with dodgy trajectory diagrams disguised in a welter of erroneous figures. James DiEugenio and Harold Weisberg have demolished this book so effectively that for me to do the same would be futile. DiEugenio also attacks the actor Tom Hanks who bought the film rights to another book that tried to put back the historical clock, Vincent Bugliosi's *Reclaiming History*. Hanks egged on the historian Stephen Ambrose, an Establishment yes-man if ever there was one, to give the project some gravitas. Everybody in that camp was outraged and appalled by Oliver Stone's film *JFK* in 1991, in which the various plots and sub-plots were revealed.

Bugliosi was the lawyer who represented Charles Manson and his 'family' over the Tate-LaBianca murders. Given that Manson was not actually present at either murder, and that his conviction rested on the highly dubious legal catch-all of 'felonious enterprise' (as it is known in Britain) another jury might easily have found Manson not guilty. Bugliosi's book on all this – *Helter Skelter* – makes compelling reading, but of course both it and *Reclaiming History* (2007) were written by a ghostwriter.

Posner and Bugliosi were, in effect, rewriting the Warren Commission, beefing up the 'integrity' of the grandees who formed the panel, praising the oily work of their fellow lawyers and dismissing any naysayers as cranks, drunks and liars. But the astonishing thing about these books is that mainstream American media *raved* over them. Random House published, the *New York Times* sang the books' praises. Could anything be more respectable than that?

Why? Why is the mainstream media still touting this nonsense after all these years? Why did the Dallas police, the FBI and the CIA cover their tracks so carefully? Part of the answer is self-preservation. Twenty minutes after the shooting, Earle Cabell, Dallas's mayor, was standing in Parkland Hospital in shock and muttering to himself, 'It didn't happen! It didn't happen!' and that is exactly how the conservative media and politicians and the debunkers have carried on since. They have buried their heads in the sand and refused to accept the obvious. Why? Because it is safe. If a lone nut shot the president, that is deplorable, but what can be done in such a situation? The world just gives itself a shake, comes out with that lamest of pronouncements – 'Lessons have been learned' – and moves on. But if the president was shot by three men in a military-style ambush orchestrated and paid for by any organization in the corridors of power, what does that say about American society? *Any* society? It is simply too horrible and terrifying to accept, so the Bugliosis and Posners of this world get away with it and Lee Harvey Oswald, against all the evidence, remains the bogey man of our time.

Let us leave the last word, ironically, to J. Edgar Hoover, Kennedy-enemy, deviant-watcher and one of the most repellent men in recent American history. When he was on holiday late in 1964, he told a friend who had asked him who *really* killed Kennedy – 'If I told you what I really know, it would be very dangerous to this country. Our whole political system could be disrupted.'

Select Bibliography

Aaronovitch, David, *Voodoo Histories*, Jonathan Cape, 2009

Belfield, Richard, *The Secret History of Assassinations*, Magpie Books, 2008

Benson, Michael, *Who's Who in the JFK Assassination*, Carol Publishing, 1993

Buchanan, Thomas, G., *Who Killed Kennedy?* Secker and Warberg, 1964

Bugliosi, Vincent, *Reclaiming History*, W.W. Norton & Co., 2007

Cottrell, John, *Anatomy of an Assassination*, Frederick Muller, 1966

Cox, Alex, *The President and the Provocateur*, Oldcastle Books, 2013

Dale, Iain, *The Presidents*, Hodder, 2021

DiEugenio, James, *The JFK Assassination*, Skyhorse Publishing, 2016

Fitzgerald, Ian, *The Deep State*, Arcturus, 2023

Fleury, John, *The Assassination of Fidel Castro*, Absolute Crime, 2013

Garrison, Jim, *On the Trail of the Assassins*, Penguin, 1988

Greenberg, Bradley and Parker, Edwin, (eds.), *The Kennedy Assassination and the American Public*, 1965

Groden, Robert, *The Killing of a President*, Bloomsbury, 1993

Hersh, Seymour, *The Dark Side of Camelot*, Harper Collins, 1998

Holzman, Michael, *Spies and Traitors*, Weidenfeld & Nicholson, 2021

Kessler, Ronald, *The Sins of the Father*, Hodder and Stoughton, 1996

La Fontaine, Ray and Mary, *Oswald Talked*, Pelican, 1996

Lewis, Jon E., (ed.), *The Mammoth Book of How it Happened in America*, Robinson, 2003

Lifton, David S., *Best Evidence*, Carroll and Graf, 1980

Livingstone, Harrison, and Groden, Robert, *High Treason*, Carroll and Graf, 1998

Mayo, Jonathan, *The Assassination of JFK: Minute by Minute*, Short Books, 2013

Menninger, Bonar, *Mortal Error*, Sidgwick and Jackson, 1992

Moore, Jonathan J., *Shot, Stabbed and Poisoned*, New Burlington, 2018

Patterson, James and Fagan, Cynthia, *The Kennedy Curse*, Arrow Books, 2021

Phillips, Tom and Elledge, Jonn, *Conspiracy: A History of Bollocks Theories and How Not to Fall for Them*, Wildfire, 2022

Posner, Gerald, *Case Closed*, Random House, 1993

Sample, Glen and Collom, Mark, *The Men on the Sixth Floor*, Sample Graphics, 2011

Scheim, David E., *The Mafia Killed President Kennedy*, W H Allen, 1988

Scott, Paul Dale; Hoch, Paul L.; Stetler, Russell, (eds.), *Assassinations*, Penguin, 1976

Shenon Philip, *A Cruel and Shocking Act*, Little, Brown, 2013

Sifakis, Carl, *Encyclopaedia of Assassinations*, Headline, 1993

Smith, Matthew, *JFK: The Second Plot*, Mainstream Publishing, 1992

Smith, Matthew, *Who Killed Kennedy?*, Mainstream Publishing, 2013

Southwell, David, *The Kennedy Conspiracy File*, Sevenoaks, 2012

Steers, Edward Jr, *The Lincoln Assassination Encyclopaedia*, Harper Perennial, 2010

Summers, Anthony, *Conspiracy: Who Killed Kennedy*, Fontana, 1980

Weisberg, Harold, *Case Open*, Carroll and Graf, 1994

Weisberg, Harold, *Whitewash*, Skyhorse Publishing, 1965

Wills, Gary and Demaris, Ovid, *Jack Ruby*, Irish Pess International, 1967

Index